Combatting Modern Slavery

Combatting Modern Slavery

Why Labour Governance Is Failing and What We Can Do About It

Genevieve LeBaron

polity

First published in 2020 by Polity Press

Polity Press
65 Bridge Street
Cambridge CB2 1UR, UK

Polity Press
101 Station Landing
Suite 300
Medford, MA 02155, USA

ISBN-13: 978-1-5095-1366-6
ISBN-13: 978-1-5095-1367-3 (pb)

A catalogue record for this book is available from the British Library.

Library of Congress Cataloging-in-Publication Data

Names: LeBaron, Genevieve, author.
Title: Combatting modern slavery : why labour governance is failing and
    what we can do about it / Genevieve LeBaron.
Description: Cambridge, UK ; Medford, MA : Polity Press, 2020. | Includes
    bibliographical references and index. | Summary: "A compelling exposé
    of the failings of corporate anti-slavery initiatives"-- Provided by publisher.
Identifiers: LCCN 2020000089 (print) | LCCN 2020000090 (ebook) | ISBN
    9781509513666 (hardback) | ISBN 9781509513673 (paperback) | ISBN
    9781509513703 (epub)
Subjects: LCSH: Forced labor. | Slavery--Prevention. | Employee rights. |
    Labor laws and legislation.
Classification: LCC HD4871 .L43 2020 (print) | LCC HD4871 (ebook) | DDC
    331.11/73--dc23
LC record available at https://lccn.loc.gov/2020000089
LC ebook record available at https://lccn.loc.gov/2020000090

Typeset in 11 on 13pt Sabon
by Fakenham Prepress Solutions, Fakenham, Norfolk NR21 8NL
Printed and bound in Great Britain by TJ International Limited

For further information on Polity, visit our website:
politybooks.com

Contents

Acknowledgements

While writing this book, I have benefited from dozens of conversations with colleagues and friends. My special thanks go to, in no particular order: Andrew Crane, David Blight, Tim Bartley, Janie Chuang, Luc Fransen, Jennifer Clapp, Daniel Mügge, Claire Cutler, Jane Lister, Ben Cashore, Elena Shih, Nicola Phillips, Vivek Soundararajan, Laura Spence, V. Spike Peterson, Jamie Peck, Michael Bloomfield, Peter Dauvergne, Mark Anner, John Hobson, Scott Nova and Brian Burgoon. Extra special thanks go to J. J. Rosenbaum for her detailed and incisive suggestions on a draft of Chapter 4, and Penelope Kyritsis and Tom Hunt for their excellent insights on a draft of the full manuscript. I am also grateful to two anonymous Polity reviewers for their helpful feedback.

My colleagues and friends at the Sheffield Political Economy Research Institute (SPERI), especially fellow members of our Corporations Reading Group, have made writing this book exciting and a less lonely task than it would have been otherwise. They helped me to sharpen ideas and tackle parts of the global economy that I wouldn't otherwise have been bold enough to write about. Thanks especially to Andrew Gamble, Colin Hay, Andreas

Rühmkorf, Michael Jacobs, Scott Lavery, Jon Gamu, Liam Stanley, Andrew Hindmoor, Tony Payne, Owen Parker, Natalie Langford, Ellie Gore, Remi Edwards, Ed Pemberton, Patrick Kaczmarczyk and Charline Sempéré. I feel lucky to have such wonderful colleagues who reciprocate my enthusiasm for researching labour and corporations.

I'm hugely grateful for all of the support I've been given over the years by the Department of Politics and International Relations at the University of Sheffield. My heads of department, Nicola Phillips and Andrew Hindmoor, and colleagues have been a profound source of encouragement since I joined the department in 2013. In the last few years, I have been especially lucky to be mentored by fellow women professors Ruth Blakeley, Rosaleen Duffy and Charlie Burns. The department has made this book possible in myriad ways, from research assistant funding to encouraging big-picture thinking and pluralism with respect to theory and methods.

For funding the research that underpins and informs this book, I am grateful to: the United Kingdom Economic and Social Research Council, Social Sciences and Humanities Research Council of Canada, the British Academy for the Humanities and Social Sciences, and the Joseph Rowntree Foundation. I am also grateful to Laine Romero-Alston, who, while at the Ford Foundation, supported and built a wonderful community of scholars and organizations pushing for better labour standards and building worker power in global supply chains. I was lucky to be part of this community as editor of the openDemocracy site 'Beyond Trafficking and Slavery', through which I met many of the key collaborators and friends who have been an important source of encouragement and expertise as I've written this book.

I wrote the proposal for this book and its early chapters during a fellowship at the Gilder Lehrman Center (GLC) for the Study of Slavery, Resistance and Abolition, within The MacMillan Center at Yale University. I am so grateful to colleagues and staff at Yale and the GLC for their tremendous hospitality and support of my research, especially David Blight, David Spatz, Michelle Zacks, Daniel Vieira and Melissa McGrath. The GLC also formed, and serves as the home of, the Yale University Modern Slavery Working Group, which has been hugely formative in my thinking on the topics within this book and has given me new friends within this odd field.

For part of the time I have been writing this book, I have been an editor of the academic journal *Review of International Political Economy*. Editing the journal and working with fellow editors Jacquie Best, Paul Bowles, Rachel Epstein, Juliet Johnson, Ilene Grabel and Lena Rethel has shaped my thinking on political economy in important ways.

Some of the data collection for the research discussed in this book was conducted collaboratively with colleagues, including Andrew Crane, Luc Fransen, Nicola Phillips, Andreas Rühmkorf, Peter Dauvergne, Ellie Gore and Jane Lister. I am grateful to these collaborators for their many insights, which have hugely shaped my thinking.

For their wonderful research and fact-checking assistance, I thank the ever-brilliant Penelope Kyritsis, Remi Edwards and Charline Sempéré. I am also grateful to the terrific professional service teams within the Department of Politics and International Relations and SPERI at the University of Sheffield, especially Sarah Cooke, Sarah Beddow, Katie Pruszynski, Wendy Birks, Helen Cutts, Greg Morgan and Melissa Nance.

I am grateful to Louise Knight, my amazing editor at Polity, and her colleagues Nekane Tanaka Galdos and Inès Boxman. Without their incisive advice, patience and persistence, this book simply wouldn't have happened, never mind taken the shape that it finally did.

Thanks to everyone who has participated in the research contained within this book, especially the workers, who have the most to lose and often place themselves at considerable risk to share their stories and visions for change.

Thanks to my friends for the adventures, laughter, kindness, mountains, poetry, good books and starry nights they bring to my life: Rosie, Rhodri and Rupert Evans; Matthew Tann; Mark Ayyash, Chris Hendershot and Lori Crowe; Ross Bellaby, M. J. Summers and Pepper; Liam Stanley; Jonna Nyman; Jamie Johnson; Jane Lister; Shawn Arquinego; Leila Monib; Joanna Dafoe; Erin Rutherford; Julia Doherty, Brett Wilhelm, Mags and Vespa; the Kates; Travis Wayne; and Alan Nasser, Lydia Nasser and Julia Garnett.

My greatest thanks are reserved for my family. They know who they are and how much I love them. Especially my Mom.

1

Who Does Labour Governance Work For?

In April 2013, the Rana Plaza factory building collapsed near Dhaka, Bangladesh, killing more than 1,100 garment workers and injuring around 2,500 people. The workers were making clothes for western brands, including Benetton and Disney.[1] Industrial accidents are unfortunately not uncommon in the garment industry, though the high death toll of Rana Plaza caught the world's attention and ignited calls for corporate accountability for workers in global supply chains. A few years after the accident, a court in Bangladesh charged 38 people with murder.[2] But some key players within the Rana Plaza disaster have largely evaded scrutiny: the people behind the ethical certification schemes, social audits, and corporate social responsibility (CSR) initiatives that failed to prevent the disaster in the first place.

Although the Rana Plaza disaster has been widely reported in the media, far less frequently noted is the reality that the building itself contained two factories that had been recently checked by social auditors hired to monitor factory conditions on behalf of brand companies. It has been reported that a few months before the building collapsed, a large German certification company called

TÜV Rheinland completed a social audit for the textile factory Phantom Apparel Ltd located within Rana Plaza. It used a widely respected standard, the Business Social Compliance Initiative (BSCI) certification, which incorporates core labour standards from the International Labour Organization (ILO) to confirm that factories met requirements around labour standards such as minimum and living wages and absence of child and forced labour.[3]

Following its audit, the TÜV Rheinland auditor noted that there were some 'improvements needed' in the factory, but reported no issues to do with child labour, overtime, freedom of association or the rapidly deteriorating building that housed Phantom Apparel. Yet, in the aftermath of the collapse, journalists began to reveal that the audit report had missed major problems. Children were working in the factory; their dead bodies found in the rubble made this undeniable. Forced overtime was also common and there were serious dangers to worker health and safety at Rana Plaza, such as the obviously compromised building structure.[4] A few days after the collapse, the *New York Times* reported that, in addition to Phantom Apparel, operations at another BSCI-registered factory – New Waves Style – had also recently been passed.[5] How could these social audits have missed and failed to fix such major problems, including those that led to the factory's collapse?

In addition to passing recent social audits, the Rana Plaza building was covered by an array of CSR initiatives, in the same way that much of the global garment sector has been since the late twentieth century. Many of the companies implicated in the collapse champion the safe workplaces and high labour standards achieved through their CSR efforts. A year before the disaster, Disney's 2012 glossy 128-page citizenship report, for instance, noted, 'We believe that acting responsibly is an integral part of our brand', and detailed their extensive efforts to foster 'safe, respectful, and inclusive workplaces' within their global supply chains, among other issues.[6] Benetton, which sourced 266,000 shirts from Rana Plaza in the months before the building collapse, is well known for its social commitments, such as fighting HIV and promoting multiculturalism.[7] Given that companies like these, with established CSR programmes, sourced from Rana Plaza, how could they not have been aware of the problems?

The Rana Plaza factory didn't sit outside existing governance systems used to detect and address labour exploitation and dangers to worker health and safety. Rather, it sat right at the centre of these. Bangladesh is the second largest exporter of apparel. It is home to a workforce that has been making clothes sold by well-known brands for decades. Companies with celebrated CSR programmes sourced from Rana Plaza. Respected auditors using stringent social standards developed by credible organizations had recently inspected it. If existing systems to detect and address labour exploitation in the global economy had been working, the Rana Plaza collapse would never have happened. But it did. And the fact that such catastrophic problems with Rana Plaza were inaccurately reported and left unaddressed, killing and injuring thousands of workers, raises profound questions about the credibility and effectiveness of the labour governance systems in place to combat forced labour and safeguard labour standards in global supply chains.

What is Labour Governance?

In this book, I use the term 'labour governance' to capture the public and private standards regulations, responses and forms of power (including rules, norms and actions) that surround labour standards in the global economy, including its worst forms, which are frequently referred to as forced labour and modern slavery.

Within this, I primarily focus on what is called 'transnational private regulation' within the academic political science literature.[8] This term refers to rules and authority within the global economy designed to transcend constraints associated with nation-states, amidst the cross-border movement of labour and capital. Over recent decades, as the limits of national regulation to govern a globalized economy and multinational companies has become clear, nonstate actors have taken on new roles as regulators within global supply chains, setting and enforcing standards around labour, the environment and other issues.

Transnational private regulation includes CSR. As I've described elsewhere, along with my co-authors Jane Lister and Peter Dauvergne, as part of the trend towards private transnational governance, 'corporations have sought power and authority to make their own rules, and with this have implemented private supply chain governance mechanisms – including multistakeholder initiatives (MSI), standards, certifications, and codes of conduct – which purport to manage and solve environmental and social problems'.[9] But it also includes actors and dynamics beyond CSR, such as binding agreements between trade unions, workers and business actors, codes and standards developed by civil society, and a plethora of other initiatives designed to govern labour standards.

I also use the term labour governance to encompass more traditional forms of state-based regulation, enforcement and power relations, which CSR frequently attempts to take an end run around. This includes national and local laws, such as those pertaining to wages and health and safety, and their enforcement or lack thereof. There is no doubt that laws pertaining to labour standards and workers' rights are routinely not enforced in some contexts and are sometimes accompanied by competing social norms. But as sociology professor Tim Bartley has argued, in contrast to scholarly portrayals of governance in our globalized world as something that has totally bypassed states, in most places, 'one is more likely to find a plethora of half-enforced and contradictory rules than a true regulatory void'.[10] I include these public regulations and forms of power where they are relevant to the conditions of vulnerable workers and labour abuse.

Finally, the term labour governance also refers to international conventions related to labour standards, and to corporate accountability, such as those passed by the European Commission or the ILO, or included within trade agreements.

Not all labour governance fits neatly into either 'public' or 'private' governance. Indeed, perhaps increasingly, as governance actors champion a 'smart mix' of public and private regulation, many initiatives incorporate elements from both categories and are therefore hybrid. An example of a hybrid governance instrument is what is often referred to as 'home state' regulation, through which countries seek to change the behaviour of corporations headquartered within their borders by spurring private governance activity. For instance, recent home state regulation focused on transparency and forced labour is hard law, enacted by states, but it is designed to create change by stimulating corporations to bolster their own labour standards in global supply chains through tools and steps they choose themselves, which include social auditing, codes of conduct and ethical certification.[11]

My definition of labour governance is intentionally broad. While law scholars have traditionally focused on national law, and business scholars often confine their focus to CSR, I am keen to capture both public and private as well as their intersections, as they are relevant to severe labour exploitation in the global economy. All of the forms of governance described above shape the conditions that workers face in contemporary global supply chains. And failures in both public and private governance lie behind the prevalence and patterns of labour exploitation today. So only a broad definition can capture the trends and dynamics I'm interested in here.

With so many actors contributing to labour governance, and given that it takes so many forms today, one might think it would be strong and well developed. But although labour governance is a crowded and complex space, this flurry of activity and effort hasn't yielded a world free of labour exploitation. Contemporary labour governance systems are plagued by deficiencies.

A string of recent incidents suggests that there are problems with prevailing initiatives to combat modern slavery, tackle labour exploitation and create safe and decent working conditions in global supply chains. To name just a few of dozens of examples of the gaps recently exposed in ethical certification schemes, forced labour has been discovered on some tea plantations ethically certified by Fairtrade and Rainforest Alliance.[12] Child labour and producer poverty are well documented at the base of ethically certified coffee supply chains in Mexico, linked to major brands.[13] The list could go on and on, and many more examples are shared later in this book. The reality, in sharp contrast to the idyllic photos of agricultural fields and happy workers found on ethical certification websites promoting fair trade and conscious consumerism, is that workers covered by well-developed labour governance systems are frequently mistreated and vulnerable to abuse. Incidents such as the discovery of widespread slavery in the Thai prawn industry, which supplies to Walmart, Tesco and Costco, Apple's detection of endemic debt bondage at its major subsidiary factories in China, and the skyrocketing death rate for workers constructing stadiums for Qatar's World Cup have all drawn international attention to the severe labour exploitation that continues to prevail in the face of supplier codes of conduct, ethical auditing and other CSR initiatives. As investigative journalists and workers expose more and more problems with labour abuse in global supply chains, it's hard to overlook the fact that the labour governance systems we rely on to detect and address abuses are falling dramatically short.[14]

What is Modern Slavery?

Since the early years of this century, modern slavery has become a buzzword for policymakers, businesses, civil society organizations and the media as a movement of modern-day 'abolitionists' has arisen to combat contemporary practices they consider a modern iteration of the 'old' slavery that thrived before legal abolition in the nineteenth century.[15] Different people and organizations use the term 'modern slavery' to mean slightly different things, but most see it as encompassing situations in which victims are forced to work as a result of violence or intimidation, including forced labour, debt bondage and child labour.

Modern slavery is a slippery concept, because even the people that use the term can't agree on its boundaries or exclusions, and, when pressed for a definition, tend to emphasize that modern slavery takes a plurality of forms. John Bowe captures the modern slavery literature's basic stance on defining the term: 'It is helpful to think of slavery in the modern world as something like a resistant disease, refusing to die off, constantly metamorphosing into new guises.'[16] Some scholars and activists include hugely varied practices within the boundaries of modern slavery; for some, all forms of sex work, forced marriage and child sexual exploitation are slavery. But proponents of the concept have cautioned against dwelling on precise definitions. As Kevin Bales and Ron Soodalter put it: 'We know that slavery is a bad thing, perpetrated by bad people.'[17]

The concept of modern slavery, and the real-world 'abolitionist' movement purporting to combat it, have been widely debated within the academic literature. Concerns include that the modern slavery framing (1) obfuscates the true nature of the problem, (2) is a fig leaf that bolsters the credibility of corporations, anti-feminist and anti-immigration politics, (3) reflects paternalistic tendencies of western humanitarianism and

(4) de-politicizes and naturalizes labour exploitation and disempowers workers.[18] Law professor Janie Chuang has powerfully shown that the elevation of the causes of 'modern-day slavery' and human trafficking has caused 'exploitation creep', focusing attention and responsive legislation on extreme forms of abuse, while normalizing and distracting from the forms of labour exploitation that are widespread in the global economy.[19] Julia O'Connell Davidson, a vocal critic of the modern slavery concept and movement, has noted that contemporary abolitionists see modern slavery as constituting 'a uniquely intolerable moral wrong' 'that can be separated from other social and global ills for purposes of practical intervention and for purposes of quantification'.[20]

I dislike the term modern slavery. Those who use it tend to place way too much emphasis on criminal justice solutions and not nearly enough on the political economic root causes of the problem, the dynamics that give rise to a supply of people vulnerable to forced labour and businesses built to systematically profit from it. They tend to assume that one can cut an easy line around victims of modern slavery and those stuck in more routine or minor forms of labour exploitation, when in fact, as I discuss in Chapter 2, that's much harder to do than one might think. Modern slavery discourses tend to portray people as helpless victims waiting to be rescued, when, in reality, no matter how vulnerable they are, those in forced labour situations, migrant workers, trafficked workers, always have agency. Indeed, one (of many) strange things about the modern slavery field is that almost nobody bothers to speak to workers themselves. More often than not, they are assumed to be too oppressed to speak for themselves and are then patronized by the imposition of solutions they've had no say in.

As well, businesses do sneaky things when they say they are combatting modern slavery. They use the antislavery cause to focus our attention on an evil, monstrous crime occurring in the shadows of supply chains, so that we don't pay attention to the scam they are perpetrating in broad daylight: business models that perpetually and endemically make massive profits through human suffering and exploitation. The language of modern slavery keeps people focused on the base of the supply chain, rather than on those up at the top, who are stockpiling more cash than they know what to do with, giving out huge bonuses, acquiring other companies and growing year on year. As I argue throughout the book, there is a reason that businesses are combatting modern slavery instead of labour exploitation; the former can be portrayed as a randomly occurring and individualized crime, attributed to individuals' moral shortcomings and greed, while the latter is more systemic. With modern slavery, businesses can be the heroes that save the day, but when we talk about labour exploitation, they are the culprits.

For these and many other reasons, I dislike the term modern slavery. In fact, I dislike the term so much that in 2014 I co-founded a website, the 'Beyond Trafficking and Slavery' section of openDemocracy.net, and edited it for three years in order to move the conversation about severe labour exploitation beyond 'the empty sensationalism of mainstream media accounts of exploitation and domination, and the hollow, technocratic policy responses promoted by businesses and politicians'.[21]

So why, you might be wondering, have I used this term in the title of this book? I have called it *Combatting Modern Slavery* for two reasons. The first is that I am interested in exactly that – what it is that business actors, civil society and policymakers are doing when they say they are combatting modern slavery. Since the early 2000s, huge amounts of resources and energy have been poured into this cause, from the halls of the United Nations (UN), to documentary films, to nongovernmental organization (NGO) efforts to rescue 'slaves' from abusive workplaces. Because these efforts encompass very diverse actors with different visions of the problem, such activities can only be summarized using the language they use themselves

– that of modern slavery. This is especially true of the business activity that is at the forefront of this abolitionist movement. Companies like Apple, Unilever, The Coca-Cola Company and Amazon have all recently taken up the cause of combatting modern slavery. They are partnering with NGOs to design 'blueprints' for how governments, civil society and the private sector can collaborate to tackle the problem. They are investing millions in programmes to audit and promote fair recruitment in global supply chains and are publishing colourful modern slavery and human trafficking reports documenting their efforts. Companies are championing the cause of modern slavery at World Economic Forum (WEF) meetings, launching business networks against it, and paying consultants, assurance and advisory firms, and NGOs lots of money for their advice on how best to combat modern slavery within their supply chains. What they actually mean by that term differs from company to company and initiative to initiative, and sometimes the term isn't defined at all. I'm interested in the impact that the focus of businesses and policymakers on combatting modern slavery rather than on addressing labour market issues is having on labour governance. As I argue in Chapter 3, the fact that businesses and governments are combatting modern slavery and not labour abuse and exploitation is in fact part of the problem.

After all, when you scratch beneath the surface of antislavery initiatives, you realize not all of them relate to labour issues: they are about everything from crime to sexual abuse to migrant smuggling. And yet, efforts to combat modern slavery are having a profound impact on labour governance. So that's what I'm keen to point out with the title: that we need to understand and pay attention to efforts to *combat modern slavery*, ask whether and under what conditions they align with or undermine a labour perspective and a workers' and migrants' rights agenda, and to understand how the rise of activities to combat modern slavery are reshaping labour governance. In this book, I use the term modern slavery to describe activities that are self-described by businesses, policy actors and others as relating to modern slavery. Otherwise, as I explain further in Chapter 2, I opt for more specific, clearly defined and less nebulous terms such as 'forced labour'; this book is fundamentally about the severe forms of labour exploitation and the corporate structures, ownership patterns and supply chain dynamics that have made them an endemic part of the global economy.

The second and overlapping reason that I've called the book *Combatting Modern Slavery* is that I have written it with the hope of persuading those who see themselves as doing just that that they fundamentally misunderstand the nature of the problem and are in fact advancing solutions that don't and won't work to help the people they'd like to see helped. By using the term 'modern slavery' in the title, I hope to attract readers whose aim is to combat modern slavery from within their jobs, whether they work in governments or corporations or NGOs, or through their activism or scholarship. If you are one of those people, welcome! I hope that reading this book will help you to see the problem differently and to channel your efforts into more effective strategies for change.

Regardless of the terminology that is used to describe the problem, there can be no doubt that severe labour exploitation is a major problem in the world economy; it is known to be widespread in many sectors, especially agriculture, the garment and footwear industries, domestic work and hospitality, construction and the extractives sector. While statistical data on forced labour is shaky at best, the ILO estimates that 24.9 million people were victims of forced labour in 2016 and that the private sector's use of forced labour generates US$150 billion per year in illegal profits gives a good sense of its scale.[22] But whether corporate antislavery efforts are making a dent in the problem is less apparent.

As calls for greater corporate accountability have increased in recent decades, initiatives to address the labour exploitation fuelled by discount-driven consumer markets have exploded. Many of these initiatives focus on combatting modern slavery. Governments have passed new regulations to address labour abuse and modern slavery and to bolster transparency in global corporate supply chains. Corporations have invested millions in new CSR programmes and have expanded 'ethical' auditing initiatives, certification and the civil society partnerships they rely on to monitor labour standards. MSIs like the Sustainable Palm Oil Initiative and the Better Cotton Initiative are touted as solutions to sector-based labour problems. Ethical certification schemes like Fairtrade promise to build better futures for the world's workers. Yet, by most measures, and across many sectors and regions, severe labour exploitation continues to soar.

Why Global Labour Governance Is Failing

Why aren't these governance efforts working? And what type of supply chain governance is needed to protect the world's most vulnerable workers?

The answers, as this book will reveal, are complex and vary across different sectors, type of governance initiative, and parts of the world. But stepping back, it is clear that two mutually reinforcing problems stand in the way of improving labour standards in global supply chains: both the design and the implementation of contemporary labour governance are severely flawed and limited, in ways that benefit individuals and organizations profiting from exploitation, and fail to protect workers.

Most public and private initiatives to combat modern slavery and bolster labour standards in global supply chains are designed to omit the portions of supply chains in which the most severe forms of labour exploitation are known to thrive. Focused on the large 'Tier 1' suppliers (those that hold contracts directly with and take orders from brands and retailers), corporate and government programmes rarely address labour supply chains – the unregulated networks through which contingent and sometimes forced and trafficked workers are recruited, transported and supplied to businesses by third party labour agents – nor the 'shadow factories' (unregistered and undisclosed production sites that are used to meet orders on time and evade compliance) in which unauthorized production takes place. They tend to create loopholes around the most vulnerable workers within supply chains, rather than seeking to protect them. Indeed, in spite of the widespread recognition that severe exploitation is accelerating in the bottom tiers of supply chains, among labour subcontractors, in unauthorized factories, in the informal sector and in home-based work, recent labour governance initiatives tend to conceal and disclaim responsibility for these spaces and relations of exploitation rather than bring them to light.

In addition to their design flaws, the implementation of labour governance initiatives is similarly deficient. In recent years, most countries have scaled back public labour inspectorates and given businesses more authority to enforce private labour standards and laws. A booming private industry of accounting firms, social auditors and supply chain analysts has emerged to monitor and enforce labour standards, and verify conformance to CSR standards, often in collaboration with NGOs. Yet, while the enforcement industry has helped corporations to generate media- and consumer-friendly metrics and reports and bolster the credibility of their aspirational goals, it has led to very little concrete improvement in the detection, reporting and corrective action of severe labour exploitation.

These flaws, I will argue, are not coincidences. Rather, as civil society actors work to raise labour standards in the global economy, powerful business interests are fighting to preserve the status quo of a retail-driven economy that is heavily dependent on labour exploitation. Today's corporations are hardwired to maximize profits for their shareholders and executives, to monopolize and to grow, and built into this wiring are enormous risks and dangers to workers. To preserve their profitable business models, corporations are leveraging strategic control over the design and implementation of public and private supply chain governance initiatives. And they are wielding power in governance arenas – from policy processes within national governments, to global forums and organizations like the ILO – to stave off restrictions on their production practices and increases in legal liability. In short, industry actors are speaking out of both sides of their mouths when it comes to labour governance. They are championing causes like safe workplaces and worker voice and initiatives to combat modern slavery even as they are, at the same time, quashing laws and conventions that would spur real and long-lasting change to labour practices in the global economy.

The overall result is that, by creating an illusion of effective governance and buy-in to incremental improvement, CSR is doing more to cover up labour problems in global supply chains than it is doing to fix them, or even bring them to light. No doubt, there are some cases where corporate initiatives have led to improvements for some workers with respect to some issues, like better health and safety standards. But, as this book will reveal, overall the trend is towards the legitimization and reinforcing of prevailing business models and endemic exploitation. The issues that matter most in terms of protecting workers and improving their conditions – wages, forced overtime, forced labour, collective action rights – are rarely altered by existing private governance programmes. In short, efforts and initiatives to govern global labour standards are working to enhance corporate growth and profit, but are failing workers and civil society actors seeking to raise labour standards in the global economy.

This Book's Approach

Hundreds of academic journal articles and books examine individual labour governance initiatives and the micro-conditions for their successes and failures. This body of research gives us insights into the opportunities and challenges surrounding individual cases – for instance, the implementation of ISO 26000 (a social sustainability standard) by an orange juice company in a region of Algeria, or an NGO's efforts to address the plight of rug-weaving families in a city like Delhi. These studies have helpfully analysed operational issues associated with the design, uptake, merits and shortcomings of various private, public and hybrid initiatives within various sectors and geographical contexts, as well as relationships between stakeholders, such as activists and firms, in standard-setting processes.[23]

The academic literature on the design and effectiveness of individual labour governance initiatives has yielded important insights about whether and under what conditions supply chain governance initiatives do or do not work to make improvements across a range of issue areas, how they can be improved through redesigning procedures and implementation, and how the interactions between public and private governance systems can be optimized to yield better outcomes.[24] But these studies often lose sight of broader questions about whether or not labour governance initiatives are actually solving the problems they've been established to address, like living wages, safe working conditions and protecting workers' rights to collective action. On-the-ground effectiveness is seldom analysed. Furthermore, most scholars focus on case studies, with few investigating the net and combined results of individual labour governance initiatives, such as whether they are solving – or even marginally improving – the world's major labour market challenges, like forced labour and poverty wages in global supply chains.

This gap is rooted in a common conceptual limitation within the literature on private governance and labour standards. Namely, that scholarship tends to be technical in its focus, treating labour governance initiatives as objective and neutral instruments that can be pushed towards better performance. Debates around the effectiveness of initiatives like ethical certification, MSIs, social auditing and other supply chain governance efforts tend to take for granted the notion that such measures can be tweaked to resolve any current shortcomings.[25] For instance, as political scientists Matthew Potoski and Aseem Prakash see it, 'the theoretical and policy challenge is to identify the program characteristics that can *ex ante* predict program efficiency'.[26] However, these technical and predictive approaches tend to overlook the role of structural power dynamics within the global economy, as well as the broader politics that surround labour governance initiatives, which pose fundamental obstacles to improving these systems.[27]

In this book, I take a different approach. After 20 years of CSR, I argue that it is time to confront the reality that industry-led efforts are not neutral and that nudging them towards better performance won't solve the problems of labour exploitation in the global economy. Corporate actors' longstanding resistance to transforming labour governance initiatives in light of their well-documented flaws begs us to ask bigger, more political questions. Specifically, I question the interests, power and forms of profitability that are safeguarded and reinforced through CSR approaches to setting and enforcing labour standards. I examine the fundamental governance question surrounding the growing adoption of industry-led labour governance initiatives: that of *who* these initiatives *are effective for*. Are current systems designed and equipped to find and resolve labour abuses in supply chains, or are they set up to spur corporate profitability, protect business models, generate reassuring metrics for investors and shareholders and help already massive companies to grow even bigger?

Throughout this book, I draw on primary and secondary research that I conducted between 2012 and 2019 on the effectiveness of labour governance initiatives in a range of geographical contexts, including China, India,

Ghana, Switzerland, the United States (US) and the United Kingdom (UK). This research has involved case studies encompassing a range of sectors, including consumer goods, agricultural products, construction and garments. It has also covered an array of labour governance initiatives, including labour-related disclosure legislation such as the UK Modern Slavery Act, CSR programmes including company and supplier codes of conduct, ethical certification schemes and various forms of social auditing. My primary research has involved hundreds of interviews with business actors, including corporate executives; representatives of certification bodies, social audit firms and accounting firms; producers; suppliers at various stages along the supply chain; exporters; and industry associations. It has also involved interviews with government and international organization officers, trade unions, civil society and workers' organizations. In addition, I draw on interviews and surveys conducted with workers within global supply chains. This includes research with vulnerable workers at the base of global supply chains, such as more than 1,200 tea and cocoa workers, some of whom have been subjected to forced labour.[28] Detailed case studies and methodologies for my various research projects have been published elsewhere as academic journal articles and reports.[29] My goal in this book is to combine and consolidate the insights within these various studies about the failures of labour governance and prospects for improving it.

In addition to drawing on original field-based empirical data from my recent research, to develop my arguments about the current state of global labour governance, I also draw on desk-based research completed specifically for this book, comprising a study of: (1) the 25 top retail and manufacturing companies (by annual sales), including their structure, ownership dynamics, supply chain, corporate social responsibility policies and workforces; (2) the business actors and dynamics of the recruitment and enforcement industries; and (3) key trends within the global labour market, including through national government and international organization statistics databases. Information has been drawn primarily from company websites, consulting firm websites, international organization and government websites, and reports, as well as industry databases such as Factset and the World Bank Enterprise Survey.

My aim is to synthesize this body of data to advance an argument about the state of contemporary global labour governance and to stimulate debate about why governance systems are failing to protect the world's workers. I aim to reflect on the serious but too often not spoken about obstacles that currently limit efforts to eradicate labour exploitation from the global economy – namely, corporate power, interests and ownership structures, and the ways that those affect governments and civil society – and to shift the debate on governance effectiveness from technical considerations to questions of politics. My broad approach, sweeping across a number of case studies, sectors and contexts, has the advantage of allowing me to reflect on the big picture of what's going wrong with prevailing public and private governance systems to combat labour exploitation, delving into global political economy issues that are frequently overlooked in case studies. This wide-angle approach does have drawbacks: I will no doubt overlook some of the microlevel dynamics of individual initiatives as well as the full extent of variation across geographic contexts, sectors and types of initiative. Yet, a narrower approach would miss too much of the story of global labour governance and the breadth of challenges that need to be overcome to protect twenty-first-century workers.

Corporations as Cause and Solution to Labour Abuse

A few decades ago, corporations were widely considered to be the *cause* of problems like sweatshops, poverty wages and child labour. Throughout the 1990s and early 2000s, activists, workers, trade unions and civil society organizations vehemently protested the globalization of production, offshoring and the lack of restrictions on multinational corporations' activities. Mass demonstrations and general strikes raged, drawing attention to issues like water and electricity privatization, outsourcing and patterns of foreign investment. This social movement, often described as the anti-globalization movement, countered the rapidly unfolding globalization regime, which it saw as facilitating corporate greed and profit at the expense of the public. Much of the movement's energy was targeted at challenging the mounting role, rights and benefits of corporations within global capitalism and, especially, their exploitative labour practices.[30]

A key contention of the anti-globalization movement was that corporations were causing labour abuse as they laid off workers and outsourced and offshored production activities to supplier firms in the global South. For corporations, one of the great benefits of using supplier firms is that they could set up relatively anonymous sweatshops, shielding brands from the legal and reputational consequences. However, at the same time as brands sought to distance themselves from these abusive labour practices, activist efforts and a raft of journalistic exposés sought to close the gap between consumers and the adults and children sewing their clothes, making their jewellery and assembling their sports equipment in appalling conditions. In 1996, for instance, a photo essay in *Life Magazine* introduced American consumers to the Pakistani children as young as 10 who were sewing their Nike soccer balls for around US$0.60 per day under 'horrible conditions', to use Nike chairman Phil Knight's own regretful words following the incident.[31] The next year, Nike was in the spotlight again when 'it was revealed that workers in one of its contracted factories in Vietnam were being exposed to toxic fumes at up to 177 times the Vietnamese legal limit'.[32]

Activists pushed for a range of solutions to the problems of offshoring and accelerating indecent work. Some called for an end to outsourcing, while others pressured the UN to create an international convention to impose corporate liability for labour standards. Still others pressured policymakers and international organizations like the International Monetary Fund (IMF) and World Bank to make trade and investment treaties more equitable by building in guarantees that a certain share of the value produced would remain in the countries and in the pockets of workers who contributed to the production of goods, even when the goods were sold elsewhere. While activists, workers and unions mobilizing for workers' rights often differed on preferred solutions, they shared a united vision of the cause: that corporations and political elites were advancing a model of capitalist globalization allowing businesses to freely exploit vulnerable workers in poor countries desperate to attract foreign investment, and this was facilitating a global race to the bottom in labour standards and workers' rights.[33]

Nearly three decades later, corporations have made serious strides in positioning themselves as *solutions* to problems like labour abuse and poverty in the global economy rather than the *cause*. No doubt some activists and civil society organizations continue to bemoan corporate profits and greed, and many still would identify companies as the cause of exploitative labour practices within their supply chains. But at the same time, corporations have achieved sizable legitimacy and authority as problem-solvers for labour exploitation in supply chains. Today, they are just as likely to be discussed as part of the solution to problems like modern slavery, forced labour and a lack of labour law enforcement as they are to be spoken about as the cause of such problems. And many civil society, government and international organization actors have embraced their new role, arguing that what's right for workers and society is compatible with what's right for businesses' bottom lines. Indeed, this 'business case' for abolishing slavery is a crucial rationale for many initiatives to combat modern slavery.

Corporations Save the World's Workers

In sharp contrast to the era in which Nike's reliance on child labour was first exposed, corporate actors today play a central role in global labour governance. As already mentioned, multinational corporations (MNCs) like Nike, Apple and Nestlé have enacted a vast array of voluntary initiatives to detect, address and prevent labour exploitation in their supply chains. Companies at the helm of global supply chains include within their codes of conduct specific requirements for suppliers concerning labour standards and use elaborate indexes to score suppliers on labour practices and noncompliance. They develop CSR initiatives, such as Mondelēz International's Cocoa Life programme. And they write about these in their annual sustainability reports and modern slavery statements, which are produced to comply with recent legislation to spur greater transparency over global supply chains.

In an effort to prevent the embarrassment of incidents like Nike's child labour scandal, companies now monitor labour standards in global supply chains using social auditors. Most companies hire third party (but typically still for-profit) auditors to monitor working conditions in portions of their supply chains, usually focusing on Tier 1 suppliers. Nike notes in its 2018 *Statement on Forced Labor, Human Trafficking and Modern Slavery* that it conducted 471 audits and assessments in fiscal year 2018.[34] Some companies push the cost of auditing onto suppliers, requiring them to hire auditors and submit results. As Coca-Cola describes it, 'all of the bottling operations and authorized suppliers selling more than $60,000 annually to the Coca-Cola system are required to complete a third-party audit and share the audit results with The Coca-Cola Company'.[35] Many companies also monitor working conditions by providing hotlines for workers to report abuse and by administering mobile phone surveys to workers – measures they describe at sustainability conferences and in their CSR reports as 'technology-supported worker engagement'.

In addition, companies seek to address modern slavery through ethical certification schemes like Fairtrade and Rainforest Alliance. As companies have battled media and activist attention towards bad labour practices in their supply chains, many have increased the proportion of their business covered by ethical certification schemes. Some have even achieved full certification. As Tata Global Beverages describes one of its tea brands, Tetley, for instance:

> At the start of 2010, Tetley announced its commitment to purchase all of the tea for its branded tea bag and loose tea products from Rainforest Alliance Certified™ farms. We are pleased to report that in FY17/18, 100% of all Tetley branded black and green tea (*Camellia sinensis*) and red/rooibos tea (*Aspalathus linearis*), including flavoured and decaffeinated varieties, sold by TGB is Rainforest Alliance Certified™.[36]

Ethical certification schemes like Fairtrade can be costly investments. Starbucks, for instance, reports it has paid US$16 million in Fairtrade premiums alone since 2000, as well as US$10 million to 'Fairtrade licensing initiatives that support the international certification system (FLO-CERT), producer services and awareness building around the benefits of Fairtrade'.[37] Big profitable companies can afford the cost of certification; some companies are now double or even triple certifying their supply chains, combining schemes like Fairtrade, Rainforest Alliance and Organic. But for suppliers, who are frequently expected to bear the costs of becoming certified, the price can be exorbitant. One garment factory owner recently declared that, given their high cost for little value and the need to use them in order to stay in business, 'the certification systems are the mafia'.[38]

In addition to auditors and ethical certification companies, corporations also engage a range of other industry actors to support their new and accelerating efforts to combat modern slavery. Big audit firms like Deloitte, KPMG, Ernst & Young and PricewaterhouseCoopers are hired by brand companies and manufacturers to provide assurance and advisory services related to transnational labour governance, ranging from supply chain mapping, advisory and risk assessment in relation to labour standards to the establishment of key performance indicators (KPIs) around human trafficking and child labour.[39] Deloitte even partnered with an antislavery NGO, Free the Slaves, to publish a report called *The Freedom Ecosystem: How the Power of Partnership Can Help Stop Modern Slavery*, in which the benefits of soft-law incrementalism and corporate–NGO partnerships are touted. 'Rather than seeking silver bullets', the authors urge, 'organizations looking to contribute to the eradication of slavery should aim to take incremental steps to improve the status quo.'[40]

In addition to working in partnership with consultancy firms, and on their own, corporations are collaborating to promote industry-led solutions to labour abuse through industry associations. The Consumer Goods Forum, for instance, which is made up of 400 retailer and manufacturing companies within the consumer goods industry and works to 'promote more business growth, business efficiency and positive change',[41] has recently developed a social resolution on forced labour, which it is advancing by supporting companies to make voluntary commitments and raise awareness.[42] The Global Business Coalition Against Trafficking brings together major companies, including Google, Amazon, Microsoft, Carlson and The Coca-Cola Company, to 'harness the power of business across all sectors to prevent and reduce modern slavery, and support survivors, through collaboration, guidance, and shared resources'.[43] These are just a couple of the dozens of recently formed industry collaborations that industry actors claim will help to save the world's workers.

As companies have come to occupy greater space within transnational labour governance, NGOs have largely accepted CSR as a legitimate means of finding and addressing labour abuse within supply chains. Despite corporations' past misconduct, many labour and human rights NGOs are increasingly willing to partner with them towards creating bespoke initiatives to assess standards and improve social and labour conditions in their supply chains. To name just a few examples, Unilever has collaborated with Oxfam to better integrate smallholders within its supply chains;[44] Marks & Spencer collaborates with and funds initiatives for modern slavery charity Unseen;[45] and another antislavery charity, Hope for Justice, is partnering with UK retailer Morrisons to develop 'due diligence and resilience' for the company.[46] Some NGOs partner with several corporations at once. For instance, Free the Slaves currently lists Google, Deloitte and AmazonSmile among its partners and sponsors on its website.[47]

Within global governance arenas, too, corporations are joining coalitions made up of labour and social NGOs to tackle labour governance challenges. The UN Global Compact – advertised as 'the world's largest corporate sustainability initiative'[48] – brings around 10,000 companies together with thousands of NGOs, academic organizations, foundations and trade unions.[49] Of all the voluntary industry initiatives, the UN Global Compact is the one that would have been most unimaginable at the height of the anti-globalization movement. Then, the notion that trade unions and anticorporate NGOs could collaborate and share conference rooms with the oil and mining companies, the big-box retailers, apparel and footwear brands, and food and beverage corporations that they were naming and shaming, protesting and campaigning against would have surely seemed impossible.

In addition to these multistakeholder initiatives, corporations have initiated bilateral partnerships with international organizations. UK retailer Tesco, for instance, partners with UNICEF to 'improve opportunities for tens of thousands of children in Indian tea communities and reduce their vulnerability to trafficking and abuse'.[50]

Partnerships between corporations and big business are springing up not just in response to industry initiatives. They are also working the other way, with global governance actors seeking out opportunities to work with and influence business actors. The ILO, for instance, launched the Global Business Network on Forced Labour and Human Trafficking, which it describes as a 'partnership between the ILO, multinational and domestic enterprises, employers' organizations, and business associations in the call to drive action on forced labour and human trafficking deeper into the supply chain and across industry and sectors'.[51] Business partnerships with international organizations are further linking companies to civil society organizations and policymakers.

Through all these voluntary efforts, corporations have positioned themselves as part of the solution to the problems of modern slavery and labour abuse more broadly – and have made more complex, if not wholly distanced themselves from, their earlier reputations as uncaring, profit-hungry monsters who cause labour abuse through reckless purchasing practices, planned ignorance and a lack of transparency around working conditions within their supply chains. In short, they have made sizable gains in their efforts to shed their sociopathic reputations – to paraphrase the key insight of law professor Joel Bakan's well-known book (subsequently made into a film), *The Corporation*[52] – as entities in pathological pursuit of profit and power.

The countries in which MNCs are headquartered and incorporated, often called their 'home states',[53] have done little to challenge the rise of CSR as a credible solution to labour exploitation in global supply chains. Rather, home states have reinforced this status quo through a recent wave of transparency legislation that does little more than codify existing CSR programmes, social auditing and ethical certification.[54] The growing body of labour-related disclosure legislation, which includes the 2015 UK Modern Slavery Act and the 2012 California Transparency in Supply Chains Act, might at first glance appear to be a stringent and serious state response to the problem of forced labour. However, as I substantiate in Chapter 3, most pieces of transparency legislation simply require that companies report on efforts they are taking to address and prevent modern slavery, human trafficking and other forms of severe labour abuse in their supply chain.[55] This has fuelled social auditing and certification, but, as I discuss later in the book, there is little evidence that it has actually reduced the prevalence of forced labour.

There are typically no penalties for noncompliance and no enforcement provisions. As such, compliance rates are low. For instance, a civil society coalition estimates that between 12,000 and 17,000 companies are within the scope of the UK Modern Slavery Act, but only around 3,000 companies had published statements on the Modern Slavery Registry website by the end of 2017. Large numbers of these are of low quality and do not comply with the requirements of the Act.[56] As one NGO representative explained, 'If you look at the number of reports that have been published, there are obviously a lot of businesses that aren't doing anything ... That compliance gap is quite worrying.'[57] With few exceptions, recent legislation to combat modern slavery has reinforced the dominance of industry-driven solutions to labour abuse in supply chains, rather than fundamentally transformed, displaced or improved it.

Some NGOs, governments and lawyers are pushing back against these trends, reminding policymakers and the public that companies often overpromise and under-deliver when it comes to social and labour standards and causes. But overall, as this brief snapshot illustrates, the trend is towards an increased reliance on corporations and CSR governance to eradicate forced labour and curb exploitation. The sheer flurry of activity alone has helped to deepen the legitimacy and authority of corporations as 'problem-solvers' for labour exploitation in supply chains – as has the acceptability conferred on corporate efforts by governments, international organizations and NGOs.

This Book's Arguments and Structure

In this book, I argue that efforts to combat modern slavery through CSR are failing. After all, what do the vast array of labour governance initiatives described above have in common? The initiatives are almost entirely driven by industry actors. They are all voluntary and are not legally binding or enforceable, and there is little public oversight or accountability over these private efforts. CSR is failing because prevailing labour governance initiatives do little to nothing to disrupt corporate business models, leaving fully intact poverty wages, the low prices that companies pay suppliers, the short contract windows and unpredictable orders imposed on businesses lower down the chain by businesses higher up, and other drivers of labour exploitation. And they mostly fail to empower workers, or even to involve them in basic ways; only very rarely do industry-led labour governance solutions involve or meaningfully integrate workers in shaping, negotiating and operating initiatives.

Corporations have positioned themselves as champions of labour governance for a number of complex reasons, and their motivations vary across company type, scale, size and sector. Overall, though, it's clear that big business has forged a model in which they can have strategic control over the design and implementation of labour governance initiatives. As one company CSR executive described of Walmart's CSR efforts:

> By adopting the process that said, 'We got it, this is our ball, we're going to do something about supply chains'

... Walmart, on behalf of the entire retail industry said, 'This is our problem. This isn't a government regulatory problem. This isn't China's problem, this isn't Vietnam's problem. This is our problem. We have the power, resources, and ability to deal with it and we will.'[58]

At the same time as companies have increasingly claimed that the ball of labour governance is in their court, states have stopped or struggled to enforce the labour laws on their books. Indeed, the rise of corporate auditing and CSR has coincided with the decline of state-based labour law enforcement and inspections in many jurisdictions. In countries across the global North and South, state-based labour law enforcement is now low to nonexistent. In the US, for instance, employers are very unlikely to be inspected by the Department of Labor. Economist Gordon Lafer has estimated that 'an employer would have to operate for 1,000 years to have even a 1 percent chance of being audited by Department of Labor inspectors'.[59] As labour abuse has continually been framed as something perpetrated by 'bad apple' and 'rogue' employers and criminal actors within the private economy, states have increasingly sat at the sidelines, except where they are afforded opportunities to rush in and lock up the really bad guys, heroically liberating victims of human trafficking and modern slavery.

But just because corporations have built labour governance initiatives and are pouring loads of money into them – money which, incidentally, is not being paid in taxes to government or as wages to the workers earning well below the poverty line in global supply chains – does not mean that these governance initiatives are designed or implemented in ways that meaningfully protect workers. By contrast, as I will discuss in Chapter 2, a growing body of research suggests that industry-led labour governance initiatives are failing to meet their stated aims and are doing little to solve workers' most pressing challenges; they rarely achieve their aspirational goals of creating supply chains characterized by safe workplaces free from forced labour or predatory recruitment fees and characterized by women's empowerment. When the design and implementation of industry-led labour governance initiatives is examined and compared against patterns of labour exploitation in global supply chains, it is unsurprising that many fail to yield concrete improvements. After all, business initiatives rarely tackle the root causes that give rise to exploitation in supply chains, and tend to structure systems to skirt around and cover up – rather than shed light into – the worst abuses.

How could there be such dire problems when rich and powerful companies are channelling their resources into addressing labour abuse through CSR, supplier codes of conduct, social auditing and ethical certification schemes, and many consumers are paying more to buy products advertised as ethically made? To understand how things have gone so badly wrong in global supply chains, we need to take a step back and look at the bigger picture of labour exploitation and deficiencies in labour governance.

In this book, I analyse four core challenges in contemporary labour governance. I argue that, first, there is a mismatch between the patterns of labour exploitation in global supply chains and the design of labour governance initiatives and their enforcement. Second, changing patterns of corporate ownership, organization and scale – and industry actors' growing political power – is making them more and more ungovernable. Third, a sizable governance gap surrounds the booming recruitment industry, through which workers are supplied into global supply chains. Finally, a profitable enforcement industry has arisen, with vested financial interest in monitoring tools and programmes, and no financial interest in actually solving problems. These are profitable and advantageous for industry actors, but seldom lead to accurate depictions of labour standards or concrete improvements for workers.

In the remainder of this section, I'll briefly outline each of these four challenges, which are taken up, respectively, in Chapters 2–5, and then highlight the book's key conclusions, which are developed in Chapter 6.

Labour exploitation in global supply chains

Labour exploitation is endemic in several industries and global supply chains today, including more minor forms like wage theft and forced overtime, as well as the worst forms of labour exploitation typically described as forced labour, human trafficking and modern slavery. The worst forms of exploitation tend to thrive more in some portions of supply chains than in others, and among certain types of businesses.[60] Further, there are predictable and stable patterns regarding the workers who become vulnerable to it.

As I substantiate in Chapter 2, labour exploitation does not occur randomly or spontaneously in global supply chains. Rather, it is a logical outcome of the ways that contemporary supply chains are set up, and, more broadly, of the high-volume, low-cost business model of retail production that powers the global economy. It can be linked to political economic drivers. These include both the factors that trigger a business demand for forced labour, as well as those that create a supply of workers who become vulnerable to it.

On the demand side, a variety of pressures that lie at the heart of global supply chains as they are currently constituted create a demand among businesses for exploited labour. These include irresponsible sourcing practices, which put severe cost and time pressures on suppliers, leading to steep financial penalties for delayed orders and missed deadlines. This can lead to risky practices like unauthorized subcontracting, and to outsourcing along both product and labour supply chains, which makes oversight over labour standards difficult, in part because it fragments responsibility for workers across multiple businesses and agents.[61] As the architects of global supply chains, MNCs bear sizable responsibility for business pressures experienced by suppliers, and the forms of exploitation that result from them. If they were serious about tackling labour exploitation, rather than setting up elaborate CSR programmes, corporations would alter their business practices.

On the supply side, across recent decades, political economy dynamics have created a supply of workers who are vulnerable to forced labour and overlapping forms of exploitation. These include: poverty, including among workers in lucrative supply chains; discrimination on the basis of social identity, such as race, gender and sexuality; lack of labour protections, which means that many workers face barriers to collective action and the exertion of their rights; and restrictive mobility regimes, which leave migrant workers unprotected. These dynamics have intensified in the latest era of global capitalism, as political elites and business actors have transformed the rules of the global economy in ways that privilege the profitability of businesses.

Understanding the complex political economy dynamics that give rise to labour exploitation in global supply chains is vital if we are to grasp the weaknesses within prevailing initiatives to tackle it. In particular, it is essential to understand the disjuncture between the patterns of labour exploitation and the design and enforcement patterns of industry-led initiatives, which tend to circumvent the portions of supply chains in which exploitation is known to manifest and thrive.

Corporate power and the state

Understanding the changing nature and organization of corporations at the helm of global supply chains, and their deepening political power, is also essential to understanding why contemporary labour governance is failing to yield concrete improvements.

As corporations merge, monopolize and grow, they are exerting heightened control across broad global industrial sectors of production and consumption, and gaining even further power to dictate labour conditions within global supply chains. Further, changing patterns of financialization, corporate ownership and market speculation are introducing new and deeper pressures for corporations to produce profits for their shareholders. Under these circumstances, the value created within global supply chains is increasingly concentrated at the top, among investors and shareholders, and as profit.

At the same time, industry actors – including brand and retail firms, as well as big asset managers, big auditors and industry associations – are becoming increasingly proactive in initiating and shaping public regulations on supply chains, at the national and subnational levels, as well as in international conventions. In addition to longstanding lobbying activities, corporations are now seconding employees to national policy organizations, pioneering and funding civil society coalitions to stop slavery and human rights abuses by business, and integrating CSR initiatives into their long-term growth strategies. Yet, at the same time as they champion CSR initiatives to combat modern slavery and promote worker voice, industry actors are part of regulatory coalitions to fend off stronger labour laws and their enforcement. The result is that even the governance actors and initiatives we generally consider to be 'public' are often highly influenced by corporate power.

As I argue further in Chapter 3, the deepening political power of corporations is allowing them to leverage strategic control over supply chain governance initiatives, and especially those intended to bolster labour rights and reduce exploitation. It is staving off more radical reforms on corporate production activities, and it is undermining and co-opting civil society efforts to increase corporate liability and accountability for the worst forms of labour exploitation. It also troubles prevailing academic conceptualizations about the clean division between public and private, market and state, which has implications for solutions to these problems.

The recruitment industry

As part of the broad political economy dynamics outlined earlier in the book, a booming recruitment industry has emerged within global supply chains, posing major problems for the enforcement of global labour standards. A high and growing proportion of victims of labour exploitation – and especially victims of forced labour and human trafficking – are not part of companies' core workforces. Rather, they are supplied through long and complex labour supply chains and employed by labour market intermediaries like agencies or brokers. Yet, recruiters and third-party agencies are very poorly regulated, and are inadequately covered (where included at all) in market-based labour governance initiatives. Indeed, as I will argue in Chapter 4, recent governance initiatives may even be fuelling exploitation by the recruitment industry as suppliers facing increased scrutiny by brands are turning to recruiters and labour agents as a strategy to outsource risk and cut costs.

A key part of the story of why labour governance is failing relates to this recruitment industry. In particular, it lies in the dynamics of labour supply chains, how recruiters and agents within them facilitate the transnational supply of vulnerable workers, and the role of the industry in anchoring labour exploitation within the global economy. Due to flaws in both design and implementation, contemporary efforts to govern labour standards have tended not to touch the recruitment industry, and, in doing so, have missed highly vulnerable and exploited workers.

The enforcement industry

Another set of industry actors that pose a crucial challenge to efforts to upgrade and improve working conditions worldwide is the enforcement industry. As mentioned, as part of the broader shift towards the privatization of supply chain governance, industry actors and NGOs have taken on roles as 'monitors' and 'enforcers' of labour standards in supply chains. But while private supply chain monitoring tools and programmes are highly profitable for accounting firms, NGOs and other industry actors involved in selling them, these seldom lead to concrete improvements for workers. Retail and brand companies leverage highly strategic control over the design and implementation of auditing programmes, including over new 'beyond audit' initiatives. As such, the ability of these programmes to detect and report exploitation and spur corrective action is limited. In the words of one UK audit firm employee, the majority of supply chain monitoring programmes 'are not trying to find things out, they're trying to prove that something is not there'.[62]

As I will argue in Chapter 5, the enforcement industry is helping to conceal rather than solve the most urgent labour issues in supply chains. Taken as a whole, it is misrepresenting the nature of labour conditions and practices, not only doing little to help workers, but actively misleading consumers and policymakers about their plight. The enforcement industry is helping corporations to legitimize and grow their businesses, in part by generating media- and consumer-friendly metrics and reports that are helping to stave off pressure from civil society groups and reassure investors. But it is doing little to solve the urgent problem of labour exploitation in supply chains.

Corporate Fairytales vs. Worker Power

Understood in this way, industry-led labour governance initiatives are not simply neutral mechanisms that can be nudged towards effectiveness. It's not enough to simply say that CSR efforts aren't working. Too often, this insight then immediately leads to conversations about how existing programmes could be improved, overlooking major structural flaws such as the fact that most leave business models off the table for change, fail to confront corporate power and cannot overcome the reality that industry actors are lobbying to undermine the very causes they also promote through CSR. There is no doubt that it may be possible to make small improvements by tinkering around the edges of MSIs or ethical certification schemes. But this won't correct the larger problem – that workers are largely unprotected and labour standards are dramatically underenforced in the contemporary global economy. Corporations may be undertaking efforts to improve and monitor labour standards in supply chains and fight problems like modern slavery. But by most measures, existing public and private initiatives are creating little concrete progress towards solving problems like forced labour, poverty wages, forced overtime and health and safety.

What should we make of the vast range of CSR initiatives to improve labour standards, and the compelling stories that companies tell us about these? In the conclusion of the book, I argue that we should understand corporate accounts of industry-led labour governance initiatives as fairytales. They are detailed, happy and compelling stories about magical mechanisms and events in faraway lands. But they are very unlikely to be true. And they are equally unlikely to become true in the future.

The longer that it takes for us to accept that, in spite of the undoubtedly good intentions of those involved in audit programmes, social benchmarks, ethical certification schemes and CSR programmes championed in corporate reports and company modern slavery statements are structurally flawed, the longer it will take to reclaim the regulatory space, power and tools that are necessary to promote credible and effective labour governance. The reality is that these corporate-led governance programmes are working just as they are intended: to improve corporate reputations, and to give us the impression that the problem of labour abuse in supply chains is slowly disappearing, so we don't fight for alternatives that would challenge the status quo of highly profitable business models that rely on labour exploitation.

Contemporary governance efforts are failing to protect the world's most vulnerable workers. And, the prospect of strengthening labour governance initiatives appears bleak. Powerful business interests are fighting to preserve the status quo of a retail-driven economy rife with labour exploitation by undermining the power of unions and workers. They are transforming public regulatory agencies and processes, and realigning the balance of power in civil society and in international organizations. These trends ultimately leave workers with less power, and fewer and less influential social forces fighting for their protection and rights. The key problem in engineering governance initiatives that will effectively strengthen and enforce labour standards in supply chains, therefore, is a political problem rather than a technical one.

Ultimately, as I argue in this book, labour exploitation cannot be eradicated by corporate fairytales. Since the start of this century, CSR has yielded few concrete improvements in terms of labour standards. As a growing body of evidence suggests, across several social and labour issue areas, there are serious gaps between CSR promises and actual outcomes. These gaps will only continue to grow as corporations continue to monopolize and seek to wrench ever more profit from their supply chains. CSR has failed.

In the absence of meaningful progress through industry-led solutions, a new approach is needed. Recognizing that corporations are actively creating and maintaining governance gaps regarding labour standards in supply chains should prompt policymakers, NGOs and unions to change their understanding of corporate accountability and liability. The growing evidence that core elements of global supply chains – including subcontracting, outsourcing, uneven value distribution, financialization and monopolization – fuels severe exploitation compels us to consider whether eradicating labour exploitation will require more profound change to contemporary business models than is generally considered in debates about supply chain governance. It also requires fresh and innovative thinking about how to protect workers in the twenty-first century. The critical challenges are how to transition from industry-driven to worker-driven solutions, and how to overhaul business models and the economy so that workers have more secure employment, living wages and the power to exert their fundamental rights – these are the factors that are well documented to protect workers from exploitation within supply chains.

2

Labour Exploitation in Global Supply Chains

Most countries outlawed slavery in the nineteenth century. Yet, the business of forced labour continues to boom in today's global economy. Workers subjected to severe labour exploitation grow, pluck and dry the tealeaves that we drink. They dye and spin the cotton that goes into the clothes that we wear. They produce the sugar and cocoa beans that get mixed into Hallowe'en and Valentine's Day candy. They take care of our children and grandparents and clean our houses, cars and hotel rooms.[1] Indeed, as much as we may despise the fact that workers are often treated harshly, cheated out of pay and face severe constraints on their mobility as companies compete to deliver us cheap goods and services, most of us still participate in the economy that depends on their exploitation.

In a world of unprecedented wealth and global mobility for billionaires and MNCs, it is shocking to realize that people are forced to work and are even violently abused by employers. This often happens in sectors that are highly lucrative. In the fishing industry, for instance, where exports were estimated to be worth US$143 billion in 2016,[2] the *Guardian* reported in 2014 that 'large numbers of men bought and sold like animals and held against their will on fishing boats off Thailand are integral to the production of prawns (commonly called shrimp in the US) sold in leading supermarkets around the world, including the top four global retailers: Walmart, Carrefour, Costco and Tesco'.[3] The investigation alleged that workers routinely faced 'horrific conditions, including 20-hour shifts, regular beatings, torture and execution-style killings'. Why are workers being so badly abused in global supply chains? And how are businesses getting away with it?

Activist campaigns and media reports tend to give the impression that forced labour can emerge anywhere and at any time – popping up in a Malaysian electronics factory one day, tomato fields in Italy the next, and your neighbour's backyard the day after that. They make it appear that workers become vulnerable to forced labour because they are simply unlucky, or because they have fallen prey to the tricks of violent and immoral employers or recruiters. A US Department of Homeland Security campaign against forced labour and trafficking cautions that, 'traffickers use force, fraud, or coercion to lure their victims and force them into labour or commercial sexual exploitation'.[4] Because antislavery activists tend to see forced labour as something that happens at the hands of individual perpetrators, many envision a solution in finding and locking up the bad guys. For instance, Kevin Bales and Ron Soodalter urge that 'the best defense against modern-day slavery is a vigilant public. Be a nosy neighbor.'[5]

Such explanations are superficial and misleading. Forced labour is, undoubtedly, a form of human rights abuse and, on one level, it is true that individuals are responsible for enacting it. But contrary to received wisdom, forced labour is not randomly occurring and cannot simply be attributed to individuals' moral shortcomings or greed; spying on our neighbours will do little to stop it.

Although often overlooked in the academic and civil society literatures on modern slavery, the reality is that individuals who perpetrate forced labour are embedded in larger structures. They are often part of businesses, which are connected to other businesses through supply chains, which sit within the global capitalist economy. We can only understand these dynamics – including why illegal labour exploitation has become such a predictable and stable feature of global supply chains – if we take the business dynamics of forced labour seriously.

Across many sectors and countries, forced labour is an endemic part of contemporary business models.[6] There are coherent patterns regarding the political economic circumstances that make forced labour viable and profitable, as well as the factors that render people vulnerable to it. There are also patterns regarding the perpetual failures of CSR programmes to prevent, detect and address forced labour in global supply chains. After all, the *Guardian*'s shrimp exposé wasn't about workers hidden away in some far-flung and highly informal corner of the global economy; rather, it focused on workers within an 'ethically certified' supply chain. Following the *Guardian* investigation, one of Aldi's suppliers pointed the finger at GlobalGAP, 'a non-governmental organization that sets voluntary standards for the certification of agricultural products around the globe',[7] which companies rely on to guard against these sorts of abuses (and associated brand damage) in their supply chain. To grasp why and how forced labour arises and why businesses so often get away with it, we need to understand how global supply chains are structured and why efforts to govern them fall short.

Two key trends, I argue in this chapter, are especially important for understanding why forced labour occurs in the contemporary economy: the business demand for forced labour; and the failure of CSR initiatives to curb this demand. Before exploring these, I first discuss the definition of forced labour used in this book.

What Is Forced Labour?

As mentioned in Chapter 1, governments and businesses tend to use the term 'modern slavery' as a catch-all to describe severe labour and sexual exploitation. I avoid the term in this book, except when referring to scholarship or initiatives that use it, because it is nebulous and inconsistently defined. I instead use the term 'forced labour', which is clearly defined within international law. The definition of forced labour was put forward by the ILO in the Forced Labour Convention of 1930, which reads: '"Forced or compulsory labor" shall mean all work or service which is exacted under menace of any penalty for its non-performance and for which the worker concerned does not offer himself voluntarily.'[8] This definition is widely recognized to encompass a variety of practices, including slavery, debt bondage, serfdom and human trafficking.[9] It excludes some state-imposed forms of forced labour, such as military conscription and prison labour.[10]

The ILO definition of forced labour is succinct, but has sometimes been interpreted in limited ways, two of which are especially important. First, it has been interpreted to exclude economic coercion – such as threat of destitution or starvation – as a valid form of compulsion rendering labour involuntary. While physical, psychological and financial coercion are deemed to be causes of involuntary labour, the ILO's Committee of Experts have made it clear that economic coercion is not. As they write:

> An external constraint or indirect coercion interfering with a worker's freedom to 'offer himself voluntarily' may result not only from an act of the authorities ... but also from an employer's practice ... However, the employer or the State are not accountable for all external constraints or indirect coercion existing in practice: for example, the need to work to earn one's living.[11]

The problem is that burgeoning empirical evidence suggests that many victims of forced labour remain in exploitative situations due to the fact that they have no viable economic alternative. In several recent studies of forced labour and overlapping forms of exploitation, including my own, workers have noted that staying in their job – no matter how exploitative, no matter how little they are paid, and no matter how badly they are treated by an employer – is preferable to the alternative, which could include starvation or death for them or their family members because they lack alternative means of obtaining subsistence. In some industries, such as agriculture, workers are routinely taking home earnings far beneath the poverty line and live in remote communities where there are highly limited options for earning money; in such situations, starvation is not hyperbole but, rather, a credible threat. As an MNC executive I recently interviewed admitted, when I asked what would happen if his company stopped sourcing cocoa from Cote d'Ivoire, 'people would starve, to be frank'.[12] My conceptualization of forced labour in this book thus recognizes that economic coercion is an important dynamic that can preclude a worker's exit from a labour situation in which their freedom is severely curtailed. As I substantiate later in the chapter, in contrast to media and activist depictions that suggest victims of forced labour are captured or physically constrained, in reality, workers often exhibit considerable agency in entering and remaining in coercive labour relations, which further complicates the ILO's conception of 'involuntariness'.[13] I seek to explore and highlight this complexity in this book.

The second limit of the ILO definition of forced labour relates to the tick-box approach that some researchers have taken to demarcating workers who could be considered victims of forced labour from those who are not. While it's easy to imagine in theory that workers fall into two categories (forced and not forced), in the real world it is often very difficult to pinpoint the threshold between what might be considered forced labour from what might be considered very exploitative labour that doesn't quite amount to forced labour using the ILO definition. For instance, in a large study I did of around 1,200 workers at the base of tea and cocoa supply chains, I found there to be considerable overlaps in the experiences and conditions of workers in both categories. I also found that individuals tend to move between the categories of forced labour and severely exploitative labour within their lives, and sometimes multiple times in a matter of years, making forced labour difficult to isolate.[14] By glossing over this complexity in an attempt to focus solely on forced labour, researchers miss key aspects of how forced labour arises and is experienced in the real world, and its grounding within more minor forms of labour exploitation.

The challenge of determining whether someone is or isn't a victim of forced labour is intensified by the reality that forced labour often comes about in mundane ways. It can take just one contingency – a child getting sick, a worker having a heart attack, a family growing and needing more food – to push a worker from regularized abuse into the more severe forms of exploitation known as forced labour. In such situations, a worker will frequently borrow money from whoever will lend it to them; if this is a manager or employer charging usurious interest rates, the worker is suddenly pushed into debt bondage or another form of forced labour.[15] The moment at which a worker becomes a victim of forced labour is often not characterized by remarkable and extreme circumstances like kidnapping, deception by traffickers, or the manipulation and exploitation of children, but, rather, by the quiet exchange of cash or signing of a contract. As such, it can be difficult to isolate.

Because the boundary between forced labour and other types of exploitation is porous, contingent and tricky to demarcate, in this book I am interested in forced labour as well as overlapping relations of exploitation. This includes a focus on how severe forms of exploitation such as forced labour interface with more minor forms of exploitation, such as wage violations, limits on freedom of association and freedom of movement, and gender-based violence. Scholars like Janie Chuang and Alessandra Mezzadri have persuasively argued that forced labour is the tip of the iceberg of exploitation faced by workers in the contemporary global economy, and that the overwhelming media and scholarly attention on it is normalizing and distracting us from far more widespread forms of labour exploitation.[16] This has been confirmed in my research. I adopt a wide-angle lens in this book, encompassing both the tip of the iceberg (forced labour) and the iceberg itself (more minor forms of exploitation), and am interested in their overlaps and intersections.

The Business Demand for Forced Labour

Forced labour, and labour exploitation more broadly, does not occur randomly or spontaneously in global supply chains. Rather, it is a logical outcome of the way that contemporary supply chains are set up. The global retail production model characterized by low-cost, high-volume and high-turnover goods triggers a predictable business demand for forced labour and exploitation. Pressure on supplier firms to produce goods for very low prices in short time windows combine with broader political dynamics such as low levels of labour law enforcement and unionization to create a business climate in which suppliers can use forced labour as a strategy to deliver orders and stay afloat in increasingly competitive markets. As business professor Andrew Crane has put it, forced labour has become a 'viable management practice for many enterprises, despite being universally condemned as unethical and indeed criminalized in most jurisdictions and under international law'.[17]

The specific business pressures that create a demand for forced labour vary across sector, type of business, supply chain structure, governance model, geography and institutional context.[18] Yet, looking across these, key dynamics at the heart of how global supply chains are currently set up persistently drive demand for labour exploitation.

Outsourcing

Most companies with global supply chains don't own the production facilities that make their goods. Walmart, for instance, sources from more than 100,000 direct suppliers.[19] These direct suppliers source parts and materials from other suppliers; for instance, an electronics supplier might buy graphic cards that go in a laptop computer from a business further down the chain, and so on, all the way down to the raw materials that go into the component parts. Most contemporary *product supply chains*, meaning 'the discrete stages that a product goes through to transform it from raw materials to a finished product', are made up of several tiers of production.[20] A single company's supply chain can involve hundreds of thousands of businesses. Nestlé, for instance, has more than 165,000 direct suppliers and sources ingredients from 'more than 13 million farmers across 86 countries around the world'.[21] According to the UN Conference on Trade and Development, around 80 per cent of global trade currently flows through supply chains coordinated by transnational corporations.[22]

In addition to subcontracting parts of the production process to other firms, suppliers may also rely on labour market intermediaries (often described as labour agencies or labour providers), which creates another form of outsourcing – outsourcing along the *labour supply chain*. The labour supply chain consists of 'the employment relationships that a worker goes through to arrive at the worksite'.[23] Some labour supply chains are quite short, where workers are directly recruited and employed by the business they are working for. However, sometimes these chains involve multiple tiers, made up of labour agencies, recruiters and others who might be supplying workers to producers. As Apple described of their labour supply chain:

Some of our suppliers work with third-party labour agencies to hire contract workers from countries such as the Philippines, Thailand, Indonesia, and Vietnam. These agencies, in turn, may work through multiple sub-agencies: in the hiring country, the workers' home country, and, in some cases, all the way back to the workers' home village.[24]

As I discuss further in Chapter 4, Apple recently acknowledged that heavy subcontracting along its labour supply chain was leading to 'bonded servitude' for some workers, since intermediaries often charged them predatory fees; so Apple now requires suppliers to cover recruitment costs.[25]

Outsourcing along both product and labour supply chains fragments responsibility for workers and makes it challenging for social auditors, civil society organizations and labour inspectors to monitor labour standards. The complexity and lack of traceability it introduces makes it easy for businesses to get away with abuse because it's hard to follow products and identify which workers and businesses are associated with them. In addition, outsourcing legally distances large and powerful businesses from suppliers' business practices and shields them from legal liability and reputational damage. Given these advantages for companies, it is perhaps unsurprising that, as the *Financial Times* describes it, 'outsourcing of non-core business has become a key trend of the past half century and is being pursued with renewed vigour in the 21st century'.[26]

This trend is not advantageous for workers. Outsourcing has put considerable pressure on labour standards and is closely correlated to the worst forms of exploitation. Research across diverse industries, including electronics, fishing, agriculture, garments and construction, suggests that forced labour tends to occur in outsourced portions of supply chains.[27] For instance, Nicola Phillips and Leonardo Sakamoto conducted a large study of forced labour in Brazil, which includes statistical analysis of data involving 'more than 21,000 workers released from conditions defined as "slave labour" between 2003 and 2009', as well as on-the-ground investigations of garment and agricultural supply chains that found that forced labour tends 'to occur in those parts of the production process that are associated with outsourcing practices'. The study found that 'outsourced activities such as sugar cane, soybean, cotton or coal (and also in urban sectors such as garments), are routinely associated with a higher incidence of "slave labour"'.[28] As the study documents, outsourcing and labour exploitation go hand in hand.

This is confirmed by quantitative data. For instance, Supplier Ethical Data Exchange (Sedex), an organization that facilitates the sharing of sourcing data between companies,[29] has studied more than ten years of its own data to assess where risks of noncompliance, including forced labour, are most likely to take place. Analysts found these to be concentrated in the lower tiers of the supply chain, with 18 per cent more incidence of labour standards noncompliance in Tier 2 and 27 per cent more in Tier 3. They also found that the nature of the problems become worse in the outsourced lower rungs of production.[30]

Similar links between outsourcing and forced labour have been made along labour supply chains, especially where intermediaries are providing labour at or around a minimum wage.[31] Where labour supply chains are long and complex, and especially where labour market intermediaries are charging fees to workers for their services – such as a recruitment or job-finding fee, or for housing or transportation – workers are vulnerable to exploitation, including debt bondage, restrictions on mobility, illegal wage deductions, predatory fees and threats of penalty. In one study of the UK food, construction and cannabis industries, which I conducted along with my colleagues Jean Allain, Andrew Crane, and Laya Behbahani, we found that forced labour frequently enters into supply chains through informal subcontracting amongst labour market intermediaries.[32] Research across several industries including the food, construction, tourism and garment industries and domestic work in many parts of the world points to similar conclusions.[33]

Why exactly does outsourcing open the door to forced labour in supply chains? Two reasons are especially important. In the first case, outsourcing is common in industries with high price competition between firms, where there are often thin profit margins along the lower portions of the supply chain. In these industries, businesses face severe pressure to keep their labour costs low, which gives rise to informal, temporary and contract work rather than permanent jobs. These jobs tend to come with low wages, lacking job security, limited to no health care, pension or other benefits, and workers frequently face obstacles to freedom of association. All these factors can increase worker vulnerability to exploitation.

In the second and overlapping case, it's often easier for workers provided through intermediaries to be exploited, as they tend to be overlooked by auditors and inspectors. Such workers are not included within the records of the business holding the supply contract, and they are also often moved around from job to job, which makes it hard to monitor and enforce labour standards. While outsourcing along the labour supply chain makes it easier for the large top-tier suppliers to meet their contractual obligations, they are able to do so by transferring risk and liability further down the supply chain. This opens the door to exploitation.

Such dynamics are not coincidental, but rather have come about since the late twentieth century as large companies at the helm of supply chains have sought to free themselves of the costs and responsibility of directly employing workers.[34] As David Weil explains in his book *The Fissured Workplace*: 'As major companies have consciously invested in building brands and devoted customers as the cornerstone of their business strategy, they have also shed their role as the direct employer of the people responsible for providing those products and services.'[35] As they have done so, they have put heavy pressure on the businesses that have assumed responsibility for directly employing people. It's no wonder that when recruiters and other intermediaries come knocking and promise to take the tasks of locating, recruiting and employing workers off the hands of employers – for free – employers are happy to give it a try, as I document in Chapter 4.

Fissuring workplaces increases coercion in the labour market and introduces major barriers to collective action. It makes unionization much more difficult. And it often lowers the wage floor by introducing temporary migrant workers who are willing to accept less money and worse conditions, who can replace permanent workers at a moment's notice. By curtailing workers' power to resist unfair conditions, fissuring makes it much harder for workers to come forward in the face of exploitation.

Irresponsible Sourcing Practices

Because the companies at the top of global supply chains don't manufacture goods directly, they use commercial contracts to source goods from their suppliers. Buyers for large companies wield tremendous power and control over the terms of contract and sale, especially in industries and geographic settings where there are a small number of buyers relative to suppliers. Buyers can simply switch suppliers – or even countries – if they cannot get the prices and commercial requirements they want, which makes them hard to negotiate with.[36] They use their power to impose tight production windows, steep penalties for delays and quality issues, low prices and favourable payment terms. These sourcing practices drive the business demand for forced labour and exploitation. It doesn't take a highly paid CSR consultant to figure out that suppliers typically cannot meet the requirements of buyer contracts without breaking laws and standards, including those that protect workers' legal rights, unless they simply outsource that burden further down the chain.

Lacking the commercial power to secure more favourable terms, suppliers often agree to contracts that are challenging or even impossible to fulfil without exploiting workers. Common forms of exploitation in supply chains today include: illegal wage deductions or nonpayment of wages; requiring workers to meet high mandatory quotas; making them work compulsory overtime, sometimes even multiple shifts in a row; physical or verbal abuse or discipline, and gender-based violence; harassment, intimidation and repression of freedom of association; and constraints on freedom of movement.[37] In the worst cases, as suppliers race to meet the contractual conditions imposed by buyers and deliver cheap goods on time and cope with changes – such as late amendments to order size and specifications – they turn to forced labour.

There is clear evidence of this in the garment industry, where production has been sped up in recent years by the rise of fast fashion. A decade ago, it would take about six months for runway fashions to make it onto store shelves. Retail stores typically planned their merchandise offerings around four seasons. However, today retailers have up to 'a 52 seasons cycle, with a new product line every week'.[38] Irresponsible sourcing practices associated with fast fashion – such as time and cost pressures, unstable orders, shrinking quantities, and the shifting of commercial risk onto suppliers – are fuelling the presence of child and forced labour in supply chains.[39] To name just one of dozens of examples, the BBC reported in 2016 that child refugees from Syria were making clothes in Turkey for British brands Marks & Spencer and ASOS; these workers complained of being exposed to hazardous chemicals, poor working conditions and very low wages.[40] Within the UK, a study of Leicester's garment industry found 'evidence of serious and endemic labour rights abuse',[41] with workers earning around £3 an hour, less than half of the national minimum wage. Workers complained of verbal abuse, threats, humiliation and inadequate health and safety standards as they worked long hours to meet low-cost orders with extremely tight production windows.[42] Even a 2018 article in *Vogue* magazine identifies fashion as 'one of five key industries implicated in modern slavery'.[43] The industry's illegal labour practices are inextricably linked to its business model.

In addition to introducing risks of forced labour directly within businesses, irresponsible sourcing practices open the door to risks of forced labour elsewhere along the supply chain. A good example of this is suppliers' use of unauthorized subcontracting. Indeed, as an attempt to cope with growing demands and falling prices from buyers, top-tier suppliers sometimes subcontract parts of their orders to other firms. These factories – which are sometimes referred to as shadow factories – are often unregistered and not listed with the government or trade associations. Labour exploitation and forced labour form a core part of their business model. Workers within them are 'especially vulnerable because they are invisible to regulators and their employers operate on such slim margins that they cannot invest in even basic safety equipment or procedures'.[44] Shadow factories are not formally part of a buyer's supply chain, so they remain off the radar of auditors, inspectors and MNCs.

One MNC executive I interviewed in 2017 described how garment companies found evidence of unauthorized subcontracting amidst the Rana Plaza disaster described in Chapter 1. As he explained:

In the first days [after the disaster] the CEO or founder of Inditex [which owns Zara] wrote to every employee and said don't worry, none of the garments that we make were made in that factory. Two weeks later he had to write and apologize to all of the employees because journalists had been going through the rubble and found t-shirts with Zara labels. No part of Inditex was dealing with the company that owned Rana Plaza.

It was a case of a supplier subcontracting to a supplier they didn't know.[45]

Workers within shadow factories now comprise sizable portions of the labour force in some industries and parts of the world. A 2015 study of key garment industry production regions of Bangladesh, for instance, found that '32% of the 479 factories surveyed were informal subcontractors; 91% of informal factories produced at least partly for export'.[46] In addition to illegally subcontracting to shadow factories, suppliers also engage in unauthorized subcontracting directly with informal and unregulated workers, such as home workers and those engaged through platform sourcing, who are often hired for short tasks and paid in cash.[47]

In short, while companies at the top of global supply chains may not be directly responsible for exploiting workers in their supply chain, they bear sizable responsibility for creating a business demand for forced labour and exploitation further down the supply chain. Through irresponsible sourcing practices, they leverage their massive market power to maintain and grow their profit margins, while forcing suppliers to absorb shifts in production costs and falling prices. Then, in spite of the massive profits they generate through these practices, they often pay suppliers late, pay them less than expected and impose steep penalties, such as for quality deficiencies. In 2016, for instance, UK retailer Tesco was found, by the supermarket ombudsman, to have 'knowingly delayed paying money to suppliers in order to improve its own financial position'.[48] These commercial practices have devastating impacts on labour standards.

As will be explored further in Chapter 3, across many goods and commodities there is now substantial evidence that labour costs have fallen so low that producers are clearly exploiting workers. For instance, current affairs magazine *Maclean's* investigated the value distribution attached to a shirt sold in stores for CAD$14 and reported that retailers paid CAD$5.67 for it, while the total value that went to workers was only CAD$0.12.[49] When suppliers and workers receive such a low share of the value attached to goods, labour exploitation isn't optional; it becomes a necessity. As one South African apple farm owner put it: 'The only ham left in the sandwich is our labour costs. If they [the buyers] squeeze us, it's the only place where we can squeeze.'[50] The harsh reality is that companies are sourcing goods at costs too low to allow suppliers to obey laws, including those stipulating a minimum wage, which creates a predictable demand for labour exploitation in supply chains.

A Supply of Vulnerable Workers

On its own, the growing business demand for forced labour doesn't in itself give rise to exploitation. For labour exploitation to thrive, as it currently does in the global economy, business demand must intersect with a supply of workers who are poor, lacking in state and union protections, and facing constraints on their ability to exert rights, such that they find it challenging to contest their conditions or find better, more decent work. Over recent decades, growing business demand for forced labour has been paralleled by the rise of a highly vulnerable workforce. Across many countries and sectors, workers often have little choice but to take on risky and exploitative work because it's the only way to make a living. Indeed, as business actors and political elites have reformed the rules of the global economy to bolster the profitability of business over recent decades, they have also created a sizable workforce vulnerable to forced labour. While the characteristics of this workforce vary across sector and geography, some broad trends are revealing.

According to the ILO, more than 201 million people in the global economy were unemployed in 2017.[51] That year, 42 per cent of the overall labour force – 1.4 billion people in the global economy – were in 'vulnerable employment', meaning they were 'subject to high levels of precariousness' and with limited or no access to social protection schemes.[52] Only a quarter of workers in the global economy were on permanent contracts, with 75 per cent employed on 'temporary or short-term contracts, working informally often without any contract, are self-employed or are in unpaid family jobs'.[53] Worldwide, the UN estimates that more than 218 million children are working, with large swathes caught in 'hazardous work', defined as tasks that jeopardize the child's physical or mental well-being.[54]

Across many countries and sectors, wages have persistently declined in recent decades, even in the formal economy. In 2013, over half the workforce within the emerging economy members of the G20 continued to live around or below the poverty line.[55] Working poverty rates (which refer to those living on less than US$3.10 per day) are alarmingly high in some parts of the world. In sub-Saharan Africa, for instance, nearly two-thirds of workers are in working poverty, as are nearly half of the workers in southern Asia.[56] Working poverty isn't just a feature of labour markets across the global South, but of the global North, too. For instance, a 2015 UK study of workers in London found that the city's 'working poor' had increased by 70 per cent over the previous decade.[57] While poverty is still too often imagined to stem from a lack of success in finding employment, in fact, it is now common even for workers in lucrative supply chains to be earning well below the poverty line. In a study I conducted of more than 1,200 tea and cocoa workers in 2016–19, for instance, I found that tea workers were earning as little as 25 per cent of the poverty line amount (US$3.20 per day), while cocoa workers' wages were around 30 per cent of the poverty line amount (US$3.20 per day).[58]

Poverty, as well as labour market disadvantage and discrimination, plays out along lines of gender, race, caste, class, migration status, sexuality and other individual-level factors. A wide body of evidence shows that women and girls, indigenous people, migrants, ethnic minorities and other socially, politically and economically marginalized groups are disproportionately subject to the worst forms of labour exploitation.[59] One of the thousands of possible examples, a report by workers' rights organizations entitled *Gender Based Violence in the H&M Garment Supply Chain*, documents the unequal violence encountered by women garment workers in H&M supplier factories across Bangladesh, Cambodia and India.[60] It found that factory owners have a preference for women workers, who then face severe and overlapping forms of exploitation, including physical violence and abuse; sexual harassment; coercion, threats and retaliation; verbal abuse; and restrictions on freedom of movement and association. One worker describes how her gender makes it easier for employers to get away with these illegal practices: 'They can't do the same thing to a man. The manager, supervisor, floor-in-charge, master – if they go after a man, they fear being beaten by them after work.'[61] This example is characteristic of life within global supply chains, where businesses seek out workforces that they hope will be acquiescent and won't have a strong understanding of their rights or the social power to resist exploitation.

As will be discussed further in Chapter 4, pools of vulnerable people are not just found in the private economy, but in state-sponsored programmes as well. Over recent decades, many countries have tightened restrictions on immigration. For unskilled workers in particular, 'guestworker' programmes are increasingly the only way of working legally in richer countries. For instance, in the US, the H-2A visa programme allows seasonal agricultural workers to enter the country for one year at a time, renewable for up to three years. The number of workers in this programme has risen steadily, from 31,892 in 2005 to 134,368 in 2016.[62] But such programmes often leave workers open to abuse; according to the US National Guestworker Alliance, guestworkers are frequently unable to change employers, are subjected to coercion rooted in their immigration status (such as threats to call immigration or the police) and to gender-based violence and blacklisting as well as threats of these, and face constraints on their ability to exert rights.[63]

Labour unions are a crucial source of support and power for workers. However, over recent decades, union membership has declined sharply in dozens of countries around the world, leaving workers with less ability to fight for better working conditions, push for enforcement of existing labour laws, and access justice in cases where exploitation has taken place. A recent ILO study of unions across 48 countries found an average drop of 4.6 per cent between 2008 and 2013.[64] In some countries, the drops are far more dramatic. In the Russian Federation, for instance, trade union rate density went from 43.7 per cent in 2006 to 30.5 per cent in 2015. In Indonesia, rates dropped from 36.4 per cent in 2001 to 7 per cent in 2012.[65] Of course, even where unions are present, workers can still face barriers to collective association and exertion of rights. And a major problem across sectors and states is that workers who complain about abuse face retaliation from their employers.

Many states have slashed labour protections and labour law enforcement in recent decades, leaving workers even further unprotected. In most countries, the budget and size of labour inspectorates has been reduced. Overstretched inspectorates are struggling to keep up with formal businesses, never mind patrol the vast informal sectors where forced labour is most common. Inspectors are often poorly paid and, like private social auditors, are vulnerable to corruption. Further, where businesses are caught violating standards, the consequences are often negligible. In Bangladesh, for instance, the penalty for violating the labour code is only US$325.[66] In the absence of robust state protections, it is more difficult for workers to report exploitation, and easier for businesses to perpetrate it with impunity. And the impact of laws and regulations is further undermined by the fact that workers frequently cannot exert rights because they aren't adequately protected from retaliation.

The supply of workers vulnerable to exploitation has arisen from complex political economy dynamics, which have unfolded as elites have re-regulated the global capitalist economy in ways that have allowed MNCs to pile up vast sums of money and seize tremendous profit and power.[67] We need to understand these dynamics, and how they intersect with the business demand for forced labour to grasp the patterns of labour exploitation in supply chains.

Designed to Fail

In the face of rising public and policy concern about the social costs of global supply chains, since the start of this century there has been an explosion of industry and civil society initiatives to improve business practices, combat modern slavery and set and enforce private labour standards. These include multistakeholder initiatives like the International Cocoa Initiative and Forest Stewardship Council; individual company CSR initiatives, including responsible sourcing policies and supplier codes of conduct; ethical certification schemes like Rainforest Alliance and Fairtrade; and bilateral partnerships between NGOs and corporations.

There is some evidence that these initiatives can have incremental positive effects, nudging towards improvements in health and safety or helping to fund schools or medical care for workers and their children. But a growing body of research suggests that, overall, industry-led labour governance initiatives are failing to make meaningful progress towards major challenges like raising wages and detecting, eradicating and preventing forced labour in global supply chains. The reasons for this are complex and vary across sector and type of initiative, as is explored throughout this book. Here, I'd like to highlight just one key reason that so many initiatives fall short: there is a mismatch between the design of these initiatives and the actual pattern of forced labour in global supply chains.

Take ethical auditing, the tool that companies purport enables them to identify, correct and solve social problems in their supply chains. Ethical auditors are hired and paid for by MNCs (or sometimes, by their suppliers) to verify compliance with MNCs' supplier code of conduct and other voluntary standards. These typically include standards prohibiting the use of forced and child labour, requiring that suppliers pay locally mandated minimum wages, and uphold worker health and safety. For instance, Walmart notes that their audits seek to verify that, amongst other things, 'workers are properly paid for the work they do; labour is voluntary; facilities comply with employment age laws and standards; working hours are not excessive and are consistent with local laws and standards'.[68]

Given the steep decline of state-based labour inspection, social auditors now comprise the main group of people monitoring labour standards in global supply chains. Yet, most companies only audit a portion of their Tier 1 suppliers. The Coca-Cola Company, for instance, notes in its 2016 *Modern Slavery Statement* that it has 3,500 direct suppliers that 'are subject to potential audit', and claims in its *Human Rights Report 2016–2017* that it completed 2,789 audits in that same year.[69] In other words, they are auditing only a portion of their suppliers. As I elaborate in Chapter 5, by focusing on Tier 1 suppliers, companies tend to exclude subcontractors and labour market intermediaries further down the supply chain, as well as shadow factories, which are far more likely to use forced labour.

In the last couple of years, some companies have begun to acknowledge the limits of this approach and that audit design isn't fit for the purpose of tackling forced labour. British retailer Tesco, which now recognizes the limits of this approach, describes the problem as follows:

Historically we sought to address human rights issues primarily through an ethical audit programme of our direct supply base. However, this approach was limited, both because audits do not always identify hidden or systemic issues such as modern slavery, and because the most serious risks of human rights abuses tend to occur further down the supply chain.[70]

Yet, most companies are not as open or reflective about the limits of this approach and it remains standard across several industries. This leaves the businesses most likely to use forced labour in global supply chains uninspected, and the most vulnerable workers in supply chains beyond the pathway of audits. As one business actor described the gaps in the social auditing regime: 'I'm going to go audit the crap out of your coop coffee bean company to make sure you're actually paying the farmers. Who checks to see if the farmer is paying the pickers? Nobody!'[71]

Ethical certification schemes similarly exclude vulnerable workers within supply chains. For instance, in the cocoa industry, certification schemes tend to focus on working conditions and rights for cocoa farmers. Yet, the most vulnerable workers at the base of the supply chain – including seasonal, temporary, informal and contract workers – are not covered by the standards. As a representative of one ethical certification scheme explained to me: 'Hired labour of smallholders is still an area we can't reach … we don't have a system for that.'[72] By creating loopholes around the most vulnerable workers, many ethical certification schemes effectively disclaim responsibility for the people in global supply chains most likely to be subjected to forced labour.

Industry antislavery initiatives tend to skirt around and cover up the portions of the supply chain where the worst abuses are likely to be found. These initiatives may be doing some good, but they are also reinforcing the endemic business demand for forced labour in supply chains by giving the impression that labour standards are being effectively and independently monitored and enforced. In fact, a careful reading of the fine print around these programmes – such as in companies' UK modern slavery statements – reveals that this is happening only in highly limited and superficial ways. That CSR initiatives are championed as a primary solution to the problem of labour exploitation, yet continuously fall short and are never seriously reformed, is an important dimension of why forced labour is an endemic problem in global supply chains.

The Global Business of Forced Labour

Forced labour does not occur randomly within global supply chains. Rather, it is a logical outcome of how those supply chains are set up, and of the fast-paced, low-cost global retail economy more generally. Certain types of businesses have a coherent and stable demand for forced labour and exploitation, driven by dynamics at the heart of global supply chains, such as uneven value distribution, unstable demand, short lead times and razor-sharp profit margins. The pressure on top tier suppliers to provide orders on time, at cost, and while adhering to MNCs' codes of conduct that prohibit illegal labour practices, has driven outsourcing and a displacement of bad practice further down product and labour supply chains.

Just as there is a predictable business demand for forced labour, so too do CSR initiatives predictably fail to detect and address the issue. There is a serious disjuncture between the patterns of labour exploitation in global supply chains and the design and enforcement patterns of CSR initiatives like social auditing and ethical certi-fication. These initiatives frequently avoid the portions of supply chains where the worst forms of exploitation are known to manifest and thrive. It is therefore unsur-prising that many fail to yield concrete improvements with respect to their aims of combatting modern slavery and protecting workers from exploitation. By most measures, over the last two decades CSR initiatives have created little concrete progress towards solving problems like forced labour, poverty wages, forced overtime and dangerously lacking measures to protect health and safety.

Understanding the political economy dynamics that surround forced labour in supply chains is vital if we are to understand why prevailing initiatives are failing to tackle it. The changing nature and organization of the corporations that are the architects of global supply chain, and their two-faced stance both as champions and defeaters of governance initiatives to protect workers, form a big part of the story.

3

Corporate Power and the State

In 2018, two companies crossed the once unimaginable threshold of being worth a trillion dollars in market value: Apple and Amazon.[1] Microsoft passed the mark a few months later, becoming the third company to join the $1,000,000,000,000 club.[2] To depict how astonishing a figure a trillion dollars is, an infographic in the *New York Times* showed that it would take combining 111 other large companies – including Gap, Nordstrom, Ralph Lauren, Western Union, Viacom, Mattel and Macy's – to reach Apple's market value.[3]

The swelling ranks of the trillion-dollar club reflects the rise of powerful 'superstar' companies and 'mega-firms'. These terms are frequently invoked as nicer, less politicized ways of describing corporate monopolies. Indeed, the term monopoly is often avoided, perhaps because it has a negative connotation. Very large corporations and monopoly corporations have long been seen as a threat to democracy, ordinary people, consumers and small businesses. The term conjures up images of US President Franklin D. Roosevelt's quest in the 1930s to break up powerful corporations and banks that 'had concentrated into their own hands an almost complete control' of the economy, such that the US had become a country in which 'opportunity was limited by monopoly'.[4] Indeed, amidst the economic depression of the 1930s, the US government began to expend considerable effort breaking up and limiting the power of large corporations.

In the view of both President Roosevelt and, later, President Harry Truman, monopolies eroded democracy, limited opportunities for small business and undermined the livelihoods of workers and farmers. Truman went so far as to claim that monopolies caused the economy to 'fall under the control of a few dominant economic groups whose powers will be so great that they will be a challenge to democratic institutions'.[5] From Roosevelt to Eisenhower, US presidential administrations blocked mergers and enacted antitrust and antimonopoly legislation to limit the power of corporations. But by the 1970s, the political economic climate of the country had changed and the concern about monopolies had disappeared from the presidential agenda[6] – as they had in many countries across the world.

Given the history of scorn towards large corporations in the US and elsewhere, it's not surprising that terms like monopoly and trust are less commonly used today than in earlier eras of capitalism. But the reality is that massive, undemocratic and difficult to govern corporations are back. Across a range of industries, corporate consolidation and staggering growth rates have given rise to concentrations of market share and power, such that the world economy is commanded by an ever-smaller number of increasingly powerful corporate giants. Economists, policymakers and civil society organizations are concerned about their influence on wealth and income inequality, economic stability, consumer prices and growth. Even the IMF – which is hardly an outspoken critic of big business – has sounded an alarm that corporate monopolization is adversely influencing macroeconomic outcomes.[7] Columnist David Leonhardt aptly summarized the growing unease: 'The new corporate behemoths have been very good for their executives and largest shareholders – and bad for almost everyone else.'[8]

As I argue in this chapter, these trends, and the changing nature and organization of MNCs more broadly, hold profound and often overlooked implications for labour standards and efforts to govern and improve them. I first provide an overview of the changing nature of MNCs, focusing on the financialization of corporations, corporate growth and the rise of monopolies, and the implications of these trends for labour standards. I then analyse MNCs' political behaviour in the arena of modern slavery governance, arguing that companies are becoming increasingly proactive in initiating and shaping public policy at the national level and globally. I conclude by arguing that the deepening political power of corporations is allowing them to leverage strategic control over supply chain governance initiatives, especially those intended to bolster labour rights and reduce exploitation. As MNCs stave off more radical reforms on corporate production activities, they are undermining and co-opting civil society efforts to increase corporate liability and accountability for the worst forms of labour exploitation.

The Contemporary MNC

In campaigns to hold corporations accountable for labour exploitation in global supply chains, activists often focus on brands. For instance, a campaign targeted at the tea industry might focus on brands like Tazo, Lipton, PG Tips and Pure Leaf. These brands are known to and loved by consumers, so activists figure that linking them to bad labour practices will damage companies' reputation and sales. However, consumers and activists tend to overlook one crucial change that has occurred since brand activism gained traction in the 1990s: today, these tea brands are all owned by the same MNC. Indeed, consumer goods conglomerate Unilever owns several tea brands, including all those named above, along with 400 other brands used by 2.5 billion people worldwide.[9] Long gone are the days that corporations – and their owners and labour practices – could be differentiated according to the brand names we see on the grocery store shelf.

Monopolization, and the growth and concentration of corporate power more generally, hold profound implications for labour standards and activist strategy to improve them. For instance, organized boycotts have been a tool of activists trying to shame companies into better practice for the better part of two centuries. But if the vast majority of brands are now owned by a small handful of MNCs with the same business model, whose behaviour is steered by a common group of shareholders and investors, will boycotts still be effective? Probably not, at least not if activist strategies fail to account for the ways that corporations have changed in recent decades. We need to get a grip on the nature and structure of contemporary MNCs because they are a key part of the story of why labour governance is failing, and the corporate form holds important implications for how corporations can be held accountable for labour practices within their supply chains.

Three key trends are especially important for understanding the changing nature of MNCs: corporate growth, including the rise of monopolies, the financialization of corporations, and the implications of these for labour standards.

Corporate growth and the new monopolies

Corporations have grown over recent decades. Their scale and profits now rival the GDPs of rich countries and are continuously expanding. Walmart's total revenue in 2018 was US$514.4 billion, an increase of 3 per cent from the previous year, and comparable to the GDP of Sweden. Walmart US sales grew 3.6 per cent that year, 'the highest annual growth rate in a decade'.[10] Food and drink company Nestlé exceeded US$90 billion in revenue in 2017, and is

now on track to increase its 'operating profit margin to
between 17.5% and 18.5% by 2020, up from 16.0%
in 2016'.[11] Nike's 2018 letter to shareholders celebrates
its 'unrivaled scale and scope', noting that its revenues
grew 6 per cent to US$36.4 billion.[12] Amazon went from
having 1.5 million customers in 1997 to shipping 5 billion
items with its Amazon Prime service alone in 2017.[13] The
world's largest corporations are behemoths and every year
they expand.

Single corporations now employ millions of people.
Walmart, for instance, employed approximately 2.3 million
people in 2018, a workforce that exceeds the size of the
entire population of Paris.[14] Hon Hai Precision Industry
Co. – the electronics firm also known as Foxconn – had
1.2 million workers in 2015, more than if they employed
every person living in Brussels.[15] In 2016, the Big Four
accounting firms – Deloitte, Ernst Young (EY), KPMG
and PricewaterhouseCoopers (PwC) – employed more
than 887,800 employees spread across 150 countries,
a workforce roughly the size of the population of San
Francisco.[16] In addition to having massive workforces,
today's MNCs also shape employment conditions and
livelihoods for hundreds of millions of people in their
global supply chains.

One of the ways that companies have grown so large has
been as a result of mergers and acquisitions, or corporate
or asset consolidation achieved through various types
of financial transactions. Some of the largest mergers in
recent years have been: the US$45 billion deal that merged
two food companies, H. J. Heinz Co. and The Kraft Foods
Group, into The Kraft Heinz Company;[17] the US$66 billion
deal that merged health and agricultural firms Bayer and
Monsanto;[18] The Walt Disney Company's US$71.3 billion
acquisition of 21st Century Fox;[19] chemical companies
Dow and Dupont and Amazon's purchase of high-end
grocery chain Whole Foods for US$13.7 billion.[20] Mergers
and acquisitions are one way that companies can spend the
vast profits and large sums of money they are stockpiling.

Apple, for instance, had US$245 billion in cash on hand in early 2019.[21]

As companies have grown, they have commanded larger shares of their respective markets. In most sectors, just a handful of corporations now control vast swathes of commerce. For instance, in the chemical sector, just four firms – ChemChina-Syngenta, BASF, Bayer-Monsanto and DowDuPont – hold over 60 per cent of the global market.[22] Amazon alone has around 50 per cent of the US e-retail market, and the smartphone, cloud computing and social media markets are overwhelmingly dominated by what *Forbes* calls the 'technology oligarchy', comprising Apple, Google, Microsoft and Facebook.[23] In 2012, just four companies accounted for 93.7 per cent of soda production, with The Coca-Cola Company and PepsiCo accounting for close to 75 per cent of that market.[24] According to one estimate, two-thirds of industries – not including tech industries – within the US became more concentrated between 1997 and 2012.[25] From tyres to telecoms, consumers around the world are now dependent on a few very large companies to produce their goods and provide their services. As commerce has become more centralized, the distribution of wealth and power in the global economy has been altered in profound ways.

For instance, commanding high levels of market share gives companies sizable control over the conditions under which goods are made and sold. As the number of firms within any given sector shrinks, and the sector itself becomes larger, each firm has more power and discretion, such as over labour and environmental standards, prices, and terms and conditions for suppliers and employees. Sometimes, corporations' market power spans several different industries, workforces and aspects of our lives. For instance, as legal scholar Lina Khan has described Amazon: 'In addition to being a retailer, it is now a marketing platform, a delivery and logistics network, a payment service, a credit lender, an auction house, a major book publisher, a producer of television and films, a fashion designer, a hardware manufacturer, and a leading host of cloud server space.'[26] As such, Amazon – like many monopoly companies – wields vast control over a range of industries within the global economy.

Corporate giants tend to insulate themselves from competitive pressures. As Khan has argued, reflecting on Amazon's business model – which, she argues, relies on predatory pricing tactics to achieve market dominance – 'Amazon's business strategies and current market dominance pose anticompetitive concerns'.[27] In a circular logic, being large and commanding a large market share often allows companies to increase their revenues (in part, because monopolization means there is often less price competition and companies take more in profits), and then, to grow even bigger. For instance, the *Economist* estimated in 2016 that, although the number of publicly listed companies in the US shrank between 1997 and 2013 from 6,797 to 3,485, average profits and revenues of the remaining companies grew nearly threefold.[28]

These are all important signs that the role of MNCs in the global economy is evolving. While, in 1970, experts estimate there were only 7,000 global corporations, there are now more than 100,000, with nearly 900,000 foreign affiliates.[29] Big companies have become bigger. Corporate ownership has been consolidated, driven by an increasingly powerful financial sector, including the rise of index funds controlled by huge asset management companies BlackRock, Vanguard and State Street.[30] Companies are under more pressure than ever to generate quarterly profits for shareholders. And far from carrying forward earlier US presidents' efforts to control and break up MNCs, governments are fuelling these trends as they pass regulations that redraw the relationship between corporations and states and privilege corporate rights over workers' rights within trade and investment agreements, national policy and dwindling labour law enforcement budgets.

While rarely discussed within academic or policy literatures on labour standards, financial actors and dynamics have been a driving force behind these trends. They are contributing to the pressures on companies to bring in short-term profits, grow constantly and swallow up competitors.

The financialization of the firm

Scholars of political economy, business and economics have, since the early 2000s, been documenting the impact of 'financialization' within the global economy and on global supply chains.[31] Global governance professors Jennifer Clapp and S. Ryan Isakson describe financialization as 'a process in which financial actors and financially driven motivation have taken a larger role in society, across all sectors in the economy'.[32] The financialization of corporations and supply chains is reconfiguring how they operate in several important ways.[33] Three types of financialization are especially relevant to our interests in changing patterns of MNC ownership and profitability and their implications for labour standards: the rise of new financial actors; the increasing prominence given to shareholder maximization; and MNCs' rising profits from financial assets, rather than productive activity.

In the first case, new financial actors – and especially asset management firms like BlackRock, Vanguard, State Street, Capital Group and Fidelity – are dramatically reconfiguring ownership patterns of MNCs. The University of Amsterdam's CORPNET research group has spent several years analysing the role of these firms as well as the changing patterns of corporate control and ownership more broadly.[34] They've found that financial investors are increasingly shifting money into 'passively managed index funds' which 'replicate established stock indexes' but are cheaper, and which minimize investor fees.[35] As CORPNET principal investigator Eelke Heemskerk and colleague Jan Fichtner describe, 'from 2006 to mid-2017 almost US$2.7 trillion has flown out of actively managed equity funds globally, while over US$2.6 trillion has flown into index equity funds'.[36] The Big Three large asset managers – BlackRock, Vanguard and State Street – now manage 90 per cent of all assets under management in passive equity funds.[37] These investors have a growing ownership stake in MNCs, which allows them to influence their governance and business strategies, often with limited public oversight.[38]

The CORPNET research group has found that passive asset managers contribute to decisions designed to achieve short-term financial gains amongst publicly listed firms. For instance, CORPNET researchers studied the Big Three's decision-making in relation to 17 stock indexes from nine countries, focusing on share buybacks (which deliver immediate payoffs to shareholders, and are often enacted instead of measures that would increase the long-term value of the company, such as research and development) and decisions about mergers and acquisitions. They found that the Big Three often vote in favour of short-term proposals.[39] In other words, the accelerating trend of common ownership of MNCs by passive asset management firms is one of several forces pushing them towards prioritizing short-term financial gain and expansion.

The shift towards common ownership highlights an important change in the role and interests of stockholders. While corporations are 'traditionally thought of as having unique owners that try as hard as they can to drive up their market share and profits at the loss of their competitors', in the case of common ownership, a firm is 'controlled by shareholders who also own that firms' competitors'.[40] Thus, rather than trying to enhance the success of say, Tyson Foods Inc over Archer-Daniel-Midlands Co., investors in Blackrock's index fund COW (which has funds in both of these companies, amongst others) try to 'maximize the value of their entire portfolio – encompassing competing firms in the same industries – rather than the value of any one firm'.[41] Unlike before, many investors today have a stake in the success of multiple companies within a given sector, which creates anticompetitive pressure.

In the second and overlapping case, the financialization of MNCs is characterized by the rising power of shareholders and creditors, which is pushing companies to pursue short-term financial gains and measures to raise stock prices.[42] Some of the key contours of this trend include: the transition away from long-term stockholding to short-term trading; the growth of stock buybacks; the re-regulation of markets in ways that allow for greater financial involvement and speculation; the linking of executive compensation to stock prices; and the acceleration of shareholder activism, which is driving hostile takeovers, mergers and acquisition transactions, and changes in the composition of boards.[43] These measures are designed to push companies into profit opportunities and increase their stock value, making money for shareholders.[44]

Underpinning and facilitating the rising power and prominence of shareholders are broader shifts in attitudes and regulations that relate to corporations' obligations to society. In the 1970s, economists, business and management scholars, commercial lawyers and industry and policy actors began popularizing the notion that corporations' primary responsibility lies not in any obligation to society or its workforce, but, rather, in producing profits for shareholders. For instance, as Chicago economist Milton Friedman famously wrote, 'there is one and only one social responsibility of business – to use its resources and engage in activities designed to increase its profits'.[45]

Friedman and his contemporaries challenged the whole notion that corporations have broader social obligations, a widely held view within the US since the 1930s. Along with other neoliberal thinkers,[46] he advanced a conception of the corporation as an apolitical and technocratic legal and economic entity designed for the sole purpose of maximizing shareholder value. For instance, as University of Chicago professors Frank Easterbrook and Daniel Fischel famously argued in a *Columbia Law Review* article in 1989, the corporation 'is a financing device and is not otherwise distinctive'.[47] Rather than being understood and governed as a highly powerful entity that plays a key role in the distribution of wealth and conditions of production in society, corporations over the last few decades have increasingly been explained and governed as a mere aggregation of voluntary contractual and financial exchanges. Indeed, one of the political triumphs of neoliberal theorists has been to rebrand the corporation as a technical and benign legal vehicle, rather than as a highly politicized market actor through which power is exercised over workers, wealth is created, and inequality is frequently increased – as it was portrayed by Truman and Roosevelt. As previous constraints on corporate financialization – designed to protect consumers, businesses and society – have been removed by legal and regulatory shifts, shareholder value maximization has become the driving logic of MNCs.

Finally, it is important to note that nonfinancial MNCs have rising profits from financial assets. Since the 2000s, there has been a sharp rise in nonfinancial corporations holding and profiting from financial assets.[48] According to one estimate, '30 US companies have amassed holdings of more than $1.2 trillion worth of cash, securities, and financial investments. Roughly 70 percent is held overseas', to avoid corporate taxation.[49] Corporations are increasingly making money from their portfolio incomes, such as through interest and capital gains, rather than from productive activity, which has implications for their business strategies.

Monopolization, common ownership and financialization more broadly are homogenizing forces within markets. They make it less likely that large competitor companies will have serious differences in their labour standards, since all are under the same pressures from investor and shareholders at the top of the supply chain to produce short-term profits and grow. Across many sectors, these trends are interlocking in order to drive down the value available to pay workers. They tighten structural constraints around the money that corporations pay suppliers, and that suppliers can put towards labour costs, and channel more and more value produced away from workers and to the top of supply chains.

There are few constraints on spending, of course, at the top of the supply chain, where financers and company executives and their headquarter staff, high paid consultants, lawyers and other experts, seem to enjoy bigger bonuses every year. Most of the squeezing happens further down the supply chain, where business actors and employees have far less power and leverage to contest dynamics imposed by the top. Development professor Benjamin Selwyn captured well the inequality inherent within this dynamic when he argued that 'global supply chains are not benign spheres of opportunity, but tools for increasing the exploitation of labour in both the Global North and the Global South'.[50]

Structural constraints on labour costs

The changing ownership, investment and financial dynamics of MNCs are rarely discussed in the context of labour standards. However, they are reconfiguring MNCs and corporate power in ways that profoundly impact workers and pose structural obstacles to those combatting labour abuse in global supply chains. Two consequences of these dynamics are especially important: downward pressure on labour costs and new barriers posed to corporate accountability.

In the first case, changing corporate ownership structures and the financialization of global supply chains has created heavy downward pressure on labour costs. Monopolization has given lead firms more power to command the terms of global production and MNCs are sourcing goods at razor thin margins, frequently well below the costs of production. This often leaves suppliers without a sufficient share of value to comply with the labour standards enshrined in national law and imposed through private regulation, including fundamentals like minimum wage and overtime and covering the costs of creating safe workplaces.

For instance, a major survey conducted by the ILO and joint Ethical Trading Initiatives made up of 1,454 suppliers from 87 countries – covering a broad range of sectors and nearly 1.5 million workers – found that 55 per cent of suppliers are selling goods to buyers at prices below the cost of production. Over 60 per cent of suppliers admitted that these low prices 'likely lead them into difficulties in paying workers' wages and/or overtime pay', or 'exposes them to the risk of going out of business, an extreme situation that can only lead the management to reduce labour costs by cutting wages or by evading social security contributions and labour tax in order to remain in business'.[51] Given that these predatory practices are widespread amongst buyers, and given power asymmetries between buyers and suppliers, suppliers often have no choice but to accept this situation. How do they balance the books and stay in business? They do so in two main ways: by lowering their own profits, and by underpaying and speeding up their workers and doing everything they can to keep labour costs low. This often increases their reliance on temporary, agency and outsourced workers, as we'll see in Chapter 4.

The links between the increasing power and concentration of MNCs at the top of supply chain and pressure for very low labour costs in other areas of the supply chain have been well documented. Labour relations professor Mark Anner's research on the apparel industry, for instance, has documented the price and sourcing squeeze that leads to 'persistently low pay, excessive and often forced overtime, unsafe buildings, and repression of [workers'] right to form unions and bargain collectively'.[52] Anner's survey of apparel suppliers found that 87 per cent of buyers did not put prices up following increases in minimum wage, leaving suppliers to absorb spikes in already difficult-to-manage costs. Overall, he found that the 'price squeeze has contributed to sub-poverty wages and that women workers face additional discrimination based on their gender'.[53] Anner persuasively links these trends to the growing power imbalance within global supply chains, driven by capital markets, growing concentration and oligopsony of lead firms, and shifting state policies.

As pressure for higher quarterly profits, shareholder value and executive remuneration has grown, and as companies have used their market dominance to secure lower prices, labour's share of the value created within global supply chains has shrunk. Several studies have documented this decline. A 2019 study by the Economic Policy Institute found that 'CEO compensation has grown 940% since 1978', but 'typical worker compensation has risen only 12% during that time'.[54] Some have linked the fall in workers' share of value directly to financialization, which has increased corporate dividends and interest payments, technological change and the rise of monopolies.[55] One major study of the effect of financialization on the labour share from 1995 to 2016, using firm-level data, found 'a negative effect of shareholder value orientation and subsequent wage suppression on the labour share in all countries'.[56] Other studies attribute this to corporate monopolization more broadly. There is a growing consensus that several aspects of the contemporary business and ownership model of MNCs are seriously constraining what workers are paid, and also the ability of most actors within the supply chain to comply with labour standards. In this light, it is unsurprising that a study found in 2014 that, in the US, 'corporate profits are at their highest level in at least 85 years. Employee compensation is at the lowest level in 65 years.'[57]

In addition to squeezing wages, the changing nature of MNCs is also creating new obstacles to holding corporations accountable. Massive corporations drive down standards in the whole industry because they set the bar, and they are setting it very low. Wealthy corporations have huge economic and political power, which makes them difficult to regulate. They are using their resources to launch their own antislavery initiatives, but they are rarely investing in tackling exploitation in their supply chains, such as by paying enough to allow suppliers to pay a living wage or even a minimum wage. They are mobilizing their political influence, including under the banner of combatting modern slavery, to neutralize potential threats to their dominance and profitability. Antitrafficking and antislavery initiatives have become a key way for corporations to deepen their presence and political power within the labour governance arena.

Corporations and the State

As corporate power and profits have surged, so too have industry efforts to influence regulatory processes around labour standards. Industry actors – including corporations, industry associations, corporate-funded multistakeholder initiatives, and consultants – are increasingly proactive in shaping public regulations, engaging in civil society efforts to promote labour standards in global supply chains, and launching their own antislavery and antitrafficking initiatives.

In this section of the chapter, I provide an overview of key trends, focusing on legislation and initiatives related to combatting modern slavery. I argue that as MNCs have evolved over the past several years, so too have their strategies to influence labour governance. This still sometimes takes traditional forms that we would expect – such as lobbying and lawyers, undermining and challenging protections for workers and unions, using courtrooms to set precedents in their favour, disseminating their own 'research' that challenges independent studies, and suing activists and journalists. But it also now takes a softer, less obvious and more contradictory form: corporations are launching and supporting antislavery initiatives and legislation as a way of maintaining and securing for the future the status quo of high profits and growth described earlier in the chapter.

At first glance, this claim may seem contradictory. How could corporations launching antislavery initiatives and legislation be a bad thing? Won't these eventually lead to positive change, as corporations move forward in their 'journeys' to improve standards? Certainly, such efforts may be leading to some good, like awareness raising, documenting the prevalence and nature of the problem, or pilot programmes for small groups of workers with patchy success. But these efforts have a dark side: industry actors are strategically mobilizing CSR to fight off efforts to challenge and rein in their exploitation-heavy business models. They are helping to initiate new antislavery initiatives, networks and CSR programmes and soft legislation, and they are using these strategies to co-opt, stave off and stifle serious efforts to combat labour abuse in global supply chains.

And at the same time as they are investing in new philanthropy programmes, joining and funding MSIs, and flying around the world to speak at the World Economic Forum and UN meetings, corporate executives are doing little to nothing to address the key factors that trigger forced labour in their supply chains, as documented in Chapter 2 – factors that, unlike the dynamics that much of their efforts focus on, are directly within their control to change. After all, corporations are best positioned to change the facets of their business models that give rise to these problems in the first place.

While corporate antislavery efforts may appear altruistic and harmless, upon closer examination, they form a key part of the story of why labour governance is failing.

States as the architects of corporations' growing power

But before exploring the deepening political power of corporations within the labour governance arena, it is important to clarify that the relationship between corporations and states is complex and isn't one way. Governments

are not simply being held hostage and having their efforts
to protect workers thwarted by powerful businesses,
though that is of course happening in some places. Rather,
the relationship between states and corporate power is
much more complex. Not only have states actively allowed
corporations to grow, monopolize, financialize and become
powerful, but they have also helped to facilitate and expand
MNCs' role within national and global governance.

For several decades, governments across the global
North and South have regulated the economy in ways
that have facilitated and bolstered the power and profitability of MNCs. There are of course striking exceptions;
political leaders who – like Truman and Roosevelt – have
challenged the private profits of MNCs and sought to
break up corporate monopolies. But the dominant trend
is towards enabling MNCs to profit and grow with as
little restraint as possible. This has been particularly true
since the late 1970s, when powerful states embarked 'on
a massive political economic, and ideological project of
global sweep and reach designed to free up market forces'[58]
and drive economic growth, often described as the policy
regime of neoliberalism. Over the last four decades, governments worldwide have redrawn the balance of power
between workers and employers as they've overhauled
policy relating to immigration, labour markets, unions
and collective bargaining, trade and investment, capital
mobility, and the obligations of business and employers.

Scholars like Susan Strange, Jamie Peck and Susanne
Soederberg have persuasively shown that states haven't
been passive or neutral bystanders to the changing nature
and organization of MNCs.[59] Rather, they have legally
underwritten these changes and actively promoted MNC
involvement in national and global economic policy and
decision-making. As a result, since the 1990s, a 'significant
degree of global order is provided by individual firms that
agree to cooperate, either formally or informally, in estab-
lishing an international framework for their economic
activity'.[60] Put simply, states have been – and continue to

be – the architects of corporations' growing power and involvement within the labour governance arena, not helpless victims of it.[61]

Corporate antislavery activism

Since the late 2010s, corporate actors have been flooding the antislavery governance arena. This arena previously consisted of civil society organizations, unions, governments and international organizations dedicated to combatting forced labour, modern slavery and human trafficking, with a central goal of changing business and holding corporations accountable. Today, corporations themselves sit right at the centre of the antislavery movement.

There are dozens of industry initiatives and coalitions dedicated to combatting modern slavery. One of the earliest came about in 2010, when industry leaders formed the Global Business Coalition Against Human Trafficking, which now involves The Coca-Cola Company, Amazon, Google, Microsoft, Carlson and other companies.[62] Business associations have also launched their own antislavery initiatives. The Consumer Goods Forum, for instance, which represents 400 retailers, manufacturers and service providers with 'combined sales of EUR3.5 trillion and directly employ nearly 10 million people, with a further 90 million related jobs along the value chain',[63] has recently launched priority initiative principles on forced labour. In addition, companies are initiating MSIs. For instance, representatives of industry associations representing temp agencies and labour providers formed Stronger Together, a 'multi-stakeholder business-led initiative aiming to reduce modern slavery', which involves supermarkets like Tesco, Waitrose, Aldi and Asda, and construction companies like Wilmott Dixon and Multiplex.[64]

As well as creating networks and initiatives within powerful industry associations and with big business members, industry actors have become more active in setting the agenda around these themes within international organizations. Industry representatives within the ILO have established a Global Business Network on Forced Labour and Human Trafficking. In addition, the United Nations Global Compact – which brings together 9,500+ companies based in 160 countries with national and global business associations, foundations, worker organizations and NGOs – has stepped up its efforts to combat modern slavery and eliminate forced and child labour, focused largely around Sustainable Development Goal 8.7 (end child and forced labour).[65] The Global Compact holds events on forced labour in global supply chains where companies like H&M and Intel share their perspectives on modern slavery and initiatives to combat it.[66]

Industry actors have also taken control of large swathes of funding to combat modern slavery, which was previously controlled by government. The Global Fund to End Modern Slavery (GFEMS), described on its Twitter page as a 'bold international fund catalyzing public–private partnerships to sustainably end modern slavery', has a former ExxonMobil Vice President as its CEO. GFEMS has mobilized tens of millions of dollars, including donations of £20 million from the UK government and $25 million from the US government. Committed to making modern slavery 'economically unprofitable', their framework emphasizes private sector engagement and market-based solutions, pushing those seeking funding for antislavery projects towards business collaboration.[67]

These initiatives are part of the broader trends described in Chapter 1, wherein industry actors are positioning themselves as part of the solution to modern slavery, rather than a key cause of it. No doubt, some corporate antislavery activism may be motivated by good intensions, and some of these initiatives may be accomplishing some positive change. But stepping back, and reflecting on the vast resources being channelled into these initiatives, there is a need to carefully examine surging corporate involvement within this activist space. Is industry involvement changing the solutions that civil society groups and unions are fighting for? Is it pulling resources away from governments that could be using them for more stringent policy and enforcement? And crucially, is it distracting policymakers, consumers and activists from the systemic obstacles to decent work imposed by corporations' shareholder-value maximization business model?

These questions have been understudied, at least in part, because corporations tend not to provide access and transparency with respect to the data that would be necessary to evaluate them. But there are already some signs of what Peter Dauvergne and I have called 'the corporatization of activism'.[68] Not only are some once-radical activist coalitions getting on board with incremental and business-friendly solutions like transparency legislation, but business actors are convinced that their involvement in (and funding of) the antislavery movement places firm boundaries around NGO strategy. When I interviewed a representative of an industry association antislavery initiative, I was told that civil society groups were encouraged to 'engage positively' with business: 'it's really got to be very much a carrot approach rather than a stick approach'.[69]

There is little evidence that these measures are accomplishing meaningful change or progress for workers. Overall, antislavery activism by business tends to emphasize market-based incentives, compliance approaches like social auditing and certification, the power of awareness raising campaigns, philanthropic projects for survivors, and training. It does little to nothing to challenge or change the business dynamics described in Chapter 2, which fuel demand for forced labour in global supply chains. Indeed, the flurry of business antislavery activism has done remarkably little to address the drivers of forced labour most directly within their control – practices like outsourcing, irresponsible sourcing practices and dangerously low prices.

At best, corporate antislavery activism is leading to scant improvement in eradicating forced labour. But at worst, it is counterproductive, pulling away support and resources from efforts to change corporate business models and de-legitimizing and downplaying calls for broader, more radical change. Industry actors' use of corporate antislavery initiatives and CSR to justify to policymakers why stringent legislation isn't required is a good example of how corporations are using these initiatives to exert political power and deflect more radical – and potentially effective – measures to combat forced labour and exploitation.

CSR as a political weapon

The policymaking processes leading up to the 2015 UK Modern Slavery Act are an excellent example of how superficial and ineffective corporate antislavery initiatives are used to stave off more radical reforms.

Following the 2011 UN Guiding Principles for Business and Human Rights and publication of the revised OECD Guidelines for Multinational Enterprises, activists, consumers and investors called for national and state governments to pass laws to spur corporate accountability for labour standards – and especially forced labour and modern slavery – in global supply chains. California was one of the first to do so, passing the Transparency in Supply Chains Act in 2012. Around that time, civil society efforts ramped up the pressure they had been exerting on the UK government for over a decade to launch a new governance initiative to strengthen corporate accountability for modern slavery.

Hard-law measures to increase corporate accountability for illegal activity in global supply chains have a precedent in the UK. The 2010 UK Bribery Act, for instance, established extraterritorial corporate criminal liability for bribery that occurs within a company's global supply chain. The Act contains a defence to this offence, if

companies can show that they had 'adequate procedures'
in place to prevent anyone within the supply chain from
committing bribery.[70] Early pushes for modern slavery
legislation made frequent reference to the legislative model
and precedence of the Bribery Act, and many pressed the
government to use that Act as a model.

At the beginning of the legislative process for the
Modern Slavery Act, legislators were clear that their goal
was to create effective legislation to eradicate slavery from
supply chains. There was significant consensus among
legislators (as is reflected in the Draft Modern Slavery
Bill Report) that 'voluntary initiatives alone will not be
enough to ensure that all companies take the necessary
steps to eradicate slavery from their supply chains'.[71]
As the Draft Bill Report makes clear, the government
was considering three different legislative approaches that
could be used to address forced labour in supply chains.
The most stringent model was based on the Bribery Act,
which would have created new liabilities for corporations, and the least stringent was based on the California
Transparency in Supply Chains Act, which would require
only that corporations reported on their own voluntary
CSR efforts.

In early legislative hearings, NGOs argued that the
Bribery Act model was stronger and more effective than
the California model. Commentators noted that legislation modelled on the Bribery Act would create criminal
liability for forced labour within supply chains, and make
it possible to hold corporations liable for forced labour if
perpetrated by a person 'associated' with it. However, this
model, as well as the second hardest option, was eventually
rejected by the government, which opted instead for legislation inspired by the California Act.

As I've noted elsewhere with my colleague, commercial
lawyer and law professor Andreas Rühmkorf, the Modern
Slavery Act requires some large companies to issue a
statement describing any efforts they've taken to ensure that
modern slavery is not taking place in their supply chain. It

does not establish new public labour standards; it contains no financial penalty for noncompliance; and it has no enforcement mechanism or budget. Rather than creating legal liability for forced labour, the Modern Slavery Act reinforces CSR approaches to combatting modern slavery that are already under way. As we have documented elsewhere, in an article comparing the effectiveness of the Bribery Act and the Modern Slavery Act on corporate policy and behaviour, 'the substitution of a vague reporting requirement over a more stringent model of public governance appears to have undermined [the Modern Slavery Act's] effectiveness in "steering" corporate behaviour'.[72]

What caused the UK regulatory process leading to the Modern Slavery Act to change course? Why did the toothless transparency legislative model triumph over the stringent, extraterritorial criminal liability model of the Bribery Act? No doubt, many complex factors are at play. But a crucial part of the story lies in industry actors' political mobilization and use of CSR as a tool to deflect more stringent regulation.

Indeed, initially, the push for transparency legislation came from two business networks – Global Business Coalition Against Trafficking (GBCAT) and End Human Trafficking Now. As David Arkless, co-founder of GBCAT described in an interview: 'We believe that the best way to get an act through is to write a cohesive bill, a draft bill, which takes into account all aspects of slavery in the UK … So, we've taken the California act and we rewrote it in the United Kingdom.'[73]

A 'transparency coalition' led by MNCs like Ikea and Amazon, GBCAT members, ethical investors and others emerged in the UK, championing transparency approaches and deflecting more stringent legislative models that could impose criminal offences. Over time, this coalition also came to include NGOs. As one informant interviewed in the early days of the legislative process described: 'At the moment, what you've got is a few NGOs that want to work with those businesses but they're getting flack from the other NGOs because they're working with business.'[74] Arkless's coalition continued to seek out 'a group of the top NGOs in this area, in the UK, to form a coalition to work together in a much more coherent way'.[75] Eventually, while some NGOs continued to push for stringent legislation and resisted joining forces with corporations, others came to see transparency as an incremental and achievable first step.

A major report funded by an MNC, Manpower Group and the Qatar Foundation, called *It Happens Here: Equipping the United Kingdom to Fight Modern Slavery*, was released in 2013, pushing for a UK Transparency in Supply Chains Bill. The report argued that legislation would give a 'positive message to the business world, not negatively forcing companies' hands but encouraging them to look into the problem'.[76] The government claimed that this report led to a step change in its understanding. Following its publication, a business-led coalition emerged to push for transparency in supply chains, which included several large NGOs. As Arkless described, 'we've put in place a huge business lobby, which is positive for the new act that we're going to draft, to say business wants this'.[77] The industry-led transparency coalition began to exert pressure on the government.

By 2014, most NGOs had endorsed transparency legislation. Why? The reasons are no doubt complex, but one NGO representative described their motivation: 'Businesses aren't the only ones who need to demonstrate returns. We need to be seen as making an impact, and endorsing transparency seemed like the way to do it.'[78] With both major MNCs and large swathes of civil society behind transparency legislation, more stringent options became less politically feasible.

Other corporate actors, too, exerted political power and influence during the parliamentary process that resulted in the UK Modern Slavery Act. One key group of actors consisted of the Big Four audit and accounting firms – EY, KPMG, Deloitte, and PWC. As I've documented

together with my colleague Luc Fransen, the Big Four
sought to influence the UK Modern Slavery Act by
submitting written evidence to Parliament, co-hosting
events with government and NGOs, developing legislation
and guidance, contributing financially to government, and
publicizing the Act. Like the transparency coalition, the
Big Four's activities 'clearly target and seek to align diverse
governance actors on a shared regulatory agenda anchored
within an industry-driven vision of labour governance,
rather than a vision that promotes hard-law governance
and public accountability'.[79]

Throughout the policymaking process, a key tactic that
corporate actors used to deflect stringent legislation was
to launch business-driven initiatives to combat modern
slavery, which they claimed were already dealing with the
problems identified by civil society. The Association for
Labour Providers started the 'Stronger Together Initiative'
on 13 October 2013, just as the draft Modern Slavery
Bill was making its way through Parliament. Funded by
retailers, and including a government agency and some
civil society groups amongst its partners, the initiative's
founding goal was to 'provide business with pragmatic
good practice guidance ... to help them prevent and tackle
hidden forced labour and human trafficking in their supply
chains' through awareness raising activities. During the
Parliamentary hearings on the Draft Bill, this initiative was
mentioned 15 times, usually by company representatives
arguing that legislation would be redundant since business
was already taking steps to address the problem. At one
point, Parliament asked Stronger Together representative
about the effectiveness of the initiative, and, specifically,
how many businesses within it had found and freed
victims. The representative responded: 'None have said
that they have found slaves, but 90-plus per cent who have
come on the workshops have said, "Yes, we are going to
implement the actions. We are going to put up posters."'[80]
In short, in spite of the alarmingly little that newly formed
MSIs had done to address the problem of modern slavery,

they became a key justification for why hard law wasn't required.

As Rühmkorf and I have argued elsewhere, as a result of corporate lobbying for transparency legislation, corporate actors' strategic use of CSR and antislavery initiatives, and ideological opposition on the part of some politicians, the coalition that was originally pushing for stringent legislation to hold UK corporations accountable for forced labour in global supply chains got derailed.[81] The UK Modern Slavery Act was eventually passed, but it does little more than codify existing CSR efforts to combat modern slavery and is plagued by low compliance and lacking enforcement. This wasn't the case in France, the Netherlands or other jurisdictions that passed stronger, more stringent legislation in the years following the UK's Act.[82]

The Politics of Corporate Efforts to Combat Modern Slavery

As the scale and power of corporations has soared over recent decades, MNCs have also become increasingly political. Under fierce pressure to stave off criticism that could interfere with their long-term value, brand reputation or social licence, and to improve their social and labour standards and ensure living wages and workers' rights in global supply chains, corporations have incorporated CSR into their long-term strategies. Corporations have increasingly influenced labour governance through antislavery activism – but these public-friendly and visible efforts are far from the only way in which they exert influence. After all, they still lobby, court politicians, intimidate journalists and sue governments in investor disputes.

Taking up the cause of fighting modern slavery and human trafficking allows companies to claim they are doing something to address the plight of workers within their supply chains. It helps them to strategically position their organizations as aligned with the civil society groups and activists seeking to address social problems and, especially, rampant exposés of labour exploitation within the media. But as corporations develop CSR programmes and networks to combat modern slavery and human trafficking and paradoxically lobby *for* certain models of antislavery legislation, they are undermining and co-opting civil society efforts and public legislation that could change their prevailing business models.

Meanwhile, monopoly corporations and MNCs remain fully intact, and hugely profitable for shareholders, executives and some employees. In part, their profits depend on their endemically underpaid workforces. And without a major overhaul, the shareholder-value maximization model will continue to place pressure on and decrease the share of value that goes to workers, as well as smaller businesses at the bottom of the supply chain.

Too often, CSR is understood as a benevolent or at least benign force within global governance. Indeed, scholars and journalists seeking to document corporate influence over government legislation around labour standards tend to focus on their opposition – they rarely pay attention to CSR or positively framed initiatives, like antislavery activism. But as corporations monopolize, grow and face ever more pressure to maximize value for their shareholders – and a competing, also intense pressure to stop exploiting workers – they are adopting new political strategies. CSR holds an important place within these strategies. It is helping MNCs to steer civil society coalitions and governments away from hard law and the 'stick' of binding measures to increase business accountability, and towards the 'carrot' of working together towards market-based incremental actions – which ultimately fall massively short of addressing the problem.

Activists often claim that global labour governance is broken, that it needs unblocking to operate as it is supposed to do. But – as I will substantiate further in the subsequent two chapters – in many cases, labour governance systems are in fact perfectly structured to produce the outcome that they create: workforces that can be easily exploited, and perceptions among consumers, policymakers and civil society that corporations are far more ethical and far less damaging than they are in reality. The labour governance system isn't broken – it is working very well for corporations. But, as the coming chapters on the recruitment and enforcement industries will make clear, it is badly failing the world's workers.

4

The Recruitment Industry

In the months following Hurricane Katrina in 2005, around 500 Indian men went to work in the US through the government's temporary non-agricultural guestworker programme, called the H-2B visa programme. They were recruited to work as pipefitters and welders for a marine construction company, Signal International. Nearly ten years later, in 2015, a judge awarded US$14 million in compensatory and punitive damages to five of those workers, finding that Signal, their Indian-based recruiter Sachin Dewan and their immigration lawyer had 'engaged in labor trafficking, forced labour, fraud, racketeering and discrimination'. That same year, a US$20 million settlement agreement (including $14 million in previously awarded damages) was reached to resolve 11 of the other labour trafficking lawsuits brought forward by the workers.[1] The US government also granted many of the workers trafficking visas, passed in part on demonstration of coercion in the recruitment process.[2]

According to court documents, Signal's workers had come to be in this dire situation as a result of responding to ads placed by recruitment firms in newspapers across India and the Middle East, advertising jobs with US companies.

The recruitment firms promised that qualified candidates could legally and permanently immigrate to the US with their families, an expectation that was further reinforced as workers signed 'green card agreements' during the recruitment process. To be placed in these seemingly attractive jobs abroad, recruiters charged each Indian worker between US$11,000 and US$25,000 for the green card opportunity, recruitment fees, immigration processing and travel fees.[3] Workers obtained the money they needed to pay these fees by taking on debts as well as mortgaging their property in India, understanding that their new jobs and lives in the US would allow them to pay off debts and earn more income than they could in other labour markets. Importantly, they were forced to make payments at the moment when they had little ability to validate the claims being made.

When they arrived at Signal's shipyards in Pascagoula, Mississippi and Orange, Texas, the workers discovered they weren't receiving green cards or permanent residency as promised. Instead, they were forced by their employer to each 'pay $1,050 a month to live in isolated, guarded labor camps where as many as 24 men shared a space the size of a double-wide trailer'.[4] They endured racist abuse and were disparaged by their employer for their race and national origin. Workers who complained or met with workers' rights advocates were illegally detained and threatened in a trailer by Signal's private security guards. Signal tried to unlawfully deport some of the workers. One worker attempted to commit suicide because he was so scared he'd be deported and have no way to repay the massive debt he'd taken on to get the job in the US.[5] Most of the guestworkers simply kept working for Signal, saving the company an estimated $8 million in labour costs.[6] As the court complaint explains: 'Deeply indebted, fearful, isolated, disoriented, and unfamiliar with their rights under United States law, these workers felt compelled to continue working for Signal.'[7]

The Signal case is far from being an isolated incident; it is emblematic of the dynamics through which forced labour and human trafficking frequently arise in supply chains. A large, lucrative and often overlooked group of business actors, which I describe as the recruitment industry, moves workers across national and regional borders and facilitates their work in other places. The recruitment industry is made up of businesses that generate revenue by locating, recruiting and supplying workers to employers. These businesses are both formal and informal, and include MNCs, small firms and even single individuals. Most are not just single guys with trucks and white vans as they are stereotyped to be – they are major, organized businesses. Although most consumers probably couldn't pick out the brand names or logos of most recruitment firms, the recruitment industry is big business: one recent study estimates that migrant workers around the world pay a staggering US$10–20 billion a year in recruitment fees.[8]

The recruitment industry figures centrally within contemporary patterns of forced labour and exploitation. A high proportion of victims of forced labour and trafficking for the purposes of labour exploitation are supplied through labour supply chains created by recruiters and other intermediaries, as discussed in Chapter 2. To obtain a job in another region or country, workers typically need to go through the recruitment industry, which provides a range of services and facilitates a worker's employment in another labour market.[9] Workers are often charged usurious fees for these jobs, which are justified as fees for transportation, passports, medical checks, agent fees and other expenses. The ILO global estimates on modern slavery confirm that migrant workers who borrow money to obtain jobs face increased risks of forced labour.[10]

Lacking funds to cover these costs, workers usually need to borrow money. Sometimes, loans are obtained at exorbitant interest rates and with collateral in the form of their family land or home. In other cases, recruiters or smugglers offer to cover the upfront costs and then deduct them from workers' salaries later on, frequently charging illegally high interest rates for the 'loan'. As well as charging inflated rates for services at the recruitment phase, many recruiters also require fees or extract fines during migrant workers' employment period or when they return from abroad. Across large swathes of the economy, debt incurred through the recruitment industry has become a necessary prerequisite for obtaining a job abroad, a mechanism for pushing workers into forced labour, and preventing them from leaving abusive employment relations.[11] Because workers provided through recruiters and other intermediaries are not part of companies' core workforces, but rather are moved around and supplied through long and complex labour supply chains, they comprise a shadow workforce that is especially difficult to trace and monitor.

I argue in this chapter that the recruitment industry poses serious challenges for the struggle to combat modern slavery and enforce labour standards in supply chains. Recruiters and other labour market intermediaries operating in the lower rungs of the labour market systematically profit by charging workers usurious fees for their services. Employers are turning to recruiters and labour agents as a strategy to outsource risk and cut costs, and are sometimes even promised workers at below the costs of the minimum wage. The recruitment industry is very poorly regulated and inadequately covered by labour governance initiatives; states are often financially invested in the industry. And vulnerable workers lacking alternatives are heavily reliant on recruiters to find jobs and raise their income, regardless of the fees, risks and dangers associated with the recruitment industry.

In the rest of the chapter, I analyse the barriers that the recruitment industry poses to eradicating forced labour within supply chains. In the first part, I describe the growing market for the recruitment industry and argue that it is driven by three key sets of dynamics: supply-side factors, including economic inequality, poverty and the lack of decent work in many parts of the world; demand-side factors, including prevailing business models' reliance on outsourcing and temporary labour; and government regulations that promote the recruitment industry and temporary migrant work more broadly. In the second part of the chapter, I explore the flaws in the public and private labour governance regime surrounding the recruitment industry. I argue that the recent flurry of industry-led 'ethical recruitment' initiatives – especially those in the CSR framework – is failing to rein in abusive practices and recruitment industry profits, and also failing to protect vulnerable and exploited workers.

A Market for Recruitment

Recruiters are frequently demonized by antislavery NGOs and the media. They appear in antihuman trafficking campaigns and documentaries as shadowy criminals who trick, trap and exploit vulnerable workers in otherwise well-functioning and legitimate global supply chains. NGOs often use terms like 'human traffickers' to describe the entire recruitment industry – for instance: 'Human traffickers act as different "links" in the trafficking chain. Their actions may include one or more of the following: recruitment, transportation, transfer, harbouring, receiving of trafficked persons ... Human traffickers lure their victims by using charm, lies and deception, promising a better life and opportunities to make money.'[12] They then go on to describe recruiters' use of debt bondage and other forms of control to exploit victims for forced labour and sexual exploitation. Labour market economist Philip Martin writes: 'The "unfairness" of low-wage workers paying high upfront fees for 3-D (dangerous, difficult and dirty) jobs in richer countries, and often borrowing money at high interest rates to pay recruitment costs, often makes recruiters the villains of international labour migration.'[13]

There is no doubt that some recruiters are predatory and their activities so uniformly illegal that they could be accurately described as human traffickers. But these

individuals are a small part of a bigger and more complicated problem. The recruitment industry comprises labour
market intermediaries – also called recruiters, third
party labour agencies and labour providers – consisting
of individuals or organizations that 'mediate between
individual workers and the organizations that need work
done, shaping how workers are matched to organizations, how tasks are performed, and how conflicts are
resolved'.[14] This industry is massive and profitable: the
World Employment Confederation, an industry association
comprising recruitment firms and other intermediaries,
which advertises itself as the 'voice of labour market
enablers', estimates that the employment industry was
worth €491 billion in 2016.[15]

Not all the businesses and individuals within the
recruitment industry are criminals. Many are registered
and government licensed businesses. But especially within
the bottom rungs of the labour market, it is challenging
to disentangle the 'human traffickers' and 'unscrupulous'
recruiters from the rest. The business practices that can
lead to trafficking and forced labour – such as charging
workers exorbitant fees and making it difficult for them to
exert labour rights – are widespread and actually form the
core of many recruiters' business model.[16] These practices
don't always lead to human trafficking or forced labour,
but they very often lead to some form of exploitation or
abuse. This makes parsing out the 'scrupulous' recruiters
from the exploitative ones challenging, since the reality is
that most of the businesses within this industry that are
supplying low-skilled workers on around the minimum
wage are involved in some form of dodgy practice. The
notions that the recruitment industry is either unprob-
lematic, save a few rogue individuals, or homogenously
comprised of criminal operatives are equally misleading.

Furthermore, while it is easy to demonize individual
recruiters, this focus distracts from the question of why
the market for recruitment has become so popular in the
first place. After all, recruiters wouldn't be in business if

there wasn't a consistent and widespread business demand for their services and a supply of workers willing to use them, even where they are aware of the dangers and associated risks. To understand the challenges posed by the recruitment industry and how these can be overcome, we need to understand why the market for recruitment has become so massive and entrenched in the first place.

Supply-side factors

Workers provided through the global recruitment industry regularly get hurt and are abused by employers; many die. To name just two out of hundreds of examples, in 2012, ten overworked temporary migrant workers in Canada died in a car crash,[17] and between 2012 and 2013, nearly 1,000 workers from Nepal, India and Bangladesh died while working in Qatar.[18] Even within domestic recruitment markets, internal migrants are vulnerable to exploitation and entrapment. In an age of smartphones, WhatsApp group chats and online review sites for recruiters, people looking for work are not unaware of the risks and dangers. So why do such large numbers of workers still use the recruitment industry?

As a wide body of research on labour migration in the global economy has documented, the pool of people looking for work across borders is driven by a range of political, social, economic and environmental 'push' factors. These include: displacement; crop failures; loss of land rights; lack of decent work; lack of economic opportunities; poverty; droughts, floods, fires and other environmental conditions; food and water insecurity; rising consumer prices; exposure to hazards; social discrimination or persecution; changes in welfare and social protection; and conflict and political insecurity. Migration is also driven by a range of 'pull' factors, including higher incomes, availability of better job opportunities and freedom from discrimination or persecution.[19] In this sense, labour market migration is grounded in global relations of inequality, both between countries and in the income available across different labour markets.

The market for recruitment has been actively promoted by governments, as they've encouraged workers to work abroad and send remittances home to their families. Indeed, in response to pressures associated with globalization, some governments have promoted labour migration to their workforces, in spite of the risks and dangers involved. For instance, as China and other countries promoting low-cost manufacturing have created new competition and undermined manufacturing-based development strategies in many countries in Latin America, the Caribbean and Asia, governments came to see the export of unskilled labour as a coherent and purposeful development strategy. In the 1990s, the Philippines began sending migrants through the Philippines Overseas Employment Administration, which provides health and insurance benefits, training and an ATM card that workers can use to send money back home. In the early 2000s, similarly, the Thai government turned workers into a national 'export commodity' with the hope of increasing remittance flows.[20] These strategies tend to be successful. Globally, remittances to low- and middle-income countries reached a record high in 2018, according to the World Bank, which estimates that officially recorded annual remittances to low- and middle-income countries reached US$529 billion that year.[21] In Nepal, remittances from migrant workers make up an estimated one-third of the country's GDP.[22] According to the *Financial Times*, in 2019, for the first time, 'remittances have overtaken FDI, private capital flows and aid as the largest inflow of capital to emerging economies'.[23]

Recruiters often control access to jobs in other countries, or, for in-country migrants, access to jobs in other cities, so going through them is a necessity for most low-skilled workers seeking work. Recruiters tend to recruit from rural and impoverished communities with limited economic opportunities, and where people may lack the knowledge and resources to relocate without their help. Recruiters can offer a valuable service for these workers by connecting them to employers, providing work and economic opportunities for those who really need them. But recruiters often take advantage of poverty, desperation and the lack of economic alternatives in the communities they recruit from.

For instance, when there are more workers who want jobs abroad than there are jobs available, recruiters frequently take advantage of this and offer the jobs to those who will pay them the most. Fees are routinely so high that workers have to forfeit several months of their future earnings to recruiters in order to take advantage of labour opportunities abroad – they are, in essence, buying jobs through the recruitment industry, and the costs are often steep. For instance, an ILO survey of returned migrant workers found that migrants to Kuwait had paid fees equal to four months of their earnings. It also found that Pakistani workers returning from the UAE and Saudi Arabia, who had worked 70-hour weeks with average wages of US$400 a month, had paid an average of US$3,000 in migration costs – in other words, costs equal to seven and a half months of their wages.[24]

In short, the large supply of people who need income to meet basic needs – however dangerous, risky or badly paid the work is – structurally facilitates the market in recruitment from a supply-side perspective. The lack of decent work or income-earning opportunities at home, and the lack of alternative pathways to access labour markets abroad, means that vulnerable workers frequently depend on recruiters regardless of their fees and the risks associated with them.

Demand-side factors

Recruiters and agencies providing workers around or below the minimum wage are closely associated with labour exploitation. Recruitment fees and deceptive, abusive and fraudulent practices are well documented and known to lead to situations of forced labour and human trafficking. If these are located within supply chains, they can cause reputational damage for consumer-facing businesses.[25] So why do so many businesses still rely on the recruitment industry to provide workers?

As a large body of research documents, businesses' reliance on recruiters has many drivers and varies across high and low ends of the labour market. Employers may not speak the right languages, have the social connections or government knowledge to locate their own migrant workforces. They may not want to invest the time and effort it would take to recruit their own migrant workers. Some businesses and households recruiting workers think going through recruiters offers them more accountability and more reliable and vetted workers. Governments have reinforced these factors, justifying the move from government-to-government direct recruitment to relying on third-party recruiters on the grounds that third parties are better able to operate across multiple jurisdictions and exercise oversight over migrant welfare (whereas government jurisdiction is limited to their own borders).[26] But when it comes to businesses operating in the context of supply chains, all these reasons pale in comparison to one other driver: money.

As described in Chapters 2 and 3, changing patterns of corporate ownership and production over recent decades have exerted serious downward pressure on labour costs. Suppliers under price pressures from buyers often cannot afford to maintain a permanent, local labour force – especially in the face of irregular and unpredictable sourcing patterns, seasonality and razor-thin profit margins. Instead, they have come increasingly to rely on recruiters and other intermediaries who can save them 'money, or offer additional value, for example by providing them with a flexible workforce, training workers, or taking care of (and sometimes avoiding) labour standards'.[27]

Hiring workers through intermediaries instead of directly saves businesses money in a number of different ways.

Because these workers can be hired and fired alongside orders that come in, businesses don't need to pay workers when they don't need them – for instance, in between manufacturing contracts or harvest seasons. Bringing in workers through intermediaries for short durations also prevents employers from needing to pay higher labour costs to their existing workers – such as for less desirable night shifts on a construction job, which would necessitate higher costs across the existing workforce.

The recruitment industry also offers myriad other ways to cut labour costs in various sectors and parts of the world. For instance, in the UK construction industry, intermediaries use bogus self-employment schemes to supply workers who are officially designated as self-employed, which enables them to bypass various regulations and costs.[28] In India, a recent study of recruiters and other intermediaries in the automotive sector found that profitability can be increased by means of an elaborate system of worker surveillance and by undermining their freedom of association.[29] To put it bluntly, part of the value that the recruitment industry provides to employers is expertise on how to evade and manipulate local laws across a diverse range of regulatory arenas, from pensions to unionization to immigration law. These forms of regulatory evasion and disciplining of the workforce provide a key source of cost savings for businesses using the recruitment industry.

Given the flexibility, cost savings, and reduced risk and liability associated with workers provided by intermediaries, many businesses in global and domestic supply chains now use the recruitment industry to supplement their regular workforce. As development professor Stephanie Barrientos writes:

Many supplier firms employ a core regular, combined with a casual irregular, labour force. The core labour force provides the requisite skill and training to ensure consistency and quality of output. The casual labour force provides flexibility by using temporary workers (often undertaking similar tasks to core workers) to meet variations in outputs.[30]

While these parallel workforces may even be working together on the same worksite, study after study finds that workers provided through the recruitment industry make less money and have worse working conditions than others working in the same job or business. For instance, in a study of forced labour in Malaysia's electronics sector, researchers found that the rate of forced labour among foreign workers was 32 per cent higher than those of domestic workers and 92 per cent of these foreign workers had paid recruitment fees to secure their jobs, which exceeded legal standards.[31] Another study of forced labour within New Zealand's fishing industry found that Indonesian workers provided through the recruitment industry had signed employment contracts promising them between US$250 and $500 a month, in spite of the fact that they were entitled to New Zealand's minimum wage, around US$7.50 an hour, or $1,200 a month for a 40-hour week.[32]

In short, workers provided through the recruitment industry tend to be more exploitable. They can be more easily subjected to forced overtime, wage theft, limited freedom of mobility, nonpayment of benefits and other practices that minimize labour costs and heighten control and flexibility. Recruitment industry businesses often get away with illegal practices because they are not encompassed in social audit programmes and workers are scared to report abuse, or even injuries and worksite accidents, to the authorities. In our study of the business models of forced labour in the UK cannabis, food and construction industries, my co-authors and I found that recruiters and agencies commonly minimize labour costs and generate revenue, relieve businesses of the costs and responsibilities of employment, and insulate them from risk and liability from low labour standards.[33] Because liability and accountability for illegal practices rests with the intermediary who is the formal employer, businesses can accrue the financial advantages of labour exploitation and forced labour, while keeping their hands clean of legal noncompliance.[34]

Indeed, at the bottom end of the labour market, recruiters have become such a popular feature of supply chains precisely because they can offer a workforce that will work below the legal minimum wage. They have proactively created a market for their services by going out and persuading employers that they can drop their bottom lines and provide a union-free, disciplined workforce, and they can do this for free because workers will pay the costs of their own recruitment. Recruiters provide this service to employers by having workers they can control, who will work for less than market rates, and whose ability to report abuse is often severely limited by debt, lack of access to or support from government agencies, and fear of deportation. Debts are key in contributing to undermining working conditions on the job, because workers under severe financial pressure find it more challenging to contest unfair and illegal conditions harder.

Law professor Jennifer Gordon sums up the business demand for recruiters and other intermediaries nicely: 'When multinational companies demand lower prices from their suppliers in product supply chains, tapping the human supply chain to bring in migrant labor is one way that those suppliers reduce costs to remain competitive.'[35] In short, the predictable and stable business demand for exploitable workers within supply chains gives rise to the market in recruitment.

Mobility regimes and government regulation of the recruitment industry

Plenty of politicians champion the cause of combatting modern slavery. But they tend to portray the problem as something that happens far away, overlooking the vulnerability to forced labour within their own borders caused by the ways they've regulated the labour market, immigration, business and the recruitment industry.

The recruitment industry is very poorly regulated, or, more accurately, it is regulated in ways that do little to curb the well-documented fact that it often results in forced labour and human trafficking, while doing a lot to promote a cheap and flexible labour force for businesses and empowering them to exploit it. Prevailing estimates suggest that an average of 10 per cent of labour forces in industrial countries are now made up of international migrants, and this number can be as high as 25 per cent in some countries – for example, Australia and Switzerland.[36] Migrant workers in sectors like domestic work and agriculture are frequently exempted from minimum wage laws. Migrant workers are often not allowed to access social welfare systems or benefits, even though they frequently pay into them. While temporary migrant workers schemes have long been a feature of labour markets around the world, over recent decades, many countries have expanded low-paid and low-skilled temporary migrant work programmes, while reducing opportunities for permanent immigration.[37] Furthermore, precarious forms of work, such as day labour and agency work, have become more widespread.[38]

As business has demanded flexible and cheaper workforces, the recruitment industry has surged. In the UK, since 2008, the number of recruitment agencies operating in the country has grown on average 27 per cent per year, with 5,824 new recruiters established in 2018 alone. The UK recruitment industry's turnover averages £27 billion per year.[39] In the US, staffing and recruiting industry sales increased 3.9 per cent in 2018 to US$167 billion, and staffing and recruiting companies now hire nearly 17 million temporary and contract workers a year.[40] The regulation, monitoring and enforcement of regulations related to the ever-expanding recruitment industry is weak. Many governments create ever greater opportunities for recruitment firms to profit by increasing the number of administrative steps required to bring in migrant workers, making it increasingly difficult for both employers and workers to circumvent recruiters.

Notably, a number of countries with booming recruitment industries – such as the US, the UK, Canada, Qatar, Brazil and Germany – haven't ratified ILO Convention C181, the Private Employment Agencies Convention 1997, which would prohibit recruiters and agencies from charging workers fees. And most of these countries still haven't signed the ILO's C97 Migration for Employment Convention 1949 and C143 Migrant Workers Convention 1975, which protect migrant workers – including in the US, Canada, and most Asian countries – or the UN Convention on the Rights of Migrant Workers and their Families. Meanwhile, those same countries have jumped to sign international agreements regulating goods and capital, like free trade agreements with investor-state dispute settlement provisions.

By failing to regulate and enforce regulation related to the recruitment industry, and by promoting coercive mobility regimes that leave migrants unprotected, governments are allowing forced labour to flourish.[41] In some cases, they are turning a blind eye to the abuse that happens within their temporary foreign migrant worker schemes. For instance, in the US a sizable number of the trafficking cases filed since the Human Trafficking Victims Protection Act came into force in the early 2000s have been brought by foreign-born workers with legal visas.[42] In other cases, governments run their own schemes that directly exploit workers, such as Japan's Technical Intern Training Program.[43] So, why don't governments reform these exploitative systems?

Across the board, governments promote the recruitment industry as part of a broader strategy to re-regulate the economy in ways that bolster the profitability of business and disempower workers.[44] Some governments are financially invested in the recruitment industry. For instance, in many countries, employers must apply for permission from their governments to hire foreign workers and have to pay monthly or annual fees for this privilege – or even a fee per worker. In addition, there is considerable corruption associated with government support for the recruitment industry.

Research by Freedom Fund and Verité has found that 'fraud, corruption, bribery, and other illegal practices are common features of the international recruitment of migrant workers' and that various forms of corruption, including 'pay-to-play' kickbacks, bribes and illicit payments to government officials, are common.[45] The profits generated through these forms of corruption can be sizable. For instance, in 2010, a World Bank study estimated that corruption in the recruitment industry in Nepal amounted to more than US$194.7 million per year.[46] Another study found that recruiters and employers across three migrant worker recruitment corridors (Nepal to Qatar, Myanmar to Malaysia, and Myanmar to Thailand) paid anywhere from US$115 to $600 per worker in bribes 'to fraudulently approve a host of applications or facilitate discretionary decisions including, but not limited to, foreign worker quotas, demand set attestations, visas, medical certificates, and work permits'.[47]

Here come the corporates

Abuse at the hands of the recruitment industry isn't sporadic; it is systemic and widespread. It is compelled by three key sets of drivers: supply-side drivers that make people willing to obtain work through recruiters, regardless of the dangers, risks and undesirable financial arrangements involved; demand-side drivers that make workers provided through the recruitment industry attractive for business; and government regulations that make the recruitment industry viable and profitable in spite of its well-documented links to forced labour and human trafficking.

In recent years, there has been a burst of private initiatives to encourage ethical and fair recruitment, to be discussed in the next section. So far, these have done little to tackle the problem. Most initiatives leave the recruitment industry systematically profiting from worker vulnerability with virtual impunity fully intact.

The Rise of Ethical Recruitment Initiatives

Corporations like Apple, The Coca-Cola Company, Nike, Nestlé and Ikea have started to notice the risks that the recruitment industry poses for labour standards in their supply chains. As concerns about forced labour, human trafficking and modern slavery have increased, these companies have begun to act. In recent years, a flurry of 'ethical recruitment' initiatives have been launched to deal with these problems; schemes like Clearview, for example, have emerged to ethically certify labour providers. In 2016, The Coca-Cola Company, Nestlé, Nike, Mars, Unilever, Tesco, Ikea and others grouped together to 'drive positive change in the way that migrant workers are recruited'.[48] And the Responsible Business Alliance Foundation is working to accelerate ethical recruitment, funded in part by the Walmart Foundation.

A wide array of private industry-led initiatives is now under way. These range from individual companies' CSR programmes, to training and toolkit-based initiatives, to ethical recruitment certification schemes, to business networks, to consultancy firms specializing in detecting these problems.

What are ethical recruitment initiatives and why aren't they working?

Many businesses have started to make bold pronouncements about the dangers associated with the recruitment industry and have articulated aspirations to address them. In 2016, a number of companies, including The Coca-Cola Company, Unilever, HP and Ikea, launched the Leadership

Group for Responsible Recruitment initiative, adopting the 'Employer Pays' principle, which promotes the idea that workers shouldn't pay for jobs and that employers should bear the costs of recruitment fees.[49] This initiative aims to eradicate recruitment fees by 2026.

Consultancy firms, businesses, civil society organizations and social enterprises have developed new standards, principles and codes of conduct for ethical recruitment. The World Employment Confederation (formerly CIETT International Confederation of Private Employment Agencies), an industry body representing the recruiters and other intermediaries at the global level, has developed its own code of conduct, which includes a principle of not charging workers fees.[50] Fortune 500 company Manpower Group, along with Verité, has recently developed Standards of Ethical Practice and an Ethical Framework for Cross Border Labor Recruitment, which, they claim, will 'help eliminate unscrupulous brokers' and allow 'employers to avoid entanglements with unethical sources of labor supply'.[51] These new initiatives build on existing principles, such as the Athens Ethical Principles and Luxor Protocol. The Institute for Human Rights and Business has developed the Dhaka Principles for Migration with Dignity, in collaboration with companies, recruitment agencies, NGOs and others.

Industry-led multistakeholder initiatives have also been created to tackle problems in the recruitment industry. The Stronger Together initiative, mentioned in Chapter 3, 'provides guidance, training, resources, and a network for employers, labour providers, workers, and their representatives to work together to reduce exploitation'. It includes big retailers like Tesco, Marks & Spencer, Waitrose, Aldi, Lidl and more, as well as the Association of Labour Providers, International Organization for Migration, Gangmasters & Labour Abuse Authority, and Anti-Slavery International.[52]

Sector-based supply chain governance initiatives have been created to promote ethical recruitment within particularly problematic sectors. For instance, the Interfaith Center on Corporate Responsibility's No Fees Initiative seeks to help companies create management systems to ensure that migrants within their supply chains are not forced to pay for jobs within the palm oil, seafood sourcing, electronics, apparel and extractives sectors.[53] Stronger Together currently has four sector-specific programmes, covering consumer goods, construction, agriculture in South Africa and now – thanks to a grant from Walmart – will create a responsible recruitment programme for US agriculture.

Toolkits and guidance materials are proliferating rapidly to help companies evaluate risks, develop codes of conduct and understand laws related to the recruitment industry. These include Responsible Sourcing Tools, the Responsible Recruitment Gateway, Humanity United's Help Wanted Initiative and Responsible Recruiter Online Toolkit, which is sponsored by Aldi, Morrisons and Tesco.

Some businesses and consultants now dedicate themselves to providing ethical recruitment services. For instance, FSI Worldwide brands itself as an ethical recruiter of low-skilled migrant workers, and also provides consultancy services in ethical recruitment. Complyer is a consultancy and audit firm that 'supports businesses to achieve legal and ethical labour standards social compliance'.[54] And the Fair Hiring Initiative is a social enterprise ethical recruitment agency.

Industry actors have begun to launch new ethical certification schemes for the recruitment industry. In 2017, the Association of Labour Providers and NSF International created a global labour provider certification scheme called Clearview, a 'business-driven programme harmonizing a best practice methodology to deliver a shared, consistent and global approach for the assurance and continuous improvement of safe and ethical working conditions of workers supplied by labour providers in domestic and global supply chains'.[55] The Responsible Business Alliance Foundation and one of their auditor partners, Elevate, have launched the Responsible Workplace and

Responsible Recruitment Programmes, supported by the Walmart Foundation.[56]

Companies have also launched digital reporting applications and new technology that allow businesses to engage with migrant workers in their supply chains. Part of a broader set of initiatives to promote 'worker voice' in supply chains, organizations like Ulula, Laborlink and the Issara Institute, sell tools and platforms to companies that can obtain information directly from workers about their working conditions, including about recruitment and outstanding debts.[57]

UN agencies have launched a range of public–private initiatives to promote fair and ethical recruitment. The ILO launched a Fair Recruitment Initiative in 2014, which aims to foster fair recruitment and protect workers from abusive and fraudulent recruitment and placement practices, prevent human trafficking and forced labour and reduce the costs of labour migration.[58] This initiative consists of several ongoing projects that aim to enhance knowledge on recruitment practices, improve laws and enforcement to promote fair recruitment, promote fair business practice and empower and protect workers. In 2018, the International Organization for Migration launched the International Recruitment Integrity Standard (IRIS) programme, which has been developed in collaboration with industry groups like the Consumer Goods Forum, as well as social compliance initiatives and ethical certifiers. It establishes 'a voluntary certification process for international labour recruiters'.[59]

Some of these initiatives are no doubt doing good work. They vary in scope, ambition and effectiveness, and some are more credible and rigorous than others. But stepping back, there are several common problems that limit the effectiveness of these voluntary initiatives to adequately reform the recruitment industry. Here, I will focus on three: the lack of enforcement and accountability; the failure to address the root causes of the problem; and the fact that these industry initiatives tend to sideline workers, while creating a market for high-paid consultants to monitor and certify standards.

Lack of enforcement and accountability

Most ethical recruitment initiatives are completely voluntary. They aren't legally binding, they aren't enforceable, and they create no liability amongst companies for the low labour standards and illegal actions perpetrated by recruiters. Most of these ethical recruitment initiatives have no verification or enforcement systems to check whether codes and principles are being robustly implemented by the companies involved. As such, although companies are starting to make bold commitments about cleaning up the recruitment industry, these commitments are not enforceable by workers or their advocates, and are thus of little help when workers face abuse.

Unsurprisingly, given the lack of accountability or on-the-ground enforcement of these schemes, there is little evidence to suggest that these ethical recruitment initiatives are leading to concrete results such as access to justice for workers, elimination of debts, repayment of fees or reductions in the prevalence or severity of exploitation within supply chains. Where on-the-ground effectiveness has been investigated, researchers have uncovered a host of implementation problems. An especially critical one relates to the difficulty in tackling informal recruiters in rural locations and communities. Many private ethical recruitment programmes are designed around the 'employer pays' principle and try to stop workers from paying fees to recruiters. However, these initiatives omit the informal rungs of long and complex labour supply chains, and workers are therefore often already in debt and have paid fees before contacting the programmes. As one expert put it:

The most tricky part is that even when labour recruiters want to reform their business model, normally they are

at the capital [city] level and they will say to a worker
'do not pay fees.' But by the time the worker arrives in
this agency, they have already paid. Because the worker
was recruited through a sub-agent at the village level.
The employer pays principle programmes do not reach
the informal agents in villages.[60]

As will be discussed in Chapter 5, existing private
enforcement tools like social audit and certification
programmes are of limited effectiveness when it comes
to detecting, reporting and correcting recruitment debts.
There's little reason for optimism that these new ethical
recruitment initiatives will overcome these limits.

Most companies involved in the ethical recruitment
initiatives described above are reporting on their participation in multistakeholder initiatives and standard-setting
initiatives. But very few are reporting on concrete action
they've taken to address the risks posed by the recruitment
industry. Even in the case of the most robust initiatives,
where 'worker voice' is collected, companies are doing very
little to address the abuses and exploitation that they are
uncovering. For instance, a recent study of digital reporting
tools for migrant workers found that 'few companies are
using digital reporting tools to provide concrete outcomes
for workers who identify breaches in labour standards and
other grievances' and that there are 'incentives for buyers
and suppliers to use digital worker reporting tools to delib-
erately create a misleading impression of compliance with
labour standards and recruitment requirements'.[61]

Two exceptions to this lack of action are Apple and
Patagonia, both of which have reported on forced labour
and human trafficking in their supply chains linked to the
recruitment industry, and on the actions they've taken to
address this.[62]

Patagonia found that the mills within their supply
chains were sourcing workers through recruiters, who
were charging migrant workers fees for jobs, confiscating
their passports, and opening bank accounts for workers to

deposit paychecks, setting them up so that fees could be deducted. Workers with salaries of around $630 a month were charged $7,000 in fees,[63] meaning that it was taking workers up to two years of their three-year employment contracts to pay off debts to recruiters.[64] In response, Patagonia developed Migrant Worker Employment Standards and Implementation Guidance for its supply chain, prohibiting suppliers and their intermediaries from charging workers fees or expenses over legal limits. However, Patagonia does not report on the effectiveness of their guidelines in tackling these problems, nor on whether fees paid have been refunded to workers.

Apple has acknowledged the links between forced labour and recruitment fees, and in 2015 it banned supplier factories from charging workers recruitment fees, described as leading to 'bonded servitude' for those assembling Apple's iPhones and other products in China.[65] As Apple explains in its 2015 supplier responsibility report:

> Some suppliers turn to third-party recruiters to secure contract workers. These third parties may charge excessive recruitment fees to foreign contract workers in exchange for jobs. Doing so creates an unjust system that places contract workers in debt before they even begin their jobs … We are committed to working even harder to end this form of bonded labor.[66]

Since 2008, Apple claims it has required its suppliers to refund US$30.9 million in recruitment fees and that US$616,000 was repaid to employees in 2018.[67] But it's not clear whether the company has covered these costs.

Most companies are far less open about the problem and have done less in terms of concrete actions to address the risks associated with the recruitment industry within their supply chain. If such severe abuses could thrive and be widespread in the supply chains of two consumer-facing brand companies with reputations for being industry leaders on social and sustainability issues, they are surely major issues elsewhere. Yet, there's surprisingly little evidence that companies are acting to address these problems. The actions they are taking are mostly at the level of aspirational goals and participation in multistakeholder programmes with no binding or enforceable commitments.

It is important to consider whether these private initiatives are displacing public, state-based and regulatory approaches to tackling the rising power, profits and problems associated with the recruitment industry. Ironically, the ILO's Fair Recruitment Initiative is partially funded by the US and UK governments, which have failed to ratify most of the ILO conventions that the initiative is anchored within, including C97, C143 and C181 on private employment agencies and migrant workers.[68] Several ethical recruitment initiatives have participation or funding from the US and UK governments. While it is positive that governments are engaged in addressing the abuses that stem from the global recruitment industry, there is also a dire need for these governments to address the dynamics of human trafficking and forced labour linked to the recruitment industry domestically.

Failure to tackle root causes

Most ethical recruitment initiatives tend to focus on 'training' and 'capacity building' of workers and recruiters. But they do little to address the supply or demand drivers that create a market for recruitment in the first place. They do not tackle the demand for temporary workers, the uneven value distribution, short-term contracts or price pressures that make the recruitment industry such a stable feature of supply chains. And they do nothing to tackle the power relations within supply chains or within governments, which means workers rarely have the power or freedom from retaliation that they need in order to exert their rights.

Indeed, many ethical recruitment initiatives prioritize training, guidance and 'tool-kits' for businesses. The idea is that if managers and companies understood the risks of recruitment, they would improve their policies and practices related to it. However, so long as the structural drivers of the business demand for the recruitment industry stay in place, it's hard to see how training will solve the problem.

There's little evidence that training workers about the dangers of recruitment or their rights is an effective means of reducing the prevalence of abuse. In 2019, the UK Department of International Development funded a major evaluation study of the ILO's Work in Freedom programme by a team of academics at the London School of Hygiene and Tropical Medicine. The South Asia Work in Freedom programme is a 'multi-country intervention to minimize women's vulnerability to labour trafficking in South Asia and the Middle East'.[69] The study involved major data collection over five years, including a survey with prospective and returned migrants in Nepal, a large household survey in India, and in-depth interviews with migrant women in Nepal, India and Bangladesh.

A key focus of the research was whether training prospective migrants was an effective means of protecting them from trafficking and forced labour. As part of the programme, prospective women migrants were given a two-day training, which emphasized topics like empowerment and rights, self-care, financial literacy, avoiding deception during recruitment and assistance in their destination country. The research found that training doesn't positively impact a worker's chances of exploitation, and that it could even mislead workers, for example by suggesting there is adequate assistance for those who need help in the destination country. The researchers found that,

> although women can benefit from improving their understanding of rights, women's empowerment alone is unlikely to prevent human trafficking or exploitation. Effective empowerment strategies to reduce a woman's

vulnerability to forced labour cannot rely exclusively on strategies to promote power within (self-worth and confidence) but depends on structural change creating the conditions for women to assert their power to (agency) and power with (collective action).[70]

This study provides powerful evidence to suggest that awareness raising about workers' rights isn't effective unless it's accompanied by structural changes that improve workers' ability to assert their rights.

There are some private ethical recruitment initiatives that do more than training, and do begin to tackle commercial dynamics and the sources of workers' vulnerability. However, these often experience difficulty in finding a market for their services. As a representative of one fair recruitment initiative describes it: 'It's very difficult in the current context where you have so much unscrupulous competition to move to a fair recruitment model in the low skilled sectors and to really make good profits.'[71]

Sidelining workers

A notable limitation of initiatives to promote ethical recruitment in supply chains is that very few give a central role to workers, unions or workers' organizations.

Most initiatives create or reinforce a new market for 'verifiers', 'assessors' and certifiers who are hired by companies to ensure compliance with standards. A quick scan of social audit company websites reveals that social auditors are already marketing their services in relation to ethical recruitment services. For instance, TÜVRheinland's website invites clients to 'Schedule an RBA audit today!', referring to the Responsible Business Alliance's code of conduct for social and labour conditions in the electronics industry.[72]

Certifying supply chains against unethical recruiters is a lucrative business. For instance, Clearview charges up to £5,950 as an application fee, as well as a £4,450 annual renewal fee and £985 compliance audit in year two, earning it up to £11,385 for certifying each new applicant.[73] The emerging market in monitoring ethical recruitment raises several questions about financial conflict of interest and privatization of data, and whether the growing power and profits of private experts and professionals are in the interest of workers, or merely the corporations who are hiring them. Indeed, it's not hard to see how a lucrative industry profiting from 'monitoring' the recruitment industry could create new barriers to adequately reforming it.

In addition to worries about the burgeoning industry of consultants and industry groups emerging to monitor and certify labour supply chains, which could mislead consumers and policymakers about the nature of labour standards in supply chains, another reason to be concerned about the lack of worker involvement in the design and implementation of these initiatives is the evidence suggesting that industry-led tools are not collecting accurate information from workers. For instance, a study by Elena Shih and Lisa Rende Taylor comparing various worker feedback technologies as tools to locate and address modern slavery in global supply chains, found that corporate 'due-diligence oriented technology tools were found to help control risk in supply-chain hot spots, but rarely identified modern slavery due to gaining little trust from workers, and business clients not being ready to expose or address modern slavery'. By contrast, the study found that 'empowerment-oriented worker feedback tools were found to regularly identify modern slavery, forced labour, and human trafficking and to assist exploited workers'.[74] In other words, ethical recruitment initiatives designed without input from workers and without their central involvement in delivery are less likely to be effective.

So, where are the workers? Are there any ethical recruitment initiatives that *do* involve them? Not really. But there is an important umbrella organization responding to these issues. The International Labor Recruitment Working Group (ILRWG), formed in 2011, focuses on the exploitation of guestworkers in the US. Amongst ILRWG's members are unions and worker organizations, including AFL-CIO (the umbrella federation for US unions), Centro de los Derechos del Migrante, Inc., Farmworker Justice, Jobs with Justice, the National Domestic Workers Alliance, National Guestworker Alliance, the Service Employees International Union and the Solidarity Center. The ILRWG is one of the only ethical recruitment initiatives pushing for actions that would address the root causes of the problems with the recruitment industry in the US, including an overhaul of work visa programmes, regulation of recruiters, the prohibition of recruiter fees and making employers accountable for the actions of recruiters.[75] Their principles are broader than those common within industry-led initiatives, and include freedom from discrimination and retaliation, freedom of movement while working in the US, freedom of association and collective bargaining with labour unions and organizations, and access to justice.[76]

Notably, the solutions proposed by the ILRWG are not possible for industry to execute on their own. They would require serious involvement from workers, binding regulation and state-based enforcement. This may not be as marketable to corporate foundations, but it is no doubt the sort of serious change that is necessary to address the problems of forced labour and human trafficking that thrive within the recruitment industry.

Monitoring Unethical Recruitment

The recent flurry of private ethical recruitment initiatives creates an impression that action is being taken to address the problems associated with the recruitment industry. However, the reality is that private industry-led ethical recruitment initiatives are doing more to help corporations bolster their credibility and reputations than they are doing to achieve justice for workers who have been trafficked or subjected to forced labour, address the problems of forced labour and trafficking within the recruitment industry, and protect workers going forward. While joining ethical recruitment initiatives and making aspirational commitments to various principles is helping companies to look like they are addressing the problem, they are actually doing very little to address the business dynamics that are completely within their control, which trigger the demand for the recruitment industry in the first place.

There is little evidence that these private initiatives are leading to concrete improvement in the detection, reporting and corrective action of labour abuse by the recruitment industry within global supply chains. What there is evidence of, however, is that monitoring and certifying supply chains against dodgy recruitment practices is becoming a new market opportunity just as modern slavery became in the early 2000s. New digital reporting applications and tech platforms are emerging, and are highly lucrative for consultants. But these allow companies to outsource responsibility for problems caused by the recruitment industry, and to raise their hands up in disbelief next time something bad happens in the supply chain.

While the recruitment industry is starting to be more widely recognized as an obstacle to efforts to eradicate modern slavery, the nature and scale of the problem is still widely misunderstood. NGOs and the media demonize international recruiters as rogue criminals and 'unscrupulous' businesses operating in the dark underbelly of the economy. In reality, as the Signal case discussed at the beginning of the chapter illustrates, these are often legal businesses operating in broad daylight for large, legal global companies. Governments are not helpless victims of criminal recruiters; rather, they play a key role in facilitating the recruitment industry. After all, in countries like Canada, many victims of forced labour and trafficking are working within state-sponsored temporary migrant work programmes, for intermediaries that have been licensed by the government or even for state-run employment agencies.[77] In other countries, like India or Mexico, the government turns a blind eye to private sector abuse because of the value of remittances. While antitrafficking campaigns and initiatives frequently focus on criminal agencies and organized crime, it is far more common for recruiters and other intermediaries to be legal businesses using some illegal practices than to be criminal or unregistered operators. And it is far more common for them to skilfully manipulate visa systems and laws pertaining to fees and charges than it is for them to circumvent laws entirely. The problems posed by the recruitment industry are therefore complex and difficult to detect, and cannot simply be solved by locking up a few bad guys.

The lack of progress made by the enforcement industry towards solving problems with forced labour and labour abuse since the early 2000s is a powerful warning about the lacking effectiveness of CSR approaches to tackling low labour standards.

5

The Enforcement Industry

The business of creating, certifying and auditing labour standards in global supply chains is lucrative and booming. Since the 1990s, as MNCs have faced public and government pressure to address abusive labour conditions within their supply chains, they have increasingly hired private firms and MSIs to implement voluntary, non-binding codes and workplace inspection programmes. Industry actors claim these create a mechanism to independently monitor and enforce labour standards within supply chains. But a string of recent tragedies in ethically certified and audited workplaces – such as the fire at Ali Enterprises in Pakistan that killed 300 workers three weeks after having been awarded SA8000 certification – raise major questions about the enforcement industry's role in labour governance.[1]

As MNCs have increasingly relied on the private enforcement industry to detect and address labour exploitation in their supply chains, social auditing has morphed into a multibillion-dollar business dominated by large multinational companies with publicly traded stocks, thousands of employees and highly paid CEOs. The enforcement industry is profitable for these firms, as well as for tech firms, ethical certifiers, labelling organizations, consultants and NGOs that help to create codes and programmes to check compliance. Private enforcement is costly for MNCs, but it gives them someone to blame when problems are exposed, and it shields them from criticism and liability. It also helps consumers to feel better about corporations and the goods that they buy. However, there's one key group that isn't benefiting from the booming enforcement industry: workers.

Indeed, the key problem with the enforcement industry – as a slew of recent factory fires, building collapses, instances of forced labour and gender-based violence within ethically audited and certified supply chains reveal – is that it is failing to adequately detect, report, remedy and correct labour exploitation in supply chains. This is especially true of severe forms of labour exploitation like forced labour and human trafficking. Although corporations increasingly extol the benefits of social auditing and certification in their modern slavery statements and glossy CSR reports, the reality is that these private labour governance tools are failing to protect the world's most vulnerable workers.

The enforcement industry is often presumed by academics and the public to be a neutral, technical and benign component of labour governance. Recent studies have drawn attention to shortcomings in private initiatives to enforce labour standards, but they tend to assume that the enforcement industry is incrementally improving and, since it's already in place, we may as well keep it.

I am far less optimistic about the private enforcement industry's capacity to detect and address labour abuse. And further, as I argue in this chapter, the enforcement industry is helping to conceal rather than solve the most urgent labour issues in supply chains. Far from being independent or neutral, it is an industry designed and paid for by business, to achieve business-friendly goals like enhancing corporations' brands and reputation, legitimacy and growth. Although many NGOs, policymakers and consumers take it on trust that social auditing will improve labour standards, auditing isn't actually designed or enforced in a way that would allow the big and urgent labour exploitation problems in supply chains to be solved.

Indeed, while the firms that make up the enforcement industry are often labelled independent third parties, they are commissioned, instructed and paid for by corporations and their suppliers. Corporations exert high levels of strategic control over enforcement industry tools and processes. As mentioned in Chapter 2, social auditing relies heavily on self-reporting by suppliers, focuses on Tier 1 suppliers, and tends to avoid the portions of supply chains where labour exploitation is most likely to thrive.

The information collected through the enforcement industry gives a partial and distorted picture of working conditions and the problems workers face within supply chains. Research points to serious problems and gaps between the labour standards set within the private enforcement industry and the actual working conditions on the ground.[2] Problems with the private enforcement industry are well-known by brands, auditors and certifiers, and have been since the late twentieth century. Yet, corporations maintain that the enforcement industry can be incrementally improved, with minor tweaks to audit protocols, better training and new standards and labels. This perspective seeks to gloss over the politics, profits and power dynamics of the enforcement industry, as well as the barriers it poses to eradicating forced labour and exploitation in the global economy.

The first section of this chapter elaborates on the problems with social auditing and explains why it is an inappropriate tool to detect and address forced labour in supply chains. I then examine the problems with ethical certification, pointing to growing evidence that ethical certification is failing to produce worksites free from exploitation and forced labour. Finally, I argue that these problems cannot be solved by tweaking processes within the private enforcement industry. Rather, we need to accept that the industry is working exactly as it is intended to – enhancing corporate legitimacy, growth and profits, while doing little to tackle the status quo of labour exploitation.

The Problems with Social Auditing

As part of a broader shift towards the privatization of labour standards, governance and enforcement, social auditors – and the firms, NGOs and multistakeholder initiatives that create some of the social compliance protocols they audit to – have taken on a prominent role in the global economy. Over recent decades, government labour inspectors have battled cuts to budgets and staff, and in the absence of functioning systems for ensuring worker safety and well-being, social auditors are often the only people inspecting labour standards. Social auditing is taking on a new level of importance as it is being promoted as part of corporate efforts to combat modern slavery and a tool to prevent forced labour and human trafficking in supply chains.

However, in spite of social auditors' growing importance to labour governance worldwide, to date, there has been insufficient public debate and government scrutiny of social auditing and its effectiveness in detecting labour abuse. Scholarship on the topic is sparse, and the practical dimensions and business of social auditing aren't well understood. As corporations tout social auditing – and the standards, certifications and CSR initiatives that social auditing verifies compliance to – as armour in the battle against modern slavery, it's an apt moment to examine social audits and their role within the enforcement industry.

Because MNCs select from dozens of social auditors and audit schemes, standards and protocols, there is considerable variation across social auditors and methodologies. Some social audit protocols and firms are undoubtedly more stringent and in-depth than others. But stepping back, there are consistent problems that cut across social auditing. I focus here on five: the business model of social auditors; increasingly long and complex enforcement supply chains; social auditor secrecy and lacking transparency; lacking liability for deficient and inaccurate reports; and, most importantly, the failure of audits to adequately detect and remedy labour exploitation and dangerous working conditions.

The rise of big audit firms

Social auditing is a multibillion-dollar industry. Its key players increasingly resemble the MNCs that hire them. Today, audit firms have thousands of employees, offices around the world and billions of dollars in annual revenues.

Headquartered in Geneva, one of the world's largest audit firms, SGS, 'employs more than 97,000 employees across 2600 offices and laboratories and is active in nearly every country in the world'.[3] By comparison, this is a larger workforce than is employed by many Fortune 500 companies, including Procter & Gamble (92,000 employees), ExxonMobil (71,000 employees), Coca-Cola (62,600 employees), HP (55,000 employees) and Facebook (35,587 employees).[4] SGS provides 'inspection, verification, testing and certification' services[5] and explains on their website that 'sustainability is nothing new to us. For decades we have been providing sustainability solutions and services for companies and organizations across the globe'.[6] Last year, SGS brought in 6.7 billion Swiss francs (more than US$6.8 billion) in revenue,[7] and ranked on Forbes Global 2000 List of the world's largest companies.

Competitor firm Bureau Veritas is headquartered in France and has more than 75,000 employees, about 400,000 clients, and a presence in 140 countries. It had €4.8 billion (US$5.7 billion) in revenue in 2018.[8] Bureau Veritas advertises its social audit services on its website: 'We perform customized social audits to help you to improve your organization's social and ethical performance, and to meet your stakeholders' expectations regarding your social and environmental responsibilities.'[9] Bureau Veritas undertakes social audits for more than 100 accreditations, including industry standards developed by Worldwide Responsible Accredited Production (WRAP), the British Retail Consortium and the Supplier Ethical Data Exchange (Sedex).[10]

The Italian firm RINA audits to 140+ certifications and 29,000 management systems certificates, and has 170 offices across 65 countries. It had a turnover of nearly €440 million in 2017 and reported an average growth over three years of more than 27 per cent annually. This has been driven, in part, by the increasing demand 'for ethical audits of supply chains' and 'validation of sustainability reports'.[11]

Headquartered in London, Intertek conducted 100,000+ audits in 2018 across 100+ countries and made £2.8 billion (US$3.4 billion) in revenue (with £1.67 billion (US$1.9 billion) of that revenue coming from social auditing).[12] German audit firm TÜVRheinland has 20,450 employees and conducted 10,000 social certification audits in 2018. The company generated €1.99 billion (US$2.16 billion) in revenue that year.[13] And ELEVATE, headquartered in Hong Kong, describes itself as the fourth biggest auditor, conducting 'over 12,000 assessments and audits per year with the geographic reach to 110 countries'.[14]

Share prices of the biggest publicly traded social auditors are soaring. For instance, SGS's stock price went from US$113.28 in 2001 to US$2,638.28 in 2019, an increase of 2228.99 per cent.[15] The value of Bureau Veritas's stock share price has nearly tripled since 2008.[16] And Intertek joined the Financial Times Stock Exchange 100 (FTSE 100) in 2009, and in 2017 was recognized by investors as one of the best performing stocks of the year.[17]

Across the enforcement industry, salaries are high. In 2013, National Public Radio in the US reported that Underwriters Laboratories (UL) paid the executive running its social audit business more than US$1 million per year.[18] The Fair Labor Association, a nonprofit body that sets labour standards and conducts factory audits, reported paying its CEO US$244,765 in 2017.[19] WRAP, a nonprofit that is the world's 'largest independent factory-based social compliance certification program for the sewn products sector',[20] reported paying its president US$226,255.[21]

Like other MNCs, audit firms are looking to keep their costs low and stock values and executive salaries high. This can create downward pressure on quality, for example by limiting the time auditors spend on worksites, the balance of in-person verification as opposed to self-reporting, and on the training of auditors. According to the *New York Times*, some auditors have as little as five days of training before being sent off to monitor labour standards in factories around the world. By comparison, US health and safety inspectors would need three years of training and experience before conducting a similar inspection.[22]

Long and complex enforcement supply chains

As the enforcement industry has ballooned, it has become fragmented and complex. Today, there are dozens of different audit schemes, standards and protocols that social audit firms inspect. These include audit firms' own in-house standards, corporate codes of conduct, and industry standards like SMETA, WRAP, Social Accountability 8000, RBA, BSCI, ICS and APSCA. Many industry standards select external auditors. For instance, SMETA has more than 60 accredited external auditors. These accredited auditors sometimes subcontract audits to other firms or divisions of their own firm.

The long and complex enforcement industry supply chain that has become common in social auditing today works something like this: Company A receives a tip that workers in Factory 1 are complaining about health and safety problems, including the lack of a fire escape. Company A has a Code of Conduct that sets high standards for worker health and safety, so it decides to conduct a social audit of Factory 1. Company A checks its list of approved social auditors – let's call them Companies B, C, D, E, F, G and H. Company A selects one of them and then picks an audit protocol from an even longer list of more than two dozen audit protocols, made up of acronyms like FLA, WRAP, SA8000, RBA, BSCI, ICS, APSCA and SMETA. Company A hires Company B to conduct the audit of Factory 1 according to Audit Protocol X. But then, Company B subcontracts the inspection to another company – let's call it Company Z. Company Z takes on the job, but does not actually visit Factory 1; rather, it calls up the manager of Factory 1 and chats for a while, collects some data over the phone and then gives it a pass on its social audit.

The complexity of the enforcement industry means that when things go wrong, it is very hard to pinpoint who is responsible. For instance, what happens if Factory 1, a week after Company Z has passed the social audit, burns down and hundreds of workers tragically die because there are no fire escapes? Who is responsible for failing to prevent the workers' deaths? The aftermath of the tragedy might look something like this: Company A points the finger at its social auditor, Company B, which points the finger at the company it was subcontracted to, Company Z, which points the finger at Protocol X because it didn't have a tick box for fire escapes. The designer of Protocol X blames the government, saying its voluntary protocol can't replace government health and safety regulations and it's the government's job to enforce regulation.

Ultimately, nothing happens. Nobody from Company A, B, Z, Protocol X or Factory 1 goes to jail. Nobody even gets fined or reprimanded. Everyone still gets paid and stocks continue to soar. The government in which Factory 1 is located tries to investigate what went wrong, but Company A's list of approved auditors is not public, and the companies have petitioned the court to have the audit documents sealed, hampering the investigation. So, it isn't possible to determine exactly what the audit reports did or didn't say, and who is at fault for failing to protect workers from this tragedy. All the companies remain in business and even see their share prices increase as other companies ramp up auditing in an attempt to prevent similar tragedies. The workers, however, are dead, and their families cannot even recover the pension contributions or wages they are owed by Factory 1.

This isn't a made-up story. It's an alarmingly real representation of how the enforcement industry works and the dynamics that have unfolded in the wake of recent scandals. For instance, in 2012, around 300 garment workers died and many others were injured when the Ali Enterprises factory in Karachi, Pakistan caught fire and workers were unable to escape because exits were locked, windows were barred and there was a lack of fire escapes. Just three weeks prior to the fire, the factory had passed the SAI's SA80000 certification. How did this happen? As a trade union report describes it:

> The SAI system approved the Italian company RINA to certify factories. RINA subcontracted the inspection to a local company, RI&CA, and never actually went to Pakistan to approve workplace conditions. Neither SAI, its own technical experts, nor RINA ever had visited the factory, which was not even registered with the government. Yet somehow, Ali Enterprises received global SAI certification.[23]

In another incident, an SGS audit failed to detect problems with labour abuse in a factory in Bangladesh. The abuse came to light months later as workers protested sexual harassment, beatings, wage theft and other forms of exploitation. In the wake of worker action, another inspection conducted by Verité found 'physical abuse' and 'verbal and psychological harassment' within the worksite, as well as errors in workers' wage calculations. The inspectors concluded that workers who had protested had been beaten by security guards. When SGS was questioned about what went wrong within their social audit, they pointed the finger at BSCI, saying they were merely following the BSCI's inspection protocol.[24]

In yet another incident, after a factory inspected by UL caught on fire and killed 112 workers, the *New York Times* reported that the president of UL blamed local building inspectors, since it was their job to inspect for fire escapes.[25] Because the enforcement industry is so complex and each social audit involves several different industry players, there is a lack of clarity about who holds accountability for the accuracy of audit results and certification outcomes.

Just as they do for other firms, outsourcing and cost-cutting make economic sense for audit firms. But ironically, given that social auditing is touted as a means of heightening accountability and visibility around labour standards within complex global supply chains, the auditing industry is itself now characterized by long and complex supply chains. Audit firms subcontract inspections to other audit firms, which operate according to protocols designed by still other firms. The result is that when problems are discovered within audited and certified supply chains, it is very difficult to know – and legally prove – where accountability and liability should lie.

Secrecy and a lack of transparency

Social auditors are mostly self-regulated and left to prosper with minimal accountability. There is no independent oversight or professional body dictating standards and acceptable practice for social auditors, as there is for lawyers, accountants and other professions. Social audit reports are not subject to public or government scrutiny. This allows the enforcement industry to function in a highly secretive and non-transparent way.

The information collected through the enforcement industry is confidential, since client–auditor relationships are governed by confidentiality agreements. Sometimes, data collected and audit results are not even shared with the supplier firms that are the focus of the audit. Confidentiality clauses within audit contracts can prevent information sharing of audit results and problems uncovered through audits with governments. As one highly experienced social audit informant explained: 'You really can't start going to the authorities, not if you want to stay in business, anyway.'[26] This means that when problems like forced labour are found, they are not reported to those in a position to help or advocate for workers.

The fact that companies do suppress reports of labour exploitation discovered as a result of an audit was confirmed by corporate representatives during the parliamentary evidence hearings on the draft UK modern slavery bill. During the process of gathering evidence, company representatives were asked whether they shared data on incidences of exploitation and criminality gathered through audits.[27] This question was based on a 2013 Joseph Rowntree Foundation report that I co-authored with Andrew Crane, Jean Allain and Laya Behbahani, in which we recommended that social audit firms should be required to report suspected or documented incidences of forced labour externally.

Business representatives have confirmed that they do not allow auditors to report forced labour discovered in their supply chains externally. For instance, a business was asked this question based on our research: 'The Joseph Rowntree report on forced labour suggested that social audit firms should be required to share data on incidences of suspected exploitation or criminality. Do your auditors share data outside your organisation and would you support such collaboration?' The representative answered:

Our auditors do not share specific data resulting from audits conducted on our behalf outside [our company]. This confidential relationship is essential to maintaining full and honest discussions between [our company], our suppliers and our auditors. By having open conversations, we can ensure that potential compliance issues are fully and honestly discussed so that the appropriate corrective actions can be implemented.

In other words, confidentiality clauses prevent social auditors from reporting problems they uncover to anyone except the client that commissioned the audit.

Secrecy also surrounds auditor–client relationships. Most companies explain on their websites or in modern slavery reports that audits and supplier monitoring are outsourced to third parties and independent organizations. But the firms they use are rarely listed or disclosed, making it challenging to assess how stringent and in-depth supply chain auditing programmes are, and to uncover who has been auditing when major issues are exposed.

The secrecy around auditing is a problem because auditing has become a crucial source of information about corporate labour practices; a source of information to which consumers, the public and policymakers are denied access. Furthermore, it fuels the lack of oversight and accountability in the auditing industry and makes it more likely that poor quality, misleading audits will take place without repercussions. Workers in exploitative situations discovered by auditors are often no better off, because only corporations get access to audit information.

Liability of social auditors

A string of recent lawsuits has sought to establish liability for deficient quality and inaccurate social audit reports that rubber stamp dangerous and exploitative worksites, with deadly consequences for workers. For instance, the Ali Enterprises factory fire is the subject of a civil case in Germany (against retailer KiK) and criminal investigation in Italy (against RINA).[28] Lawsuits focused on social auditor liability are also underway in relation to the Rana

Plaza building collapse; in Canada, for instance, there's a pending suit against Bureau Veritas for a factory audit that failed to note obvious problems with the building. Some retailers have also recently suggested that auditors should guarantee the quality of their audits.

At present, however, social auditors are not liable for the accuracy or reliability of their reports, nor for consequences of their failure to spot problems. Auditors I've interviewed have been keen to point out that audits don't guarantee accuracy. As one social audit firm representative put it, 'we don't say guarantee because you cannot really guarantee a lot of things'. The same audit firm representative also stressed, 'there is no guarantee. We don't use the word guarantee because especially when you speak of groups with thousands of members you know they have been inspected by the internal inspections, and a sample of them has been inspected by the external auditor who also reviews the internal management system. But it's like traffic controls, you cannot control everybody every time.'[29] Another explained, in relation to child labour: 'We can't guarantee that there is no child labour but we are making efforts to make sure that there would not be any child labour in [the] supply chain.'[30]

Social auditors' lacking accountability or liability for their audit reports is a key factor driving the proliferation of poor-quality audits. It allows for disasters to take place without anyone being held responsible. As a lawyer involved in litigation against a social auditing firm explained:

> You have social auditors coming in, certifying that everything is okay, which is false. Then you have a disaster happening and then if you try and hold liable the company in the background ... this company would argue against its own liability, arguing that they were not negligent because they relied on the auditing report. And so this is why they didn't have any reason to believe that things on the ground would be problematic and they should intervene.[31]

Lacking liability for accurate representations of worksites and working conditions is precisely what allows the enforcement industry to conceal or overlook problems with impunity.

Ineffectiveness of social auditing

The biggest problem with social auditing is that it is a largely ineffective tool for detecting, reporting, remedying and correcting labour exploitation, especially its most severe forms like forced labour and human trafficking. While auditors are keen to point out that social auditing is not intended to 'fix' things, it is nevertheless the case that as businesses champion audits as a tool to combat modern slavery, auditing is being adopted as a strategy to govern labour standards and tackle exploitation and forced labour.

The ineffectiveness of social auditing to detect and address forced labour and exploitation relates to flaws in both audit design and implementation. In the first case, corporations exert strategic control over the design of social audits. Social audit pathways are designed by the firm that commissions the audit; that firm has full discretion over which portions of the labour and product supply chains are audited, and which ones are not. As one auditor explained: 'We will audit as far down as the brand wants to go.'[32]

In spite of widespread recognition that forced labour and human trafficking are thriving in the bottom tiers of supply chains, amongst labour subcontractors and recruiters (as described in Chapter 4), in unauthorized factories, in the informal sector and in home-based work, private governance initiatives tend to disclaim responsibility for these spaces rather than audit them. Auditors I've interviewed have shared concerns that the businesses engaging them are creating audit pathways designed to circumvent vulnerable workers, focusing instead on Tier 1 factories that are less likely to risk major noncompliance.[33]

Most Tier 1 suppliers are audited so frequently that they have pioneered strategies to create superficially and temporarily compliant workspaces. It is well known within industry that factories subcontract or outsource work to unauthorized factories. For instance, one company manager explained that, following Rana Plaza's collapse, 'many of the brands that found themselves in the factory were as surprised as the next person to find their brand in there. And the immediate defence was, "We never gave work to that factory and the people who gave them the work were in violation of the contract."'[34] Suppliers also contract temporary workers through the recruitment industry, who can be left off the books, given the day off or simply let go before the audit, so they are not factored into audit results. As one auditor noted, 'there could always be another group of people' who are not encompassed within the audit.[35]

Companies control who conducts their audits. Many companies require suppliers to select auditors from an approved list of audit firms. For instance, Walmart describes on its website that it 'instructs its suppliers to obtain an audit from a Walmart-approved third-party social compliance audit program so that Walmart can evaluate the facility's compliance with Walmart's Standards for Suppliers'.[36] Other companies conduct their own audits. For instance, H&M does not hire external auditing firms, but rather uses its own team to assess potential suppliers and relies on self-reported information from suppliers.[37] As the company puts it: 'Once our business partners have passed the initial, "minimum requirement assessment" we then enable our partners to self-assess their own sustainability performance annually.'[38]

Simply put, although social auditors are often described as independent third parties, the reality is they are commissioned by businesses that design audit pathways and processes in strategic ways. Sometimes the audits are paid for by corporations, but often they are paid for by already cash-strapped suppliers as a condition for gaining or

keeping business from buyers. Although they are supposed
to be at arm's length from the businesses they audit, social
auditors often have cosy relationships with those they
are supposed to be keeping an eye on. Many auditors
I've interviewed have described their fear that too harsh
an audit will result in their firm losing business. Large
swathes of audit firms, after all, are for-profit businesses
that – just like their corporate customers – are keeping a
close eye on their bottom lines.

In addition to these design issues, the ineffectiveness
of social auditing to detect and address labour exploitation relates to problems with implementation. Audits are
widely acknowledged to be snapshot observations, giving
a glimpse into conditions on a particular day. As the head
of supplier sustainability at Philips recently described,
social audits are 'a tick-mark in a box exercise'.[39] As
another MNC head of sustainability said, 'Audits are very
limited tools. They don't tell you about yesterday and they
don't tell you about tomorrow.'[40]

The checklists auditors use often leave off crucial
dimensions of worker health and safety, as well as known
indicators of debt bondage and forced labour. For instance,
a journalistic investigation into auditing found that:

> When NTD Apparel, a contractor for Walmart that is
> based in Montreal, hired a firm to inspect the Tazreen
> factory in Bangladesh before 112 workers died in a
> fire in November, the monitors' questionnaire asked
> whether the factory had the proper number of fire
> extinguishers and smoke detectors on each floor. But it
> did not call for checking whether the factory had fire
> escapes or enclosed, fireproof stairways, which safety
> experts say could have saved lives.[41]

Further, audit checklists rarely reflect the key indicators of
forced labour within a given sector, nor equip auditors to
ask the right questions that would shed light into whether
forced labour could be taking place.

Most audit protocols fail to include key protective factors that would reduce the chances of workers becoming vulnerable to forced labour. For instance, in the garment industry, several major companies, including H&M, PVH (which owns brands like Tommy Hilfiger and Calvin Klein) and Primark, have made commitments to paying living wages within their supply chains. However, a study that I conducted with my colleagues Remi Edwards and Tom Hunt, based on a survey of 20 garment companies, found that:

> One key problem across companies was a lack of clarity about what auditors should be checking in relation to living wage commitments. Because company codes of conduct do not clearly define living wage commitments, and because auditors typically are checking that codes of conduct are enforced, it wasn't clear how auditors could be looking for and detecting potential wage violations and enforcing living wage payments.[42]

Only one company out of 20 within our study provided auditors with clear assessment criteria for monitoring whether or not suppliers were paying living wages.

MNCs decide on the timing of the audit, the frequency of inspection, and whether audits will be announced or unannounced. When audits are announced, businesses have the opportunity to change their normal practices just for the day of the audit. For instance, as an Indian tea worker described of the annual audits conducted on their plantation by an ethical certification scheme: 'For safety equipment, when the [certifier] team visits, in that period alone there is a strict process of enforcement – like wearing this strip with safety equipment. But only when [the certifier] visits.'[43]

Auditors rarely conduct in-depth interviews with workers out of earshot of their managers, from whom workers may fear retribution. There is also widespread evidence that businesses coach their workers on answers to questions that could be posed. Companies also rid their worksites of workers they worry will report problems. As one social auditor said: 'It used to be the standing joke that if you went to Alton Park, which is one of our amusement parks, on any week day, what you did find is loads of illegal workers who had been given the day off by their employers, and all the difficult ones who were likely to say things to the auditors.'[44]

Indeed, audit cheating is a major problem. Suppliers struggling to meet buyers' requests for low costs, while also needing to pass social audits to maintain their business, have developed elaborate strategies to pass audits, including double bookkeeping, unauthorized subcontracting and making superficial adjustments to their practices. Many suppliers hire former auditors as consultants to coach them on how to trick auditors. Several auditors and business representatives I've interviewed have described an ongoing 'arms race' between auditors and suppliers. Jane Lister, Peter Dauvergne and I described this 'arms race' in a recent article on sustainability auditing: 'As auditing has become more elaborate, evasion has become more efficient and sophisticated. Suppliers are adopting double sets of books, documenting false emissions (based on purchasing monitoring data), and secretly re-locating production to unknown 'shadow factories".'[45]

Audit cheating is well known to be an issue within the industry. This was acknowledged by Giles Bolton, Ethical Trading Director at Tesco, in a UK parliamentary evidence hearing. He explained: 'In countries where long working hours are endemic – for example, in a lot of China – some audit firms are quite unsuccessful at getting to the truth about real working hours. A factory owner will think that the customer wants to hear that it is all right, so they will give you a false set of records.'[46] Although this cheating and deception is widely acknowledged to be a problem by the industry, little is done about it. Unlike public labour inspectors, private auditors have no power to challenge or investigate, even when they sense they are being misled.

Corruption is another challenge within the social auditing industry. According to activist organization China Labor Watch's lawsuit against Intertek, an Intertek auditor found fraud in a factory's pay records and demanded a bribe in exchange for letting the factory pass the audit, which was paid.[47] China Labor Watch claimed in 2012 it had found at least nine cases of bribery of Intertek auditors.[48] Environmental activists claim that BSI auditors are colluding 'with palm oil companies to cover up serious violations' in their auditing of the Roundtable on Sustainable Palm Oil certification.[49]

Given these wide-ranging implementation challenges, it's unsurprising that a New York Times investigation about supply chain auditing in 2013 concluded:

> The inspection system intended to protect workers and ensure manufacturing quality is riddled with flaws. The inspections are often so superficial that they omit the most fundamental workplace safeguards like fire escapes. And even when inspectors are tough, factory managers find ways to trick them and hide serious violations, like child labor or locked exit doors.[50]

Workers are rarely interviewed by the enforcement industry in any depth, away from their managers, which means the information gathered by auditors gives a skewed view of workplace dynamics. This is compounded by the fact that auditor checklists often leave out important components of worker health and safety, such as crumbling buildings or the lack of fire escapes. As the director of an antislavery NGO put it: 'There is a whole industry of ethical auditors out there now who will find nothing if you pay them to go and find nothing.'[51]

Where social audits do identify problems, there is little evidence that problems are sufficiently or consistently reported and remedied. As already mentioned, problems uncovered in audits tend not to be reported externally due to confidentiality provisions and a lack of obligations to the public interest. While some audit firms and companies create 'corrective action' plans for suppliers, it is entirely up to the companies whether and to what extent these plans are actually implemented. As one auditor put it:

> What the audit will do is present you, the factory or the farm, or whoever, plus your principal if they are the ones who have commissioned the audit, with this is what is happening. It is then up to those people to look at how they are going to address and deal with those issues.[52]

There is a high chance that where workers are found to be in exploitative or unsafe conditions, the situation will be insufficiently addressed. For instance, an internal Walmart audit in 2000 warned its executives that 'employee records at 128 stores pointed to extensive violations of child-labor laws and state regulations requiring time for breaks and meals'. However, aside from asking various courts to seal the audit paperwork, Walmart reportedly did nothing to address the problems. As Walmart store manager John Lehman described to a journalist, 'There was no follow-up to that audit, there was nothing sent out I was aware of saying, "We're bad. We screwed up. This is the remedy we're going to follow to correct the situation."'[53]

The ineffectiveness of social auditing to fix the problems it uncovers is well known within the industry. For instance, former CSR director of a large US retailer emphasized: 'Within the social compliance world, it is now standard operating understanding that audits don't work to achieve change within organizations.' Similarly, a London-based manager at a global audit firm stated: 'An audit is a diagnostic tool; it doesn't fix things. It does not matter how many times we audit a factory, that does not mean they are going to improve.'[54]

Given their limited utility in addressing problems, some companies are finding social auditing to be an increasingly pointless exercise. Signatories to the Social & Labor

Convergence Program – including Adidas, Patagonia, Eileen Fisher, Lululemon, Marks & Spencer, and Mountain Equipment Co-op – have acknowledged that 'the industry is spending vast amounts of resources on audits, which are merely duplicative and not necessarily leading to change'.[55] Marco Baren, Head of Supplier Sustainability at Philips, recently announced that his company has abandoned auditing: 'We have done two and a half thousand audits in our company, and ... we didn't find them really productive. They didn't make any real impact in our supply chains. So we're doing something else now. We've completely abandoned old-school auditing.'[56]

Instead, many companies are moving towards self-reporting and using audits sparingly in relation to especially high-risk suppliers. As Unilever describes of its Responsible Sourcing Policy, 'Unilever will verify alignment to and implementation of the RSP's Mandatory Requirements through the use of supplier self-declaration, online assessments and – for designated high-risk countries and supplier types – independent verification including third-party audits.'[57] It is too early to say whether the shift to in-house monitoring will be a step forward or backwards for effective labour governance.

Widespread awareness of audit shortcomings

The ineffectiveness of social audits to detect and correct labour exploitation has been well known for more than 20 years. For instance, in the mid-1990s, under President Clinton, The White House Apparel Industry Partnership heard testimonies in front of the US Congress on the perils of auditing and the role social auditing and self-regulation were playing in facilitating sweatshops and child labour.[58] Trade unions opposed 'independent monitoring' through social auditors, questioning whether auditors selected and paid by business could truly be independent. Expert recommendations to the White House taskforce cautioned that 'important issues can be covered up or ignored in "independent monitoring"', and urged that 'some form of public disclosure is critical to insuring the quality of auditing'.[59]

In 2000, MIT professor Dara O'Rourke's study of PricewaterhouseCoopers found that its social audits 'had a pro-management bias, did not uncover the use of carcinogenic chemicals and failed to recognize that some employees were forced to work 80-hour weeks'.[60] O'Rourke's study received widespread attention, as did his later studies.[61]

Yet, as audit companies' profit figures attest, large numbers of companies continue to rely on audits. There has yet to be a substantive overhaul to the social auditing system, in spite of growing evidence of its shortcomings.

The Problems with Ethical Certification

Another key actor within the private labour standards enforcement industry are ethical certification programmes. Today, hundreds of products at the grocery store and in shopping malls are adorned with labels from ethical certification programmes like Fairtrade, Better Cotton Initiative and Forest Stewardship Council. According to the *Guardian*, there are more than 460 ethical and sustainability labels covering food and beverage packaging alone.[62]

Ethical certification organizations claim that by buying and selling certified products, consumers and businesses can contribute to a more just and sustainable global economy that benefits workers. For instance, Rainforest Alliance encourages consumers to 'Shop Smart' by buying its certified products, noting that 'choosing products with the little green frog seal is an easy way to help protect forests, conserve wildlife, and support communities around the world'.[63] Fairtrade's website notes: 'Fairtrade is a simple way to make a difference to the lives of people who grow the things we love. We do this by making trade fair.'[64]

These claims fuel a growing market; the sale of ethically certified products is lucrative and expands every year. For example, Fairtrade's global retail sales grew 16 per cent between 2014 and 2015, reaching £9 billion worth of Fairtrade products sold in 2017. Between 2011 and 2015, the Fairtrade-certified area of global agriculture grew by over 80 per cent, and between 2004 and 2015, Fairtrade International's retail sales surged from US$1,032 million to US$8,099 million.[65]

But just like social auditing, there is little evidence that these programmes actually work to eradicate labour abuse, improve working conditions or increase wages in global supply chains. While corporations increasingly promote ethical certification as a way of combatting modern slavery, data suggests that ethical certification isn't working to enforce labour standards and eradicate forced labour on the ground. Rather, it is helping to conceal serious labour abuses, and mislead policymakers and consumers about the labour standards used across a wide and growing range of certified supply chains.

Certifying exploitation

Ethical certification sets ambitious labour standards, for example concerning living wages, the prohibition of child or forced labour, and ensuring workers' basic needs. These standards vary across ethical certifications, some of which are more ambitious and stringent than others. Yet, a heap of recent research on the effectiveness of ethical certification schemes has found that the standards set by ethical certifiers – including some of the certifications considered the most stringent and credible – are not actually being met when it comes to working conditions on the ground. In other words, certified worksites are falling short when it comes to ensuring standards and preventing labour exploitation, including forced labour.

There is substantial evidence that wages are no better on certified worksites than on noncertified worksites, in spite of the higher standards set by ethical certification programmes around wages. A systematic review of more than 179 studies published between 1990 and 2016 showing evidence of the impact of ethical certification schemes on low- and middle-income countries found that 'workers' wages do not seem to benefit from the presence of CS [certification systems]'.[66] In eight of the studies, 'wages for workers engaged in certified production were lower than for workers working for uncertified employers',[67] and none of the studies found statistically significant positive effects on wages. Some studies even found that workers' non-waged labour standards – such as standards around health and safety, job security and freedom of association and collective bargaining – were worse on certified worksites.

Sociology professor Tim Bartley has conducted research on the SA8000 standard, which advertises itself as 'the leading social certification standard for factories and organizations across the globe'.[68] His study included survey data from 86 factories and 1,357 workers in Guangdong province, China. It found that wages in SA8000-certified factories were actually lower than in uncertified factories, and fell well short of the living wage promised in the standard.[69]

Even having multiple ethical certifications layered on top of one another doesn't guarantee that worksites will have higher standards. For instance, a study of social and ethical certification on the economic conditions of smallholder farmers in Colombia used a sample of more than 600 coffee farmers to assess the impact of certification schemes, including Fairtrade, Starbucks, C.A.F.E Practices, Nespresso AAA, 4C and Rainforest Alliance. It found that even where farmers were enrolled in multiple certification schemes, they were unable to break even and earn enough income to escape poverty. In a context where coffee farmers are struggling to make a living, the study concluded that the 'impact generated by these tools seems to be too limited to make a real difference'.[70] No doubt, this has implications for labour standards, since, if farmers are struggling, they are probably cutting corners on wages and working conditions for hired workers. The evidence is piling up that ethical certification isn't working to create fair living and working conditions. My own research confirms this, and also suggests that it's not working as a tool to combat forced labour.

In 2018, I published a major study of the impact of ethical certification on indicators of forced labour in the global tea supply chain, as part of my Global Business of Forced Labour project. The study included tea plantations certified by the main ethical certification bodies within the industry, including Fairtrade and Rainforest Alliance, amongst others, as well as tea plantations with no ethical certifications. To assess the impact of ethical certification on labour standards in the tea industry, my research team conducted interviews and a digital survey with 536 tea workers from across 22 tea plantations in two regions of India: Kerala and Assam. This research uncovered widespread forced labour and exploitation, including on certified worksites.[71]

All the workers interviewed for my study reported some form of labour abuse, including actual physical and verbal abuse, threats of physical abuse or violence, debt bondage, the underprovision of legally required goods and services, underpayment or withholding of wages, sexual violence, and retaliation and punishment for exerting their rights and participating in collective action. In the worst cases, these situations were severe enough to amount to forced labour.

Surprisingly, given that the ethical certification schemes within my study set wage standards, ensuring that workers had basic necessities like water and housing, and prohibiting forced labour, I found that whether or not a worker was working on an ethically certified worksite had almost no bearing on whether or not they were likely to experience labour abuse. In other words, working conditions were very similar on certified and noncertified worksites and fell well below the standards set by ethical certification schemes. In fact, some of the worst cases of exploitation documented within my research took place on certified tea plantations.

I found that living standards across certified and noncertified tea plantations were broadly similar, which is significant to forced labour, since just one emergency – such as needing urgent medical care – is often what pushed workers into taking on debts that were a key indicator of forced labour. Indian law requires employers in the tea industry to provide basic services for its workers, such as housing, sanitation and medical care, since the plantations are often remote and, given a history of bonded labour, low wages and ethnic violence, tea workers often face constraints on leaving the plantations. Although ethical certification schemes set standards around these services, my data suggests that ethically certified worksites are falling short of meeting these standards. For instance, nearly 25 per cent of workers on ethically certified tea plantations cited in my study did not have access to drinking water, 33 per cent lacked access to a toilet and 40 per cent did not have reliable electricity.

Certified plantations did little better when it came to wages. In both regions included in my study, certification made almost no difference to wages. In Kerala, where wages are generally higher than in Assam, tea workers received an average of 312 INRs per day on both certified and noncertified plantations. In Assam, they received 146 INRs on certified plantations and 145 INRs on non-certified plantations, in spite of the fact that three out of four ethical certification schemes within my study required that the highest legally mandated wage of 250 INRs be paid. Patterns of wage violations were also similar across certified and noncertified plantations. Fraudulent and unfair wage deductions – such as for services like electricity that weren't actually provided, or deductions for services that plantations are legally required to provide free of charge – took place on certified plantations. Over 36 per cent of workers on certified plantations reported unfair deductions from their wages, and 17.22 per cent of workers on ethically certified plantations reported that managers unfairly withheld their benefits. Some workers reported that wage violations occurred as a punishment for protesting unfair treatment or for reporting it to the union. In a context where very low wages leave workers systematically vulnerable to forced labour, breaches in ethical certification standards around wages are highly significant.

Finally, workers on both ethically certified and noncertified tea plantations experienced threats, intimidation, coercion and verbal abuse, and punitive, retributory and discriminatory actions by management for their involvement in strikes, collective action or unions.

Put bluntly, my research on tea plantations found almost no difference between labour standards and living conditions on ethically certified and noncertified tea plantations. Labour standards fell well below those set by certification schemes and often broke laws. These findings suggest that ethical certification – a mainstay of the enforcement industry – is falling short when it comes to combatting modern slavery in supply chains.

Why doesn't ethical certification eradicate forced labour?

Why do ethically certified worksites fail to achieve the labour standards they set? The reasons explaining gaps between ethical certification standards and working conditions on the ground vary across programme, industry and part of the world. But one consistent shortcoming across the board is that certifications are plagued by poor enforcement and weak verification systems.

Ethical certification systems rely on private enforcement and auditing to establish that worksites meet their standards and to monitor ongoing compliance. Some programmes use their own in-house auditors, while others allow external audit firms to verify their standards. The enforcement and verification systems attached to certification programmes suffer from the same shortcomings as were described earlier in this chapter, such as cheating and deception, limited engagement with workers and superficial box-ticking exercises. Drawing on my research on ethical certification in the cocoa and tea supply chains, I'll summarize three of the key enforcement problems that allow forced labour and other breaches of certification standards to occur.

In the first case, ethical certification schemes tend to create loopholes and exclusions around vulnerable workers within supply chains, such as informal and home workers, temporary and day labourers, and certain forms of hired labour. The specifics vary by sector and scheme, but a common problem is that ethical certification schemes create loopholes in their fine print, exempting vulnerable workers from their standard. For instance, in agriculture, many schemes certify at the level of the farmer, but do not encompass the workers hired by the farmer. As one representative of an ethical certification organization explained: 'The hired labour of smallholders is still an area we can't reach. Because you imagine, how much work it is to inspect groups of 4,000 smallholders and then to meaningfully control how they treat their hired labour ... we don't have a system for that.'[72]

A second challenge relates to the distribution of profits attached to certified products, which tend to be concentrated towards the top of the supply chain, triggering fraud at the base of the chain. Employers towards the base of the supply chain often struggle to meet the financial costs of the labour standards set by the certifiers. This was a common problem reported by both tea plantations and cocoa farmers in my Global Business of Forced Labour research project. For instance, cocoa producers reported that they were selling their cocoa beans as both 'certified' and 'noncertified', and they used the same labour standards for both – standards that fell dramatically short of those set by the ethical certification scheme they were selling into.

One farmer in Ghana explained he could not meet

the certification standards because selling certified beans didn't cover the increased costs of higher labour standards, such as doing away with certain forms of child labour or paying minimum wage. He explained that he received just 14 GHS more per certified bag of cocoa and this simply wasn't sufficient to break even, never mind meet the high labour standards demanded by ethical certification programmes. As he explained: 'If I made the comparison, the expenses [of running the cocoa farm] is more than the premium.'[73] Verification systems are so weak that they allow products made with labour standards that fall short of ethical certification standards to be sold as 'certified'.

Finally, ethical certification systems have weak and partial enforcement systems. Most ethical certifiers audit only a small portion of sites encompassed within their certification schemes. As one cocoa certifier told me:

> We are working with around 118,000 cocoa farmers so we have not been able to visit any farms as of now but groups like [certified cooperative] for instance, they have workers who are mandated to visit farmers and check plantation on our behalf but us [certification scheme] workers personally we haven't been able to visit every farmer's farm due to their numbers.[74]

Audits vary in stringency and quality, and many rely on self-reporting by producers once they have passed an initial audit. This means that ethical certifiers are not verifying on the ground whether or to what extent their standards are being met. Given how limited on-the-ground verification is, it isn't surprising that certification standards are so widely violated by employers.

MNCs that I've interviewed have been candid about the problems with ethical certification. As one MNC executive put it, 'certification is like a life insurance policy. It's not an immunization. And the certifications, like insurance schemes, vary in terms of their coverage and robustness. They give you some coverage but not immunity.'[75] Another former MNC executive told me that ethical certification schemes have 'credibility issues' and that they 'cover up systemic issues within industries' such as low margins along the supply chain.[76]

Misleading Consumers, Undermining Public Governance

Professionals within the enforcement industry are surely well-intentioned. Many forgo highly paid jobs in the corporate sector to try to make a difference. But no matter how benevolent the people staffing these programmes are, overall, the enforcement industry is a key reason why labour governance is failing.

At best, social auditing and ethical certification programmes are badly managed and executed, such that they fall dramatically short of their aims. But at worst, the enforcement industry is brokering in deception. As social auditors and ethical certifiers lend their labels, logos and stamps of approval to exploitative employers, they are profiting from the impression that they can rid supply chains of labour abuse, in spite of the mounting evidence that this is false and inaccurate. The enforcement industry is mollifying consumers who are demanding corporate accountability and ethical and sustainable products. And it is misleading policymakers about the nature of labour and working conditions within supply chains.

Concern about the misleading metrics, statistics and perceptions generated through the enforcement industry have surfaced repeatedly in my interviews with businesses, NGOs and unions. As one MNC executive noted, 'Some people are very good at hiding things. And some of the ways that people are measuring risk miss what's being hidden.'[77] Similarly, a professional association represent-ative noted in relation to the enforcement industry that 'lots of people over-claim or the claim is not accurate'.[78]

Several interviewees have also raised concerns that the enforcement industry does little to mitigate risks of labour abuse. As one MNC executive said candidly: 'At the end of the day, buyers still purchase according to the lowest price. They use the lowest bid, and as long as that happens, there are real risks.'[79] Another explained: 'You can put in place robust systems and assurances, but there is always going to be some level of failure. The question is what level of failure are you willing to accept?'[80]

But even worse than falling short of delivering on its promise is the reality that – however well-intentioned individuals working within it may be – the enforcement industry is also helping to conceal the serious problems faced by workers. By failing to report criminal activity like forced labour, evading liability for the consequences of rubber-stamping death-trap factories and rampantly abusive workplaces, and by certifying as ethical products that are made with exploitative labour practices, the enforcement industry is actually distorting the nature of problems within supply chains. Corporations are paying the enforcement industry to defend their image, and the industry is profiting from the impression it gives to consumers and policymakers that labour standards are being upheld. Yet, disaster after disaster, study after study, and worker mobilization after worker mobilization all confirm that this isn't really the case.

This isn't a problem of CSR not quite working as it is supposed to. Rather, it is a logical outcome of the way that the enforcement industry is set up and functions – to achieve business-friendly goals while doing little to solve urgent problems of labour exploitation and forced labour.

One of the greatest dangers of the enforcement industry is its potential to undermine labour governance systems that are proven to be effective means of reducing workers' vulnerability to exploitation, like government inspection and collective bargaining. As a representative of an international organization put it:

They [corporate actors] will say they're not intentionally

undermining public governance with private governance. But by not actually working on the ground to figure out how they can work with labour inspection, with labour administration, to promote what the national goals are for social and economic development, they're more likely to either be competing, or potentially undermining those public goals.[81]

Viewed in this light, the enforcement industry is not only concealing problems, but crowding out those who seek to draw attention to and remedy them.

6

Protecting Twenty-First-Century Workers

Corporations haven't taken up the cause of combatting modern slavery quietly. Today, industry representatives tell seemingly endless stories about their quest to battle modern slavery in glossy corporate brochures, in colourful human trafficking statements, at UN conferences and at elegant awards dinners for modern slavery 'influencers'.

These heart-wrenching and uplifting tales feature corporations and consultants charging in to overcome criminals and villains contaminating otherwise pristine global supply chains to rescue helpless victims of modern slavery. While the specifics of the stories vary, the hero is always CSR. From the benevolent corporate foundation funding an NGO to take on big bad recruiters, to social auditors fastidiously taming noncompliant and beastly factories, to ethical certification schemes magically defeating producer poverty, corporate social responsibility always saves the day.

Corporate stories about modern slavery are seductive and compelling. They are illustrated with colourful diagrams and metrics that convey the scale and impact of their work – for instance, total number of dollars spent on the cause, number of auditors trained and number of posters hung on walls to raise awareness. Written by marketing professionals, these stories often feature happy photographs of workers who, it is claimed, benefit from corporations' philanthropic and social programmes.

Corporate modern slavery stories are often told by impressive and sincere people – corporate employees who have no doubt spent sleepless nights working out how to persuade their companies to do the right thing, employees who have courageously convinced their bosses to position their organization within the quickly forming global alliance to combat modern slavery and human trafficking. When company representatives end their speeches and reports with inspiring calls to action to end modern slavery in our lifetimes, they no doubt believe this to be possible.

For these, and many other reasons, a lot of people believe the stories corporate actors tell about combatting modern slavery. They believe that CSR can rush in and save the day. In our complicated and often dark global economy, where the scale of human suffering and inequality is enormous and our ability to change it sometimes feels miniscule, it is tempting to put our faith in corporations to solve this urgent challenge.

But the problem is that the stories corporations tell about eradicating modern slavery aren't likely to come true. They are fairytales: detailed and compelling accounts of magical mechanisms in faraway lands, which, unfortunately, are mostly unsupported by concrete evidence. While it's hard to assess the outcome of each individual corporate story about modern slavery, since the corporations own and rarely share the necessary data, the evidence that is available doesn't support their overall thrust – that business and CSR can heroically lead the struggle against modern slavery, so government and civil society should be grateful and follow their lead. This is dangerous and untrue.

The reality is, CSR is not the hero we need to combat the problem of modern slavery in the contemporary global economy. For more than two decades, corporations have been promoting CSR as the solution to the problems of labour exploitation and dangerous workplaces. And for more than two decades, CSR has failed to deliver the safe workplaces, decent wages and freedom from harassment, coercion and exploitation that it promises. The evidence is clear: CSR simply isn't working to address labour exploitation and forced labour in supply chains.

The true beasts and villains of global supply chains are not the 'unscrupulous' recruiters and 'bad-apple' employers that appear in corporate fairytales. These guys are minor figures compared to the real villains: giant corporations that are hard-wired to produce labour exploitation as they churn out shareholder value, profits and growth at all cost and, in doing so, lower the floor of labour standards across the entire global economy. So long as this business model remains intact, we would be naive to expect an end to modern slavery – no matter how hard CSR teams nudge their businesses towards better social compliance and no matter how inspiring and aligned with our own their visions for the world corporations sometimes seem.

Workers are not helpless victims waiting to be rescued. No matter how vulnerable they are, migrant workers, trafficked workers and those in forced labour always have agency. We cannot say they are too oppressed to speak for themselves and patronize them – as mentioned in Chapter 1, these forms of abolitionism and their racial politics have been challenged by workers and scholars.[1] Businesses, NGOs and religious groups rushing in to rescue workers without their permission and without providing full information about what happens next and 'liberating' them isn't a good strategy – in many cases, abolitionist movements have created 'collateral damage', for example by stopping the movement and mobility of people who aren't being trafficked and want to move for work, and making life worse for already vulnerable people.[2]

In this concluding chapter, I argue that we need to dispel corporate fairytales about modern slavery; they misrepresent the problem and oversell faulty solutions. CSR isn't working and a new approach to labour governance is needed. This new approach needs to confront corporate power and profits, dismantle exploitative business models and adequately regulate global supply chains, including the recruitment and enforcement industries. It needs to replace industry-led initiatives with worker-driven initiatives that uphold fundamental labour rights.

Trading in Fairytales for Real Change

As a strategy to deliver higher labour standards and eradicate forced labour in the global economy, CSR is failing. The evidence is all around us. The latest academic research reveals little meaningful progress across a range of metrics, from prevalence of forced labour within supply chains to freedom of association to dangerously low wages; these problems occur even in ethically certified and audited supply chains.[3] After years of waiting, there's little data to suggest that companies are following through with implementing the promises they've made that would meaningfully address exploitation, such as paying living wages. Meanwhile, there's plenty of data to suggest that multistakeholder initiatives are falling short of meeting their aims.[4] Each week, we are flooded with journalistic exposés of forced labour and human trafficking in supply chains led by retailers and brands with well-defined and award-winning CSR programmes. Notwithstanding the patchy incremental improvements that some individual initiatives may achieve in selected issue areas, the overwhelming evidence is that CSR has barely scratched the surface of addressing severe labour exploitation in global supply chains.

So, what should we do about it? Some NGOs and academics still believe CSR will work eventually and are happy to wait around and follow corporations and certifiers on their seemingly never-ending 'journeys' towards better labour standards. Others acknowledge that CSR is ineffective, but think it's relatively benign, and worth keeping in parallel to other systems just in case it is in fact useful, or because they consider it too awkward and risky a task to draw attention to CSR's ineffectiveness. In the face of the urgent problems facing the world's workers, they argue, we need all the resources we can get; corporations are responsible for these problems anyway so it would be foolish to turn down their funding and initiatives. I am not optimistic about CSR suddenly becoming effective; this overlooks the fact that it is failing by design, as powerful business interests fight to preserve the status quo of business models that are hard-wired to produce labour exploitation. I also do not believe that CSR is nonthreatening and benign, but rather see several dangers to continuing to invest in industry-led antislavery initiatives when these are clearly ineffective.

In addition to leaving patterns of labour exploitation intact, CSR is giving rise to a whole range of perverse effects and new problems. Social auditing is privatizing data on working conditions in supply chains; as social auditor reports covered under nondisclosure agreements and commercial contracts prevail over public reporting, the enforcement industry is creating new legal barriers to accountability, liability and reporting for serious labour abuse. This makes it harder for workers to hold businesses accountable for serious problems and labour abuse, and means that workers in exploitative situations are frequently left without remedy.[5] Ethical certification programmes are misleading consumers about the prevalence and nature of forced labour, producers' living standards and labour standards more broadly in the products that they buy, and channelling hopes and efforts towards building a better world into faulty industry initiatives.[6] CSR is opening up markets for private consultants to carve off and carry out fragments of labour governance, which often does little more than facilitate corporate obfuscation of bad practices, and, in doing so, we are losing sight of and responsibility for the bigger picture. The integration of private governance into public legislation is undermining and weakening its effectiveness, and there is mounting evidence that private governance is displacing public labour governance in other arenas as well.[7] And CSR has enhanced the legitimacy, authority and power of corporations within the global labour standards governance arena to set and steer the agenda in ways that will be tricky to reverse.

As challenging as it is to do, given the politics of data and access to data in this area, we need to investigate further these dark sides of CSR. And we need scholars and journalists to keep examining CSR's actual on-the-ground outcomes in the cold light of day. We also need to break the cycle of corporate fairytales. For decades, each time convincing evidence surfaces that CSR is ineffective, corporates and consultants rush in with promises to improve their private systems, and the world waits for these changes, only to find that, once they are implemented, audit 2.0 has the same structural problems as the previous model. We've been in that cycle for too long and the labour exploitation taking place in supply chains is too widespread and urgent to allow us to stay in it any longer.

It's time to face the facts that labour violations and exploitation are constantly recurring and endemic features of global supply chains. No amount of CSR and combatting modern slavery is going to change the fact that corporations and global supply chains are hard-wired to produce labour exploitation. This doesn't mean letting businesses walk away from the cause of modern slavery or turning down their money – far from it. As I elaborate below, businesses have a key role to play in ensuring their purchasing policies and practices do not contribute to the structural drivers of labour exploitation, and in participating in and financially supporting worker-driven initiatives.

But giving up on corporate fairytales does mean pushing back on powerful interests fighting to create an illusion of governance through CSR, which consistently fails to protect the world's workers. And it means abandoning the idea that the prevailing model of global corporate production is somehow an iron law of doing business that must remain off the table for change.

How to Fix Labour Governance: Paths Forward

Addressing forced labour and human trafficking in supply chains requires us to tackle both the demand and supply factors described in Chapters 2, 3, 4 and 5 and to build a stronger global system of labour governance.

Quelling businesses' demand for forced labour will require: major transformations to business models, including the redistribution of value along the supply chain; new regulation and standards to govern labour and product supply chains; reigning in the scale and power of monopoly corporations; strengthening state regulations and international standards around wages, modern slavery, labour market intermediaries and the private enforcement industry; and stronger approaches to due diligence focused around addressing the impacts of businesses' own practices and activities on patterns of labour exploitation.

Addressing the supply of vulnerable people will require: implementing measures that are known to protect workers from forced labour and trafficking, like higher wages and permanent job contracts; bolstering the power of workers vis-à-vis businesses through unions and collective bargaining; better social, economic and labour market protection policies and programmes to address and prevent poverty and social discrimination; and overhauling the regulation of migration and the recruitment industry, and, especially, temporary migrant worker programmes.

My hope is that this book will help to shift the conversation in the modern slavery space from one about how to tinker around the edges of CSR programmes into one about how to achieve these substantive and wide-ranging structural changes. While addressing the root causes of forced labour in the global economy will be harder work than waiting for corporate fairytales to come true, building a new labour governance system is the only way to protect the world's workers. In this book's remaining pages, I sketch out key contours of these pathways forward in the hope of helping to ignite and inform these conversations. In doing so, I point to inspiring, creative and transformative work and strategy from workers and their organizations around the world, who are leading the way.

Addressing the Business Demand for Forced Labour

As long as businesses at the top of supply chains squeeze their suppliers, buy goods at and below costs of production and maintain irresponsible sourcing practices as described in Chapters 2 and 3, there will be a predictable and stable demand for forced labour and exploitation in supply chains. No amount of social auditing, ethical certification or CSR will change that. If we are going to fix the problem of severe labour exploitation, we need to dramatically transform and reconfigure existing business models, regulate supply chains and devise strategies to change the current context wherein businesses can use forced labour and labour exploitation with high levels of impunity.

Transform business models and redistribute value

While business models have been scarcely mentioned in policy and scholarly discussions of forced labour, there is an urgent need to investigate new business models that can prevent and address forced labour. No feature of prevailing business models should be off the table for discussion and change, and those that are most closely associated with the demand for forced labour, like outsourcing and shareholder value maximization, should be scrutinized especially closely. Ultimately, radically new models of corporate ownership, governance, entrepreneurship and financialization are needed to rebalance the global economy and address economic inequalities, including inequalities of power and profits between companies, their suppliers and their workforces. But this can start with smaller changes.

For example, a handful of companies have begun to address forced labour by tackling various facets of their business models, acknowledging the adverse impacts these have on labour standards. For instance, industry leaders are beginning to pay higher prices to suppliers and benchmark a percentage of this increase to cover higher labour costs or living wages; to sign longer-term contracts that give suppliers longer lead times; to ensure prices paid cover at least the costs of production; and to replace social auditing and certification with longer-term and less coercive models of collaboration with suppliers.[8]

Sector-based worker-driven initiatives demanding value redistribution along supply chains have been documented to improve labour standards. For instance, in the US, the Fair Food Program requires buyers to pay a small price premium that gets passed down to workers in the form of a weekly bonus. Nearly a decade ago, the Fair Food Program was established in the Florida tomato farming industry by the Coalition of Immokalee Workers, who organized consumers to demand that tomato buyers pay a penny more per pound of tomatoes and established a legally binding agreement with major buyers, including Walmart, Whole Foods Market, Sodexo, McDonald's, Burger King, Subway, Trader Joe's and Chipotle Mexican Grill.[9] While the Fair Food Program hasn't fundamentally transformed these companies' business models, it has harnessed their commercial weight to create a binding and enforceable agreement around labour standards in the notoriously tight margined agricultural sector, and it has triggered value redistribution from the top of the supply chain to the bottom.

The Fair Food Program sets out labour standards and mechanisms to improve conditions and wages, which are monitored by the Fair Food Standards Council through worker-to-worker education, auditing by workers, and a toll-free, 24/7, bilingual complaint line and resolution service. The complaint line is backed with prohibition of retaliation against workers who complain and staffed by investigators who help to resolve complaints.[10] When the Fair Food Program began, forced labour, sexual violence and wage theft were endemic in the US tomato industry. Today, it is widely recognized to have improved wages; significantly reduced health and safety violations, sexual harassment and wage theft; and eliminated sexual assault and forced labour. It was praised by then US President Obama as 'one of the most successful and innovative programs' in the world to combat modern slavery.[11] It has been replicated in other sectors, including garments and dairy.

These are inspiring examples of how labour exploitation can be addressed and prevented through value redistribution and business model innovation. These approaches are picking up steam, but there is a long, long way to go. Most of the companies that are considering their business models and value distribution as part of antislavery efforts are privately owned and have more leeway than those facing short-term pressures from shareholders. Indeed, the companies whose business models are most urgently in need of reform – such as the monopoly corporations documented in Chapter 3, whose policies set the bar across entire industries – have shown the least interest to date in integrating considerations around their business model into efforts to address and prevent forced labour. Furthermore, redistributions of value to date have been pretty minor. A massive redistribution of executive pay and corporate profits downward along the supply chain will ultimately be required to eradicate forced labour.

Enforce existing laws

To curtail the business demand for forced labour, countries in the global North and South need to strengthen the enforcement of labour laws that are already on their books. Labour inspectorates need to be better funded, and innovative forms of enforcement should be supported, to end the current business climate in which forced labour and exploitation thrive as a viable and profitable business model.

Some governments have already recognized this. For instance, in Brazil, under the Luis Inácio Lula da Silva government, the country created a specialized model of labour standards enforcement and a National Pact for the Eradication of Slave Labour to address the use of forced labour. Brazil's system includes a specialized enforcement unit that inspects sites suspected of using forced labour. It also includes a Dirty List for businesses that are found to have used forced labour; being placed on this list impacts businesses' ability to operate in Brazil, and to receive state loans or private credit from banks. As well, Brazil's Federal Labor Prosecution Office collaborates with the ILO towards an amazing database called the Decent Work SmartLab; it combines census, labour market and other geo-referenced data to enable evidence-based enforcement of labour standards, and it includes a Slave Labour Digital Observatory.[12]

In various parts of the US, workers' organizations and advocacy groups have collaborated with government to create 'co-produced enforcement' systems to enforce labour standards along the bottom end of the labour market. Labour relations professor Janice Fine describes co-produced enforcement as being:

> when those closest to the action, with the most information and the greatest incentives, partner with government and are accountable to government to enforce labor standards, and health and safety laws.

Under co-production, unions, worker centers, legal and community-based nonprofit organizations, and high-road firms, partner with government inspectors to educate workers on their rights and patrol their labor markets to identify businesses engaged in unethical and illegal practices.[13]

Co-enforcement tends to target high-risk industries with high levels of subcontracting, and labour market intermediaries, where laws are violated widely and frequently with impunity. This model complements and collaborates with government, rather than displacing government agencies. There are a number of successful co-produced enforcement collaborations across the US, which have been well-documented to identify issues, solve problems and assuage risks and fears for workers who speak up, and which protect them from retaliation.[14]

As well, some jurisdictions have created specialized units to enforce labour laws and prosecute businesses that violate them. For instance, in the US state of Illinois, Governor J. B. Pritzker launched 'a Worker Protection Unit within the Office of the Attorney General which will protect Illinois workers from wage theft and other unlawful employment practices'.[15] The Unit gives the Attorney General the authority to investigate and file suit against employers who violate a range of workplace laws that regulate wages, employee classification and temporary work. Similar programmes – targeting wage theft and illegal practices by employers along the bottom end and most informal segments of the labour market – are already well established in other states and cities.[16]

Of course, laws are only helpful if workers can access the protections they offer, and, as mentioned, workers frequently face retaliation from employers for exerting their rights. Retaliation can include deportation, being fired from their job, or even violence, threats of violence, and other actions that can harm workers and their family. Passing laws that protect workers from retaliation is an absolutely crucial part of addressing the business demand for forced labour.

By creating a realistic possibility that businesses breaking laws and labour standards will face consequences for these violations, bolstering labour law enforcement helps to address the business demand for forced labour and overlapping forms of exploitation.

Strengthen due diligence

A number of existing global standards, guidelines and principles have sought to make corporations more accountable for labour standards within their supply chains. These include the UN Guiding Principles on Business and Human Rights, OECD Guidelines for Multinational Enterprises, and OECD Due Diligence Guidance for Responsible Supply Chains of Minerals from Conflict-Affected and High-Risk Areas. To date, there has been limited meaningful uptake of human rights due diligence. But, if implemented in a rigorous way, the human rights due diligence framework could be a useful component of efforts to address the business demand for forced labour in supply chains.

According to the UN Guiding Principles, human rights due diligence involves 'assessing actual and potential human rights impacts, integrating and acting upon the findings, tracking responses, and communicating how impacts are addressed'. It should 'cover adverse human rights impacts that the business enterprise may cause or contribute to through its own activities, or which may be directly linked to its operations, products or services by its business relationships'.[17]

Tackling the business demand for forced labour along global supply chains through human rights due diligence would require at least three types of action. First, companies need to examine their commercial practices, business relationships and the actors within their supply chains and analyse how their core practices are linked to, and impact upon, the patterns and prevalence of forced labour and labour exploitation. In doing so, they should take into account research that documents how business models heighten risks of exploitation, including practices and dynamics like subcontracting and outsourcing, buying at the lowest cost, tight production windows and short-term contracts. There are several free open access tools that companies can use to examine their practices, including the Slavery & Trafficking Risk Template and tools available through the Business & Human Rights Resource Centre.[18]

Second, companies need to act upon their findings by altering commercial practices and relationships that create pressure towards labour exploitation within supply chains and by ensuring access to justice and remedy for workers who are affected. To date, very little action has been taken along these lines, and most human rights due diligence efforts have focused on assessing risk rather than acting upon it. The actions that businesses would need to take vary depending on their ownership structure, size, industry and the precise drivers and patterns of labour exploitation; these would probably include altering purchasing practices, building in measures and pathways for remediation and access to justice for workers in the face of abuse, and implementing protective factors like living wage benchmarks, which can help to guard against forced labour and exploitation. If rigorously implemented, these forms of human rights due diligence could constitute a step change in business action to prevent and address forced labour in supply chains.

Third, companies need to communicate the actions they've taken to address the business demand for forced labour. As mentioned throughout this book, at present, company reporting in modern slavery and human trafficking statements is patchy, inconsistent and often focused around largely irrelevant or inconsequential metrics. However, disclosing consistent and meaningful metrics about due diligence to prevent and address forced labour would be useful. This might include, for instance, supplier lists, including company names and addresses; supplier maps, including information about the labour force and wage data; information about the effectiveness of efforts taken to address labour exploitation; and action to address the structural business demand for forced labour within the supply chain.

To date, although there is a lot of excitement in civil society about human rights due diligence, business action towards it has been uneven and has yet to focus on addressing the critical commercial dynamics that are most clearly within their power to change. Strong and rigorous approaches to human rights due diligence could bend the needle towards effective corporate action to address the business demand for forced labour. This would change the current status quo in which corporations demand ethical labour practices from suppliers, but do not alter the components of their business models that undermine supplier efforts to meet these demands.

Regulate supply chains

Another feature of the failing labour governance regime that needs to be addressed to curb business demand for forced labour in supply chains is the lack of binding regulation around labour standards and liability for violations within supply chains. Indeed, global supply chains have been created and evolved in recent years precisely to evade existing workplace regulation. To date, international organizations and governments have done little to repair these gaps and modernize regulation. It is no doubt possible to address these gaps; indeed, considerable modernization and new legislation has taken place to facilitate the changing patterns of trade, investment and capital mobility. So far, however, laws have not been modernized and governance gaps related to changing patterns of labour exploitation have not been addressed. Laws and standards attuned to the contemporary realities of global supply chains are sorely needed to tackle business demand for forced labour.

Over recent years, workers, some governments and civil society groups have pushed for a global standard to establish corporate liability for labour abuse within supply chains. For instance, this was a key focus of the ILO's International Labour Conference in 2016. The basis for this standard is the recognition that – as documented in Chapters 2 and 4 – the removal of capital restrictions and changing patterns of foreign investment have facilitated the reorganization of global production into supply chains. As corporations have outsourced, offshored and sought to squeeze more profit out of value chains, while avoiding the responsibilities of employment, supply chains have come to involve thousands of suppliers, labour market interme-diaries and fissured workforces across dozens of national borders. At present, although they massively influence the conditions under which supplier firms operate and those workforces work, corporations at the top of the chain have little to no liability or legal responsibility for labour standards within their supply chains. A binding standard would change that reality, and create liability for firms at the top of supply chains around forced labour. However, employers' representatives within the ILO have consist-ently pushed back on the development of such a standard, and, as a result, this governance gap persists and urgently needs to be addressed.[19]

In spite of the lack of a global standard, national govern-ments have begun to pass various forms of legislation to address the dynamics of forced labour in global supply chains led by large corporations headquartered within their borders. Often referred to as 'home state' legislation, this body of law has yet to lead to much concrete and meaningful change, but some laws are more stringent than others and could be strengthened to spur changes in corporate behaviour.

For instance, transparency legislation has recently been passed in several jurisdictions, such as the UK Modern

Slavery Act and California Transparency and Supply Chains Act. At present, much of this legislation has low rates of compliance and there is little evidence to suggest that it is triggering meaningful change in labour standards in global supply chains. In a study that Nicola Phillips, Sara Wallin and I undertook for the ILO in 2018, we analysed the institutional design of 17 pieces of transparency legislation.[20] We found most pieces of legislation were weak, rubber-stamped existing private governance approaches, and lacked adequate enforcement provisions and penalties. As we argue in our study, however, transparency legislation could be immediately improved. If, rather than requiring companies to report on any measures they are taking and granting them the discretion to report they are doing nothing, companies were required to report on a standardized set of indicators each year, then this body of legislation could generate meaningful reporting on the specific risks of forced labour within supply chains and the actions they are taking to address these risks. In addition, companies could be required to report on the effectiveness of their efforts, rather than simply describing efforts (for example, social auditing and certification) that are well documented to be ineffective. These changes would ensure that companies reported relevant and consistent information; of course, the key question would still be what happens next to that information.

New forms of home state legislation could also help to close governance gaps around corporate liability for forced labour in supply chains. One particularly promising model is home state regulation that creates extraterritorial criminal liability for forced labour that occurs within a company's supply chains. As mentioned in Chapter 3, this model of legislation is used for other illegal practices – such as bribery – and was considered as a model for the UK Modern Slavery Act, drawing from the example of the UK Bribery Act. Creating criminal liability for forced labour that occurs within global supply chains would mean that the company at the top of the supply chain could be held criminally liable for those incidents even if they occur overseas. This style of legislation has a much higher level of stringency than prevailing models of transparency legislation and has been found to spur corporations to meaningfully change their purchasing practices and private contracts with suppliers, to include stricter language in supplier-related documents and codes of conduct and to meaningfully report on problems and solutions.[21]

Another legal strategy to close governance gaps around supply chains is to establish joint liability between corporations at the top of the supply chain and suppliers and labour market intermediaries further down the chain.[22] Joint liability regulation has been around for a long time. For instance, Senator Ted Kennedy and Representative Bill Clay introduced a 'Stop Sweatshops Act of 1996' to the US Congress, which would have amended the Fair Labor Standards Act of 1983. Amidst reports of apparel sweatshops, the Stop Sweatshops Act sought to hold garment manufacturers and retailers jointly liable for labour violations within supply chains. This included wage violations, such as delayed or nonpayment and paying below minimum wage, and the Act carried civil penalties of up to US$15,000 for failure to maintain payroll records.[23] This Act was never passed by Congress, but, in recent years, joint employer liability has again gained momentum as a solution to curtailing the business demand for forced labour in supply chains.

Across several countries, governments – including the Canadian province of Manitoba, the Netherlands and the Philippines – have begun to enact and recognize joint liability.[24] For instance, in Belgium, courts have held companies liable for abetting human trafficking in their supply chains, even where they claimed they were not legally the employer.[25] Joint employer standards have been established within the US, both by National Labor Relations Board and in local jurisdictions. In 2016, the US Department of Labor issued an Administrative

Interpretation 'reminding business entities that they may be jointly liable for minimum wage and overtime obligations towards workers even where they are not the "employer" for purposes of payroll or other common law definitions'.[26]

Legal academics and experts see joint liability as a key way to enforce labour standards by making businesses at the top of the supply chain – which have the greatest capacity to address problems and influence labour conditions further down the chain – liable for labour abuse within the supply chain. For instance, law professor Jennifer Gordon has recommended that governments implement joint liability regimes to make employers of migrant workers responsible for abuse perpetrated by labour recruiters, even when they are located abroad, and has developed detailed policy recommendations for how this could be implemented.[27] Crucially, lawyer and scholar J. J. Rosenbaum cautions that joint liability will only be effective if it comes with strong enforcement by government. As she notes, 'the power of a joint employer liability legal regime – whether USDOL, ILO or any other – rests significantly in the effectiveness of its enforcement arm'.[28]

Ultimately, new and updated regulation is needed to modernize workplace protections across a whole range of issues that determine and shape labour standards in supply chains, such as wages, labour agencies and recruiters, and the private enforcement industry. As David Weil notes, there is a need to revise 'workplace laws so that they adequately recognize the far more complex nature of the modern workplace and the growing presence of multiple organizations with roles in employment decisions'.[29] The good news is that dozens of scholars and organizations around the world are putting forth promising proposals for how to do this.[30] To name just two, Global Labor Justice has developed a series of policy proposals for strengthening labour and migrant rights in global supply chains,[31] and the European Center for Constitutional and Human Rights (ECCHR) has developed proposals to create legal liability for social auditors.[32] Global trade union federations have also begun to negotiate international framework agreements with MNCs.[33]

As long as laws around labour standards in supply chains are dated and governance gaps remain open, they will be readily exploited by employers using forced labour. Legal reforms could help to change the current context of impunity for businesses, and could spur corporations to alter commercial practices that give rise to forced labour further down the chain.

Regulate the enforcement industry

As mentioned in Chapter 5, the enforcement industry is almost entirely self-regulated. If it is going to continue to operate, it needs to be regulated by a body with a responsibility for the public good. This might include, for instance, creating an oversight body and professional codes for social auditors, liability for accuracy and failing to report problems (and a lack of measures by companies to correct those problems), and a system to require transparency in social auditing results. So long as businesses are financing the enforcement industry and companies hold the power to dictate how it operates, I am sceptical that it can be meaningfully reformed. But these changes could be done swiftly, and the enforcement industry needs to be regulated if the system is going to continue to operate as a tool of labour governance in global supply chains.

Worker-driven social responsibility

As mentioned in Chapters 1, 2 and 3, a key reason that CSR approaches to eradicating forced labour aren't working is that they are not binding or enforceable and tend to sideline workers rather than make use of their knowledge of the problem and involve them in addressing it. There is a serious need for worker-driven and binding supply chain solutions that are actually enforceable.

A promising wave of initiatives – often called Worker-Driven Social Responsibility (WSR) initiatives – offers an alternative to CSR that has been well documented to improve conditions for vulnerable, low-wage workers in supply chains:

> WSR provides a proven new form of power for previously powerless workers to protect and enforce their own rights. These rights can include – according to the circumstances and priorities of the workers driving the program – the right to freedom of association, the right to a safe and healthy work environment (including the right to work free from sexual harassment and sexual violence), and the right to work free of forced labor or violence, among other fundamental rights.[34]

WSR involves legally binding agreements between workers and brands and retailers, backed by corporations' commercial power, including financial support to suppliers that enables them to meet the labour standards established in WSR agreements. In the WSR model, violations of standards carry serious consequences because brands and retailers impose mandatory economic consequences for suppliers who fail to comply. Unlike in CSR, in WSR models, workers, unions and worker organizations play a central role in creating, monitoring and enforcing initiatives. As the WSR Network puts it:

> Monitoring and enforcement mechanisms must be designed to provide workers an effective voice in the protection of their own rights, including extensive worker education on their rights under the program, rigorous workplace inspections that are effectively independent of brand and retailer influence, public disclosure of the names and locations of participating brands and suppliers, and a complaint mechanism that ensures swift and effective action when workers identify abuses.[35]

And unlike the private enforcement industry, WSR creates transparency and accountability by publicly disclosing the businesses that are involved in WSR agreements and initiatives.

The Fair Food Program described above is a flagship example of a WSR agreement, as is the Bangladesh Accord on Fire and Building Safety. Today, WSR is accelerating quickly, with new agreements emerging covering different businesses and sectors. For instance, ice-cream brand Ben & Jerry's recently signed a WSR agreement called Milk with Dignity with farmworkers in Vermont, and, in Lesotho, trade unions, women's and workers' organizations signed an agreement with Levi Strauss & Co., The Children's Place and Nien Hsing Textile to address gender-based violence and harassment at garment factories.[36]

WSR initiatives help to address the business demand for forced labour through binding agreements that carry commercial consequences for suppliers, and by ensuring that suppliers are paid and supported enough to meet labour standards. They enable workers to play a key role in solutions to forced labour and overlapping forms of exploitation, and, in doing so, overcome many of the limits of CSR. Like all sector-based initiatives, WSR carries the risk of displacing problems – in other words, as a factory in the garment industry gets cleaned up, the problems move to another factory, or to mining or agricultural – but this risk can be mitigated through complementary forms of government regulation and enforcement, as described above. As well, some actors within the labour governance space are concerned that WSR circumvents the state and unions, and this warrants further discussion, especially where WSR operates in states that do have the capacity to enforce their own labour laws through state-based inspection.

Rebalance corporate and worker power

Ultimately, creating an effective labour governance system that protects the world's workers will depend on rebalancing the power that workers and corporations hold within national economies and the global economy.

Decades of neoliberal economic policy have tilted the scales overwhelmingly towards employers. As governments and workplace fissuring have constrained workers' rights to organize, bargain, act collectively and unionize, workers' power has been eroded. Amidst soaring income and wealth inequality, capital mobility and growing poverty and precarity for large swathes of the labour market, the power of workers has been compromised and prospects for restoring it may seem dim. But new models of organizing workers are emerging and are strengthening power and voice along supply chains. For instance, Jobs with Justice's campaign 'Change Walmart, Change the Economy' created links between Walmart employees and local community groups to transform dynamics across the supply chain through advocacy, shareholder activism and various forms of mobilization, and has helped to raise wages. Organizations like Global Labor Justice, AFL-CIO, the Solidarity Center, Worker Rights Consortium, Jobs with Justice, WIEGO and Coalition of Immokalee Workers are pioneering new forms of worker organizing fit to protect twenty-first-century workers.

Rebalancing the highly uneven power dynamics between employers and workers is key to ending the business demand for forced labour. As workers along supply chains develop new strategies to transcend fissuring, organize and trace bad and illegal practices back to brands and corporations at the top of the chain, forced labour will become far less viable as a business model.

Addressing the Supply of Vulnerable Workers

In addition to building a labour governance system that can address the business demand for forced labour, we need to curtail the supply of vulnerable workers if we are going to eradicate forced labour in the global economy.

As long as workers are poor and do not have access to decent work, they will enter into jobs and the recruitment industry, even where these are risky, badly paid and involve considerable levels of abuse, and they will face structural constraints and challenges to reporting and addressing abuse and exploitation. In the global capitalist marketplace, where money is increasingly necessary to survive, and failing to locate a buyer for your labour can mean death or destitution, substantive changes to how economies and labour markets operate are needed to curtail the supply of workers vulnerable to forced labour and human trafficking. Some key immediate priorities include social protection, implementing social and labour protection measures that are known to protect workers from forced labour and trafficking, like higher wages and permanent jobs, regulating the recruitment industry and building better protections into temporary migrant work programmes.

Living wages and social protection

As described in Chapter 2, the erosion of welfare state policies and social protections means that large swathes of the global labour market have no safety net that would allow them to survive, and so they turn to low-paid, often risky and exploitative jobs and work. We need to implement protections that reduce vulnerability to forced labour by giving people – and especially the unemployed and those on low incomes – support to make ends meet. This will help to reduce vulnerability to forced labour, especially debt bondage, as well as the forms of compression within the labour market that create situations in which workers have little choice but to work for below the minimum wage and under coercion.

Rebuilding state-based protection and welfare bolsters workers' power to say no to and to contest labour market exploitation. Recognizing the role of social protection in quelling vulnerability to labour abuse, governments, civil society organizations and workers have developed wide-ranging social, political and economic policies that create safety nets, redistribute wealth and provide public goods.

One basket of such policies and programmes delivers social protection. According to the ILO, social protection floors are 'nationally defined sets of basic social security guarantees that should ensure, as a minimum that, over the life cycle, all in need have access to essential health care and to basic income security which together secure effective access to goods and services defined as necessary at the national level'.[37] Recognizing the value of social protection for curbing vulnerability to severe labour exploitation, efforts are under way in several countries across Asia and Africa to enact and expand social protection schemes that include informal and vulnerable workers and their children, such as through child grants and unconditional cash transfer programmes.[38]

There is also growing recognition that living wages are a crucial source of protection for workers. By ensuring that workers have sufficient income to meet the needs of themselves and their families, living wages mitigate vulnerability to usurious debt, predatory recruiters and the urgent need to take on exploitative work to cover shocks. Workers and civil society groups, including Living Wage Foundation and the Fight for $15, are pushing for governments and employers to raise wage standards so they cover the costs of living. Some progress has already been made; in the UK, there are now 5,000 accredited Living Wage Employers,[39] and, in the US, more than 120 municipalities have enacted living wage ordinances.[40] Of course, to ensure that these wage levels are not met through other corner-cutting and cost-reduction strategies (for instance, raised productivity), value redistribution from the top of the supply chain to the actors paying wage increases needs to accompany them.

Much more work is needed to raise wages in the global economy, and especially at the lower end of the labour market where sub-minimum wage work, wage theft and forms of under and nonpayment have become routine. Research demonstrating that these more minor forms of exploitation create and underpin vulnerability to forced labour highlights the need for living wages. Also, it points for the need to raise wage floors across global supply chains to prevent capital flight. The Asia Floor Wage Alliance (AFWA) has advocated for a 'floor wage' in the apparel industry, which would create a living wage for garment workers in Asia. This could be replicated in other sectors and regions.

Social protection and living wage, floor wage, sectoral wage and regional wage policies are all protective factors that mitigate poverty and vulnerability to forced labour. To put it simply, allowing people to earn enough money and giving them free access to necessities like medical care reduces the supply of people vulnerable to forced labour by making it less likely that they will enter into debt bondage or risky or exploitative jobs as a strategy to meet these needs.

Expand unions and organizing

Corporate fairytales about modern slavery offer a vision of the problem and solutions in which labour abuse can be addressed without unions, workers' rights or labour organizing. But this overlooks a key component of a strong labour governance system that can address the supply of people vulnerable to forced labour.

Unions provide a crucial source of protection against forced labour to their members by bolstering labour rights and conditions, providing support to address wrongs, and through enabling collective action. They also tend to yield higher pay compared to non-unionized workplaces.[41] Many of the world's most vulnerable workers, however, are not able to join unions. Even where they are able to do so, laws that should protect them from retaliation for exerting rights are not enforced. In many countries, for instance, national labour laws formally exclude migrant workers from the ability to join and hold office in unions. This needs to be changed.

But unions provide support to vulnerable workers even where they are not members. For instance, in many industries and countries, unions provide training and raise awareness about the risks of forced labour and human trafficking and how to combat these. Organizations like AFL-CIO Solidarity Center work with local unions to educate workers who plan to migrate about labour laws and rights, and to build relationships between migrant rights organizations, governments and trade unions that can strengthen migrant workers' access to justice.[42] Similarly, across Europe, trade unions have established centres for migrant workers who may be vulnerable to forced labour and human trafficking. These centres 'are often run by migrants themselves and provide information (sometimes in the migrants' own language), administrative and legal assistance, vocational training and language classes to both documented and undocumented workers regardless of whether they are union members or not'.[43]

Unions and worker organizations also provide education and training that can reinforce workers' skills and retrain them.[44] This can reduce the likelihood of forced labour, and where workers have already experienced human trafficking or forced labour, it can mitigate the chance of this happening a second time. This is especially critical where there is limited support for victims of forced labour and trafficking, and where workers may be struggling to repay debts, overcome trauma and reintegrate into society. Many trade unions provide counselling and professional and vocational training, and some even run college courses to retrain victims of trafficking and help them to locate work in higher skilled professions.

Labour organizing also plays a critical role in preventing and addressing human trafficking and forced labour. For instance, labour organizations play a critical role in supporting lawsuits that allow workers who have experienced human trafficking and forced labour to receive support and justice. The widely championed and successful Signal case described in Chapter 4 held together amidst government surveillance, threats of violence and concerns about arrest and deportation, and was ultimately successful only because it was a worker-organizing struggle.[45]

Unions and worker organizations also play a key role in enabling workers facing abuse to come forward about problems in their job, and in supporting them to access justice. They also campaign to change the behaviour of governments, employers and recruiters, to negotiate agreements and to protect workers who report problems from retaliation.

Ultimately, forced labour is not an issue that can be solved without addressing the curtailing of labour rights and the global attack on labour unions and organizing. After all, it is not coincidental that forced labour and human trafficking disproportionately impact low-wage, informal and migrant workers, who are often the least protected and face barriers and restrictions on their ability to unionize. The failure to see forced labour and human trafficking as labour rights issues is a failure to understand the power dynamics involved – these power dynamics in the labour market have to be addressed if we are to end the supply of people vulnerable to forced labour.

Strengthen protections for low-wage and migrant work

Just as regulatory reforms are necessary to close the governance gaps that fuel a demand for forced labour among businesses, so too are regulatory reforms necessary to strengthen protection for low-wage and migrant workers to prevent and address the supply of people who are vulnerable to forced labour and human trafficking.

In many countries, workers who are most vulnerable to forced labour – such as agricultural workers, domestic workers and migrant workers – are excluded from laws and protections around labour standards, such as workplace safety, wages, overtime and freedom of association. A wide range of worker and migrant rights organizations, policy-makers and others are advocating for these exclusions to be addressed, offering badly needed rights and protection to these vulnerable segments of the labour force. In addition, they are pushing for new protections to address the specific challenges and forms of vulnerability that are typical of these forms of work. For instance, in the US, the National Domestic Workers Alliance is campaigning for a National Domestic Workers Bill of Rights that would expand US workplace rights and protections to include domestic workers, as well as create new protections, such as a domestic workers wage and standards board.[46] Legal advocates and migrant worker organizations are also working to expand the freedom of migrant workers within temporary foreign work programmes, so that they can, for example, move between employers without losing their visa, which is often described as 'portability' for migrant workers.[47]

Of course, industry is pushing back. These forms of vulnerability have been carefully cultivated and are hugely valuable for businesses. Indeed, in some cases, as documented in Chapters 2 and 3, compressing labour at levels below a minimum wage and exempting workers from workplace protection are the only ways that businesses and households are remaining afloat amidst economic trans-formation wrought by neoliberalism and the ascendency of global value chains. But whether they will acknowledge it or not, these exemptions and compressions are creating a predictable supply of workers vulnerable to forced labour and so need to be addressed if we are to eradicate forced labour from the global economy.

Regulate the recruitment industry

As documented in Chapter 4, the recruitment industry is virtually unregulated and plays a key role in forced labour and human trafficking. Ending the supply of people vulnerable to forced labour requires us to regulate and reform the recruitment industry. So long as workers are charged fees for jobs and accrue debts for expenses like transportation, administrative and visa costs, they will be highly vulnerable to forced labour and very unlikely to come forward to report problems at work.

There have been several efforts to regulate the recruitment industry over recent years. For instance, an ILO contract labour convention was proposed, but ultimately failed. Some policymakers and NGOs see the new UN Global Compact for Migration as a step forward for migrant workers around the world. However, the implementation of this Compact will only expand further the market of the recruitment industry, and makes adequate regulation of recruiters even more urgent.

Lawyers have put forward several innovative proposals to regulate the labour supply chain and recruitment industry. For instance, law professor Jennifer Gordon has argued for 'applying shared liability', which would render all of the actors within the labour supply chain potentially liable for the action of recruiters, as well as a 'statutory tort regime', which would allow for lead firms to be held responsible for creating conditions under which recruiters perpetrate harm to workers. She also documents promising existing efforts by government and NGOs in countries like Canada, the UK, the Philippines and the Netherlands, which could be replicated and deepened to regulate the recruitment industry.[48] Such reforms would go a long way to closing a crucial source of the supply of workers vulnerable to forced labour in the global economy.

Conclusion

I have argued in this chapter that far more profound changes to business models and the labour market than are typically imagined are required to eradicate forced labour. The growing evidence that subcontracting and outsourcing, uneven profit and value distribution, and the recruitment industry are fuelling forced labour compels us to consider much bigger changes to contemporary business models than are generally contemplated in debates about improving supply chain and antislavery governance. And the growing evidence that forced labour and human trafficking are not anomalies within the global economy, but relate to broader patterns around low wages, lacking protections for vulnerable workers, and restrictions on union activity and organizing, prompts us to centralize fundamental labour rights and working conditions as solutions to forced labour.

No doubt, work towards creating these changes are unlikely to be funded by the CSR fairytale departments of the world's largest corporations. But these corporations have sizable financial interests in maintaining the status quo of our current failing labour governance regime. It is only by confronting corporate interests and recognizing that CSR is working to produce outcomes desirable for large corporations, but isn't working for the world's most vulnerable workers, that we can begin to fix labour governance.

Notes

Chapter 1   Who Does Labour Governance Work For?

1 See Rebecca Chao, 'Dhaka factory collapse: How far can businesses be held responsible?', *Guardian*, 16 May 2013, https://www.theguardian.com/sustainable-business/dhaka-factory-collapse-businesses-held-responsible; Jim Yardley, 'Report on deadly factory collapse in Bangladesh finds widespread blame', *New York Times*, 22 May 2013, https://www.nytimes.com/2013/05/23/world/asia/report-on-bangladesh-building-collapse-finds-widespread-blame.html; Amy Kazmin, 'How Benetton faced up to the aftermath of Rana Plaza', *Financial Times*, 20 April 2015, https://www.ft.com/content/f9d84f0e-e509-11e4-8b61-00144feab7de.
2 Reuters, 'Rana Plaza collapse: 38 charged with murder over garment factory disaster', *Guardian*, 18 July 2016, https://www.theguardian.com/world/2016/jul/18/rana-plaza-collapse-murder-charges-garment-factory.
3 European Centre for Constitutional and Human Rights, 'Case report: OECD complaint against TUV Rheinland audit for Rana Plaza', August 2018, https://www.oecdwatch.org/cases/Case_509/1732/at_download/file.
4 European Centre for Constitutional and Human Rights,

'Complaint against TÜV Rheinland and TÜV India on possible violations of the OECD guidelines for multinational companies', OECD Watch, May 2016, https://www.oecdwatch.org/cases/Case_509/1732/at_download/file.

5 Julfikar Ali Manik, Jim Yardley and Steven Greenhouse, 'Bangladeshis burn factories to protest unsafe conditions', *New York Times*, 26 April 2013, https://www.nytimes.com/2013/04/27/world/asia/bangladesh-building-collapse.html.

6 The Walt Disney Company, *Disney Citizenship: Performance Summary 2012*, pp. 8, 78, https://ditm-twdc-us.storage.googleapis.com/FY12DisneyCitizenshipSummary_FINAL_0.pdf.

7 Kazmin, 'How Benetton faced up to the aftermath of Rana Plaza'.

8 See, for instance, Tim Bartley, *Rules without Rights: Land, Labor, and Private Authority in the Global Economy* (New York: Oxford University Press, 2018); A. Claire Cutler, Virginia Haufler and Tony Porter, eds., *Private Authority and International Affairs* (New York: State University of New York Press, 1999).

9 Genevieve LeBaron, Jane Lister and Peter Dauvergne, 'Governing global supply chain sustainability through the ethical audit regime', *Globalizations* 14/6 (2017), p. 959.

10 Bartley, *Rules without Rights*, p. 46.

11 For an overview, see Nicola Phillips, Genevieve LeBaron and Sara Wallin, 'Mapping and measuring the effectiveness of labour-related disclosure requirements for global supply chains', ILO Research Department Working Paper No. 32, June (Geneva: International Labour Organization, 2018).

12 Genevieve LeBaron, *Report of Findings: The Global Business of Forced Labour* (Sheffield: SPERI, 2018), pp. 38–42.

13 Marcus Stern, 'The human cost hidden within a cup of coffee', *The Source*, 19 January 2017, https://features.weather.com/thesource/.

14 Kate Hodal, Chris Kelly and Felicity Lawrence, 'Revealed: Asian slave labour producing prawns for supermarkets in US, UK', *Guardian*, 10 June 2014, https://www.theguardian.com/global-development/2014/jun/10/supermarket-prawns-thailand-produced-slave-labour; Annie Kelly, 'Thai seafood: Are the prawns on your plate still fished by slaves?',

Guardian, 23 January 2018, https://www.theguardian.com/
global-development/2018/jan/23/thai-seafood-industry-
report-trafficking-rights-abuses; Kate Knibbs, 'Apple
banned bonded servitude, but we aren't sure about its
rivals', *Gizmodo*, 19 February 2015, https://gizmodo.com/
apple-finally-banned-bonded-servitude-so-what-about-
it-1686291768; Wesley Stephenson, 'Have 1,200 World Cup
workers really died in Qatar?', *BBC News*, 6 June 2015,
https://www.bbc.co.uk/news/magazine-33019838.

15 See, for instance, Kevin Bales, *Disposable People: New
Slavery in the Global Economy* (Berkeley: University of
California Press, 2012 [2000]).

16 John Bowe, *Nobodies: Modern American Slave Labor and
the Dark Side of the New Global Economy* (New York:
Random House, 2007), p. xx.

17 Kevin Bales and Ron Soodalter, *The Slave Next Door:
Human Trafficking and Slavery in America Today* (Berkeley:
University of California Press, 2009).

18 See openDemocracy's *Beyond Trafficking and Slavery* hub
for debates about the term 'modern slavery'.

19 Janie Chuang, 'Exploitation creep and the unmaking of
human trafficking law', *American Journal of International
Law* 108/4 (2014), pp. 609–649.

20 Julia O'Connell Davidson, *Modern Slavery: The Margins of
Freedom* (London: Palgrave, 2015).

21 Neil Howard, Cameron Thibos and Genevieve LeBaron,
'Why we need to move beyond trafficking and slavery',
openDemocracy.net, 3 October 2014, https://www.opendem-
ocracy.net/en/beyond-trafficking-and-slavery/introduction/.

22 ILO, *Global Estimates of Modern Slavery: Forced Labour
and Forced Marriage* (Geneva: International Labour
Organization, 2017); ILO, *Profits and Poverty: The
Economics of Forced Labour* (Geneva: International Labour
Organization, 2017).

23 See, for instance, Michael Toffel, Jodi Short and Melissa
Ouellet 'Codes in context: How states, markets, and
civil society shape adherence to global labor standards.'
Regulation & Governance 9 (2015), pp. 205–223; Greg
Distelhorst and Richard M. Locke, 'Does compliance pay?
Social standards and firm-level trade', *American Journal of
Political Science* 62/3 (2017), pp. 695–711; Greg Distelhorst,

Jens Hainmueller, and Richard M. Locke, 'Does lean improve labor standards? Management and social performance in the Nike supply chain', *Management Science* 63/3 (2017), pp. 707–728; Marieke Koekkoek, Axel Marx and Jan Wouters, 'Monitoring forced labour and slavery in global supply chains: The case of the California Act on transparency in supply chains', *Global Policy* 8/4 (2017), pp. 552–530; Richard Locke, F. Qin and A. Brause, 'Does monitoring improve labor standards? Lessons from Nike', *Industrial and Labor Relations Review* 61/1 (2007), pp. 3–31; Graeme Auld and Stefan Renckens, 'Rule-making feedbacks through intermediation and evaluation in transnational private governance', *Annals of the American Academy of Political and Social Science* 670/1 (2017), pp. 93–111.

24 See, for instance, Burkard Eberlein, Kenneth W. Abbott, Julia Black, Errol Meidinger and Stepan Wood, 'Transnational business governance interactions: Conceptualisation and framework for analysis', *Regulation & Governance* 8/1 (2013), pp. 1–21; Graeme Auld and Stefan Renckens, 'Rule-making feedbacks through intermediation and evaluation in transnational private governance'; Benjamin Cashore, Graeme Auld and Deanna Newsome, *Governing Through Markets: Forest Certification and the Emergence of Non-State Authority* (New Haven, CT: Yale University Press, 2004); Hamish van der Ven, Catharine Rothacker and Benjamin Cashore, 'Do eco-labels prevent deforestation? Lessons from non-state market driven governance in the soy, palm oil, and cocoa sectors', *Global Environmental Change* 52 (2018), pp. 141–151.

25 See, for instance, Carlos Oya, Florian Schafer and Dafni Skalidou, 'The effectiveness of agricultural certification in developing countries: A systematic review', *World Development* 112 (2018), pp. 282–312; Michael J. Bloomfield and Philip Schleifer, 'Tracing failure of coral reef protection in nonstate market-driven governance', *Global Environmental Politics* 17/1 (2017), pp. 127–146.

26 Matthew Potoski and Aseem Prakash, 'Preface', in Matthew Potoski and Aseem Prakash, eds., *Voluntary Programs: A Club Theory Perspective* (Cambridge, MA: MIT Press, 2009), p. viiii.

27 See, for instance, Lars H. Gulbrandsen 'Dynamic governance interactions: Evolutionary effects of state responses to

non-state certification programs', *Regulation & Governance* 8/1 (2012), pp. 74–92; Philip Schleifer, 'Varieties of multistakeholder governance: Selecting legitimation strategies in transnational sustainability politics', *Globalizations* 16/1 (2018), pp. 50–66; van der Ven, Rothacker and Cashore, 'Do eco-labels prevent deforestation?'; Ketty Kortelainen 'Global supply chains and social requirements: Case studies of labour condition auditing in the People's Republic of China', *Business Strategy and the Environment* 17 (2008), pp. 431–443.

28 LeBaron, *Report of Findings: The Global Business of Forced Labour.*

29 These include LeBaron, *Report of Findings: The Global Business of Forced Labour*; Andrew Crane, Genevieve LeBaron, Jean Allain and Laya Behbahani, 'Governance gaps in eradicating forced labour: From global to domestic supply chains', *Regulation & Governance* 13/1 (2017), pp. 1–21; Jean Allain, Andrew Crane, Genevieve LeBaron and Laya Behbahani, *Forced Labour's Business Models and Supply Chains* (York: Joseph Rowntree Foundation, 2013); Genevieve LeBaron, Neil Howard, Cameron Thibos and Penelope Kyritsis, *Confronting Root Causes: Forced Labour in Global Supply Chains* (Sheffield: SPERI/openDemocracy, 2018); Genevieve LeBaron and Andreas Ruhmkorf, 'Steering CSR through home state regulation: A comparison of the impact of the UK Bribery Act and Modern Slavery Act on global supply chain governance', *Global Policy* 8/3 (2017), pp. 14–28; Genevieve LeBaron and Andreas Ruhmkorf, 'The domestic politics of corporate accountability legislation: Struggles over the 2015 Modern Slavery Act', *Socio-Economic Review* (2017), pp. 1–35.

30 See David McNally, *Another World Is Possible: Globalization and Anti-Capitalism* (Winnipeg, MB: Arberiter Ring Publishing, 2006); Naomi Klein, *No Logo: Taking Aim at the Brand Bullies* (London: Picador, 1999).

31 For the *Life Magazine* story, see International Labor Rights Forum, https://laborrights.org/in-the-news/six-cents-hour-1996-life-article. For Phil Knight's quote, see China Labor Watch, 'TED case study: Nike Shoes and child labour in Pakistan', *China Labor Watch*, 4 November 2010, http://www.chinalaborwatch.org/newscast/66.

32 Burhan Wazir, 'Nike accused of tolerating sweatshops', *Guardian*, 20 May 2001, https://www.theguardian.com/world/2001/may/20/burhanwazir.theobserver.

33 See, for instance, Marcus Taylor, 'Race you to the bottom … and back again? The uneven development of labour codes of conduct', *New Political Economy* 16/4 (2011), pp. 445–462; Edna Bonacich and Richard P. Abbelbaum, *Behind the Label: Inequality in the Los Angeles Apparel Industry* (Berkeley, CA: University of California Press, 2000).

34 *Nike Statement on Forced Labor, Human Trafficking and Modern Slavery for Fiscal Year 2018*, https://www.nike.com/gb/help/a/modern-slavery-act-disclosure.

35 The Coca-Cola Company, *Human and Workplace Rights 2017*, https://www.modernslaveryregistry.org/companies/19434-the-coca-cola-company/statements/28265.

36 Tata Global Beverages, *Slavery and Human Trafficking Statement for Tata Global Beverages GB Limited for the Financial Year Ending 31 March 2018*, p. 2, http://tataglobalbeverages.com/docs/default-source/default-document-library/slavery-and-human-trafficking-statement-2016-17.pdf?sfvrsn=0.

37 Starbucks, 'Responsibly grown coffee', http://www.starbucks.ph/responsibility/ethical-sourcing/coffee-sourcing.

38 As quoted in Andrew Crane, Vivek Soundararajan, Michael Bloomfield, Laura Spence and Genevieve LeBaron, *Decent Work and Economic Growth in the South Indian Garment Industry* (Bath: University of Bath, 2019), p. 29.

39 Luc Fransen and Genevieve LeBaron, 'Big audit firms as regulatory intermediaries in transnational labour governance', *Regulation & Governance* 13/2 (2018), pp. 1, 8.

40 Deloitte Consulting, *The Freedom Ecosystem: How the Power of Partnership Can Help Stop Modern Slavery 2015*, p. 5, https://www2.deloitte.com/insights/us/en/topics/social-impact/freedom-ecosystem-stop-modern-slavery.html#.

41 Skype interview with Social Sustainability Manager, industry association, 20 December 2017.

42 Consumer Goods Forum, 'Forced labour eradication key topic at sustainable retail summit', *Consumer Goods Forum*, 2 November 2016, https://www.theconsumergoodsforum.

com/social_news_updates/forced-labour-eradication-key-topic-at-sustainable-retail-summit/.

43 Global Business Coalition Against Human Trafficking, 'Our Mission', https://www.gbcat.org/.

44 Oxfam, 'Smallholder supply chains', https://policy-practice.oxfam.org.uk/our-approach/private-sector/smallholder-supply-chains.

45 Marks & Spencer, *Modern Slavery Statement 2017/18*, pp. 4, 7, 9, https://corporate.marksandspencer.com/documents/plan-a-our-approach/mns-modern-slavery-statement-june2018.pdf.

46 Morrisons Supermarkets PLC, *Modern Slavery Act Statement 2017/2018*, p. 5, https://www.morrisons-corporate.com/globalassets/corporatesite/corporate-responsibility/documents/2018/morrisons_modern_slavery_act_2018.pdf.

47 Free the Slaves, 'Sponsors, donors, partners', https://www.freetheslaves.net/about-us/sponsors-donors-partners.

48 UN Global Compact, 'Who we are', https://www.unglobalcompact.org/what-is-gc.

49 UN Global Compact, 'Our participants', https://www.unglobalcompact.org/what-is-gc/participants.

50 Tesco PLC, *Modern Slavery Statement 2017/18*, p. 14, https://www.tescoplc.com/media/392433/modern_slavery_act.pdf.

51 ILO, 'Business Networks', https://www.ilo.org/empent/areas/business-helpdesk/networks/lang--en/index.htm.

52 Joel Bakan, *The Corporation: The Pathological Pursuit of Profit and Power* (New York: Simon and Schuster, 2005); see also Mark Achbar, Jennifer Abbott and Joel Bakan (dir), *The Corporation* (New York: Zeitgeist Films, 2003).

53 LeBaron and Ruhmkorf, 'Steering CSR through home state regulation'; LeBaron and Ruhmkorf, 'The domestic politics of corporate accountability legislation'.

54 See, for instance, Phillips, LeBaron and Wallin, 'Mapping and measuring the effectiveness of labour-related disclosure requirements for global supply chains'.

55 See Michael Bloomfield and Genevieve LeBaron, 'The UK Modern Slavery Act: Transparency through disclosure', *E-International Relations*, 21 September 2018, https://www.e-ir.info/2018/09/21/the-uk-modern-slavery-act-transparency-through-disclosure-in-global-governance/.

56 CORE, *Risk Averse? Company Reporting on Raw Material and Sector Specific Risks Under the Transparency in Supply Chains clause in the UK Modern Slavery Act 2015* (2017), pp. 4 and 8, https://corporate-responsibility.org/wp-content/uploads/2017/10/171003_Risk-Averse-FINAL-1.pdf; see also Ergon Associates, *Modern Slavery Statements: One Year On* (2017), https://ergonassociates.net/wp-content/uploads/2018/01/MSA_One_year_on_April_2017.pdf?x74739.

57 Interview with NGO representative, 7 December 2017, London.

58 Interview with brand retailer, 12 July 2013, Seattle, USA.

59 Gordon Lafer, 'The legislative attack on American wages and labor standards, 2011–2012', Economic Policy Institute Briefing Paper No. 364 (Washington, DC: Economic Policy Institute, 2013), p. 29.

60 See Allain et al., *Forced Labour's Business Models and Supply Chains*; Crane et al., 'Governance gaps in eradicating forced labour'.

61 See LeBaron et al., *Confronting Root Causes*.

62 Interview with auditor, 13 March 2013, London.

Chapter 2   Labour Exploitation in Global Supply Chains

1 See Genevieve LeBaron, *Report of Findings: The Global Business of Forced Labour* (Sheffield: SPERI, 2018); Orla Ryan, *Chocolate Nations: Living and Dying for Cocoa in West Africa* (London: Zed Books, 2012); Verité, *Strengthening Protections Against Trafficking in Persons in Federal and Corporate Supply Chains* (2017), https://www.verite.org/wp-content/uploads/2017/04/EO-and-Commodity-Reports-Combined-FINAL-2017.pdf.

2 See Food and Agricultural Organisation of the United Nations, *The State of World Fisheries and Aquaculture: Meeting the Sustainable Development Goals* (Rome: FOA, 2018), p. 7.

3 Kate Hodal, Chris Kelly and Felicity Lawrence, 'Revealed: Asian slave labour producing prawns for supermarkets in US, UK', *Guardian*, 10 June 2014, https://www.theguardian.com/global-development/2014/jun/10/supermarket-prawns-thailand-produced-slave-labour.

4 US Department of Homeland Security, 'What is human trafficking?', https://www.dhs.gov/blue-campaign/what-human-trafficking.

5 Kevin Bales and Ron Soodalter, *The Slave Next Door: Human Trafficking and Slavery in America Today* (Oakland, CA: University of California Press, 2009), p. 255.

6 For an overview of business models and supply chains, see Genevieve LeBaron and Andrew Crane, 'Methodological challenges in the business of forced labour', in Genevieve LeBaron, ed., *Researching Forced Labour in the Global Economy* (Oxford: Oxford University Press, 2018), pp. 25–43.

7 GlobalGAP, 'About Us', http://www.globalgap.org/uk_en/.

8 ILO, Forced Labour Convention, 1930 (No. 29).

9 ILO, *ILO Global Estimate of Forced Labour: Results and Methodology* (Geneva: International Labour Organization, 2012), pp. 19–20.

10 Andrew Crane, Genevieve LeBaron, Jean Allain and Laya Behbahani, 'Governance gaps in eradicating forced labour: From global to domestic supply chains', *Regulation & Governance* 13/1 (2017), p. 2.

11 Committee of Experts on the Application of Conventions and Recommendations, *General Survey concerning the Forced Labour Convention, 1930 (No. 29), and the Abolition of Forced Labour Convention 1957 (No. 105)* (Geneva: International Labour Organization, 2007), pp. 20–21.

12 Interview with Head of Global Supply Chain, MNC, 10 November 2017, via Skype from Sheffield.

13 See Jens Lerche, 'A global alliance against forced labour? Unfree labour, neoliberal globalization, and the International Labour Organization', *Journal of Agrarian Change* 7/4 (2007), pp. 425–452; Jamie Morgan and Wendy Olsen, 'Forced and unfree labour: An analysis', *International Critical Thought* 4/1 (2014), pp. 21–37.

14 LeBaron, *Report of Findings: The Global Business of Forced Labour*, p. 14.

15 LeBaron, *Report of Findings: The Global Business of Forced Labour*, p. 23.

16 See Janie Chuang, 'Exploitation creep and the unmaking of human trafficking law', *American Journal of International Law* 108/4 (2014), pp. 609–649; Lerche, 'A global

alliance against forced labour?'; Alessandra Mezzadri, *The Sweatshop Regime: Labouring Bodies, Exploitation and Garments Made in India* (Cambridge: Cambridge University Press, 2016).

17 Andrew Crane, 'Modern slavery as a management practice: Exploring the conditions and capabilities for human exploitation', *Academy of Management Review* 38/1 (2014), p. 49.

18 For instance, see Crane, 'Modern slavery as a management practice'; Jean Allain, Andrew Crane, Genevieve LeBaron and Laya Behbahani, *Forced Labour's Business Models and Supply Chains* (York: Joseph Rowntree Foundation, 2013); Crane et al., 'Governance gaps in eradicating forced labour'.

19 See Walmart, *2018 Global Responsibility Report*, p. 109, https://corporate.walmart.com//2018grr/media-library/document/global-responsibility-report-2018/_proxyDocument?id=00000165-1f6b-d0cc-ab77-9febd76f0000, which states: 'Walmart has a large, geographically diverse supply chain that includes more than 100,000 suppliers around the world. Our sourcing efforts can help support local and small farmers, foster growth of women-owned business and encourage the growth of small business.'

20 Allain et al., *Forced Labour's Business Models and Supply Chains*, p. 39.

21 Nestlé, *Modern Slavery and Human Trafficking Report 2017*, p. 4, https://www.nestle.co.uk/asset-library/documents/aboutus/corporate-reporting/nestle-mod-slave-act-2017-17-april.pdf.

22 UN Conference on Trade and Development, *World Investment Report 2013: Global Value Chains Investment and Trade for Development* (Geneva: United Nations, 2013), p. x.

23 LeBaron and Crane, 'Methodological Challenges in the Business of Forced Labour', p. 33.

24 Apple, *Apple Supplier Responsibility: 2012 Progress Report*, p. 9, https://images.apple.com/supplier-responsibility/pdf/Apple_SR_2012_Progress_Report.pdf.

25 BBC News 'Apple bans "bonded servitude" for factory workers', *BBC News*, 12 February 2015, http://www.bbc.co.uk/news/technology-31438699.

26 Gill Plimmer, 'The unstoppable rise of outsourcing', *Financial Times*, 13 June 2013, https://www.ft.com/content/ee63a82c-d353-11e2-b3ff-00144feab7de.

27 For instance, see Sarah Labowitz and Dorothée Baumann-Pauly, *Business as Usual Is Not an Option: Supply Chains and Sourcing after Rana Plaza* (New York: NYU Stern Centre for Business and Human Rights, 2014), p. 6; Verité, *Forced Labor in the Production of Electronic Goods in Malaysia: A Comprehensive Study of Scope and Characteristics* (2014), https://www.verite.org/wp-content/uploads/2016/11/VeriteForcedLaborMalaysianElectronics2014.pdf; ILO, *Profits and Poverty: The Economics of Forced Labour* (Geneva: International Labour Organization, 2017)

28 Nicola Phillips and Leonardo Sakamoto, 'Global production networks, chronic poverty and "slave labour" in Brazil', *Studies in Comparative International Development* 47/3 (2012), pp. 287–315; see also Nicola Phillips, 'Unfree labour and adverse incorporation in the global economy: Comparative perspectives from Brazil and India', *Economy and Society* 42/2 (2013), pp. 174, 183.

29 Sedex, 'Who is Sedex?', https://www.sedexglobal.com/about-us/what-is-sedex/.

30 Sedex, *Going Deep: The Case for Multi-tier Transparency* (2013), p. 2, https://cdn.sedexglobal.com/wp-content/uploads/2016/09/Sedex-Transparency-Briefing.pdf.

31 See Allain et al., *Forced Labour's Business Models and Supply Chains*; Kendra Strauss, 'Coerced, forced and unfree labour geographies of exploitation in contemporary labour markets', *Geography Compass* 6/3 (2012), pp. 137–148; Louise Waite, Hannah Lewis, Stuart Hodkinson and Peter Dwyer, 'Precarious lives: Experiences of forced labour among refugees and asylum seekers in England', Research Report, University of Leeds (2013), http://eprints.whiterose.ac.uk/75949/.

32 Allain et al., *Forced Labour's Business Models and Supply Chains*; Crane et al., 'Governance gaps in eradicating forced labour'.

33 See Verité, *Strengthening Protections Against Trafficking in Persons in Federal and Corporate Supply Chains*; Steven Greenhouse, 'The Changing Face of Temporary Employment', *New York Times*, 31 August 2013, https://

www.nytimes.com/2014/09/01/upshot/the-changing-face-of-temporary-employment.html; Sivan Sadeh and Anna Cibils, 'Temporary work, permanent injuries: Realities in the food processing industries and a call to action', Working Paper, Occupational Health Internship Programme, http://www.wpusa.org/Ohip_TempWorkReflections.pdf.

34 See Leah F. Vosko, *Managing the Margins: Gender, Citizenship and the International Regulation of Precarious Employment* (Oxford: Oxford University Press, 2010); Leah F. Vosko, ed., *Precarious Employment: Understanding Labour Market Insecurity in Canada* (Montreal: McGill-Queen's University Press, 2006); Stephanie Ware Barrientos, '"Labour chains": Analysing the role of labour contractors in global production networks', *Journal of Development Studies* 49/8 (2013), pp. 1058–1071; Jennifer Gordon, 'Regulating the human supply chain', *Iowa Law Review* 102 (2017), pp. 445–504.

35 David Weil, *The Fissured Workplace: Why Work Became So Bad for So Many and What Can Be Done to Improve It* (Cambridge, MA: Harvard University Press, 2014), pp. 2–3.

36 Arianna Rossi, 'Does economic upgrading lead to social upgrading in global production networks? Evidence from Morocco', *World Development* 46 (2013), pp. 223–233.

37 See Mark Anner, 'Corporate social responsibility and freedom of association rights: The precarious quest for legitimacy and control in global supply chains', *Politics & Society* 49/4 (2012), pp. 606–639: Mark Anner, 'Monitoring workers' rights: The limits of voluntary social compliance initiatives in labor repressive regimes', *Global Policy* 8/3 (2017), pp. 56–65; Jennifer Bair, Mark Anner and Jeremy Blasi, 'Sweatshops and the search for solutions, yesterday and today', in Geert de Neve and Rebecca Prentice, eds., *Unmasking the Global Sweatshop: Health and Safety of the World's Garment Workers* (Philadelphia: University of Pennsylvania Press, 2017), pp. 29–56; Richard M. Locke, *The Promise and Limits of Private Power: Promoting Labor Standards in a Global Economy* (Cambridge: Cambridge University Press, 2013); Centre for Sustainable Work and Employment Futures, *New Industry on a Skewed Playing Field: Supply Chain Relations and Working Conditions in UK Garment Manufacturing* (Leicester: University of Leicester, 2015).

38 Khalid Nadvi and John Thomas Thoburn, 'Vietnam in the global garment and textile value chain: Implications for firms and workers' (April 2003), p. 21, https://www.researchgate.net/profile/John_Thoburn2/publication/228820176_Vietnam_in_the_global_garment_and_textile_value_chain_Implications_for_firms_and_workers/links/00b7d52232593de17e000000/Vietnam-in-the-global-garment-and-textile-value-chain-Implications-for-firms-and-workers.pdf.
39 For instance, see Jennifer Moulds, 'Child labour in the fashion supply chain', UNICEF, https://labs.theguardian.com/unicef-child-labour/; Centre for Research on Multinational Corporations and India Committee of the Netherlands, *Flawed Fabrics: The Abuse of Girls and Women Workers in the South Indian Textile Industry* (2014), http://www.indianet.nl/pdf/FlawedFabrics.pdf; Sonia Elks, 'Toughen anti-slavery laws, say UK lawmakers after fashion probe', *Thomson Reuters Foundation*, 19 February 2019, http://news.trust.org/item/20190219132328-y30xs.
40 BBC News, 'Child refugees in Turkey making clothes for UK shops', *BBC News*, 24 October 2016, https://www.bbc.co.uk/news/business-37716463.
41 Quote from Ethical Trading Initiative, 'The Leicester garment trade', https://www.ethicaltrade.org/programmes/leicester-garment-trade. See also Felicity Lawrence, 'How did we let modern slavery become part of our lives?', *Guardian*, 2 April 2018, https://www.theguardian.com/commentisfree/2018/apr/02/modern-slavery-daily-life-exploitation-goods-services.
42 University of Leicester, 'New report published on working conditions in Leicester garment sector', Press Release, 18 February 2015, https://www2.le.ac.uk/offices/press/press-releases/2015/february/new-report-published-on-working-conditions-in-leiceser-garment-sector; Centre for Sustainable Work and Employment Futures, *New Industry on a Skewed Playing Field*.
43 Clare Press, 'Fashion identified as one of five key industries implicated in modern slavery', *Vogue*, 23 July 2018, https://www.vogue.com.au/fashion/news/fashion-identified-as-one-of-five-key-industries-implicated-in-modern-slavery/news-story/4cbd8bdc1168f3925bc8cbc96b1f6e6e.

44 Sarah Labowitz and Dorothée Baumann-Pauly, *Beyond the Tip of the Iceberg: Bangladesh's Forgotten Apparel Workers* (New York: NYU Stern Centre for Business and Human Rights, 2015), p. 4.

45 Interview with Head of Global Supply Chain, MNC, 10 November 2017.

46 Labowitz and Baumann-Pauly, *Beyond the Tip of the Iceberg*, p. 4.

47 For instance, see Paul Oyer, *The Independent Workforce in America: The Economics of an Increasingly Flexible Labour Market*, Upwork, 2016, https://s3-us-west-1.amazonaws.com/adquiro-content-prod/documents/paul_oyer_the_independent_workforce_in_america.pdf; The iLabour Project, 'The Online Labour Index', http://ilabour.oii.ox.ac.uk/online-labour-index/.

48 Supermarket ombudsman, quoted in Emma Simpson, 'Tesco knowingly delayed payments to suppliers', *BBC News*, 26 January 2016, https://www.bbc.co.uk/news/business-35408064. See also Matthew Weaver, 'Tesco under investigation by new regulator over dealings with suppliers', *Guardian*, 5 February 2015, https://www.theguardian.com/business/2015/feb/05/tesco-faces-investigation-over-how-it-pays-suppliers; Alex Renton, 'British farmers forced to pay the cost of supermarket price wars', *Observer*, 2 July 2011, https://www.theguardian.com/environment/2011/jul/02/british-farmers-supermarket-price-wars.

49 Rosemary Westwood, 'What does that $14 shirt really cost?', *Maclean's*, 1 May 2013, https://www.macleans.ca/economy/business/what-does-that-14-shirt-really-cost/.

50 Kate Raworth and Thalia Kidder, 'Mimicking "lean" in global value chains: It's the workers who get leaned on', in Jennifer Bair, ed., *Frontiers of Commodity Chain Research* (Stanford, CA: Stanford University Press, 2009), pp. 165–189.

51 ILO, *World Employment Social Outlook: Trends 2017* (Geneva: International Labour Organization, 2017), p. 1.

52 ILO, *World Employment Social Outlook: Trends 2017*, p. 2.

53 Katie Allen, 'Most of the world's workers have insecure jobs, ILO report reveals', *Guardian*, 19 May 2015, https://www.theguardian.com/business/2015/may/19/most-of-the-worlds-workers-have-insecure-jobs-ilo-report-reveals.

54 UN, 'World Day Against Child Labour', https://www.un.org/en/events/childlabourday/background.shtml.

55 Shawn Donnan and Sarah O'Connor, 'World's leading economies warned over "global jobs crisis"', *Financial Times*, 9 September 2014, https://www.ft.com/content/39c266f4-3826-11e4-a687-00144feabdc0.

56 ILO, *World Employment Social Outlook: Trends 2017*, p. 2.

57 Dave Hill, 'Number of London's "working poor" surges 70% in 10 years', *Guardian*, 21 October 2015, https://www.theguardian.com/society/2015/oct/21/number-of-londons-working-poor-surges-70-in-10-years.

58 LeBaron, *Report of Findings: The Global Business of Forced Labour*, p. 3.

59 For instance, see Alliance 8.7, *Global Estimates of Modern Slavery: Forced Labour and Forced Marriage* (Geneva: International Labour Organization, 2017).

60 Asia Floor Wage Alliance et al., *Gender Based Violence in the H&M Garment Supply Chain: Workers Voices from the Global Supply Chain, A Report to the ILO 2018*, p. 4, https://asia.floorwage.org/workersvoices/reports/gender-based-violence-in-the-h-m-garment-supply-chain.

61 Asia Floor Wage Alliance et al., *Gender Based Violence in the H&M Garment Supply Chain*, p. 53.

62 US Department of Labor, 'H-2A jobs certified and visas issued, 2005–2016', https://www.epi.org/blog/h-2a-farm-guestworker-program-expanding-rapidly/#_note1.

63 National Guestworker Alliance, 'Raising the floor for supply chain workers: Perspective from US seafood supply chains' (2016), p. 58, https://asia.floorwage.org/workersvoices/reports/raising-the-floor-for-supply-chain-workers-perspective-from-u-s-seafood-supply-chains.

64 ILO, 'Labour relations and collective bargaining', Issue Brief No. 1 (Geneva: International Labour Office, 2017), p. 9.

65 ILO, 'Trade union density rate (%)', https://www.ilo.org/ilostat/faces/oracle/webcenter/portalapp/pagehierarchy/Page27.jspx;ILOSTATCOOKIE=aAUTXKwV0fDe1FuJkTJtamubW8R3l26yRY6znQOJihrlCgLVmEik!1567639201?indicator=ILR_TUMT_NOC_RT&subject=IR&datasetCode=A&collectionCode=IR&_adf.ctrl-state=d0w2ezikt_50&_afrLoop=2201134441052634&_afrWindowMode=0&_afrWindowId=null.

66 ILO, 'Observation (CEACR): Follow-up to the discussion of the Committee on the Application of Standards' (2014), http://www.ilo.org/dyn/normlex/en/f?p=NORMLEXPUB:13 100:0::NO::P13100_COMMENT_ID:3189623.

67 For an overview of key trends, see Susan Strange, *States and Markets* (London: Bloomsbury, 2015); Susan Strange, *The Retreat of the State: The Diffusion of Power in the World Economy* (Cambridge: Cambridge University Press, 1996); Jeffrey Harrod and Robert W. Cox, *Power, Production and the Unprotected Worker* (New York: Columbia University Press, 1987).

68 Walmart, 'Audits', https://corporate.walmart.com/article/audits.

69 Coca-Cola Company, *Modern Slavery Statement 2016*, p. 2, https://www.coca-cola.co.uk/content/dam/journey/gb/en/hidden/PDFs/human-and-workplace-rights/Modern-Slavery-Act-Statement-FY2016-Coca-Cola.pdf; Coca-Cola Company, *Human Rights Report 2016–2017*, p. 13, https://www.coca-colacompany.com/content/dam/journey/us/en/private/fileassets/pdf/human-and-workplace-rights/Human-Rights-Report-2016-2017-TCCC.pdf.

70 Tesco PLC, 'Our approach to human rights in our supply chain', https://www.tescoplc.com/reports-and-policies/our-approach-to-human-rights-in-our-supply-chain/.

71 Interview quote from Genevieve LeBaron and Jane Lister, 'Ethical audits and the supply chains of global corporations', SPERI Global Political Economy Policy Brief No. 1 (Sheffield: SPERI, 2016), p. 3.

72 Interview with Monitoring and Evaluation Officer, Ethical Certification Organization, 22 November 2017.

Chapter 3   Corporate Power and the State

1 David Streitfeld, 'Amazon Hits $1,000,000,000,000 in value, following Apple', *New York Times*, 4 September 2018, https://www.nytimes.com/2018/09/04/technology/amazon-stock-price-1-trillion-value.html?action=click&module=inline&pgtype=Homepage.

2 David Chau, 'Microsoft (briefly) becomes the world's third trillion-dollar company', *ABC News*, 25 April 2019, https://www.abc.net.au/

news/2019-04-25/microsoft-market-value-soars-to-1-trillion-us-dollars/11046038.

3 Jon Huang, Karl Russell and Jack Nicas, 'Apple's value hit $1 trillion. Add Disney to Bank of America and ... you're halfway there', *New York Times*, 2 August 2018, https://www.nytimes.com/interactive/2018/08/02/technology/apple-trillion-market-cap.html?auth=login-smartlock.

4 Franklin Roosevelt, quoted in Stacy Mitchell, 'The rise and fall of the word "monopoly" in American life', *The Atlantic*, 20 June 2017, https://www.theatlantic.com/business/archive/2017/06/word-monopoly-antitrust/530169/.

5 Harry Truman, quoted in Mitchell, 'The rise and fall of the word "monopoly" in American life'.

6 Mitchell, 'The rise and fall of the word "monopoly" in American life'.

7 See Federico J. Diez, Daniel Leigh and Suchanan Tambunlertchai, 'Global market power and its macroeconomic implications', Working Paper 18/137, June (Washington, DC: International Monetary Fund, 2018), https://www.imf.org/en/Publications/WP/Issues/2018/06/15/Global-Market-Power-and-its-Macroeconomic-Implications-45975.

8 David Leonhardt, 'The monopolization of America', *New York Times*, 25 November 2018, https://www.nytimes.com/2018/11/25/opinion/monopolies-in-the-us.html.

9 See Maggie McGrath, 'Starbucks to sell Tazo tea brand to Unilever for $384 Million', *Forbes*, 2 November 2017, https://www.forbes.com/sites/maggiemcgrath/2017/11/02/starbucks-to-sell-tazo-tea-brand-to-unilever-for-384-million/#43a3f9ec7d78; Unilever, 'About Unilever', https://www.unilever.co.uk/about/who-we-are/introduction-to-unilever/.

10 Dennis Green, 'Walmart CEO Doug McMillon just released his annual letter to shareholders', *Business Insider*, 23 April 2019, https://www.businessinsider.com/walmart-ceo-doug-mcmillon-annual-shareholder-letter-2019-4?r=US&IR=T; World Bank Data, 'Sweden', https://data.worldbank.org/country/sweden.

11 Nestlé, *Good Food, Good Life: Annual Review 2018*, p. 2, https://www.rns-pdf.londonstockexchange.com/rns/3341V_3-2019-4-5.pdf. See also Nestlé, *Annual Report 2017*, pp. 1, 8, https://www.nestle.com/asset-library/documents/library/documents/annual_reports/2017-annual-review-en.

pdf; Fortune Global 100, 'Nestlé', https://fortune.com/global500/nestle/.

12 Nike, *Letter to Shareholders 2018*, https://s1.q4cdn.com/806093406/files/doc_financials/2018/ar/mark_parker_letter.html.

13 Amazon, *To Our Shareowners*, p. 5, https://ir.aboutamazon.com/static-files/4f64d0cd-12f2-4d6c-952e-bbed15ab1082; Louise Columbus, '10 charts that will change your perspective of Amazon Prime's growth', *Forbes*, 4 March 2018, https://www.forbes.com/sites/louiscolumbus/2018/03/04/10-charts-that-will-change-your-perspective-of-amazon-primes-growth/#7e3e73e73fee.

14 Walmart, *2018 Annual Report*, p. 14, http://s2.q4cdn.com/056532643/files/doc_financials/2018/annual/WMT-2018_Annual-Report.pdf; Insee, 'Paris – estimated population as of January 1, 2019', https://www.insee.fr/fr/statistiques/1893198#consulter.

15 Brian Merchant, 'Life and death in Apple's forbidden city', *Observer*, 18 June 2017, https://www.theguardian.com/technology/2017/jun/18/foxconn-life-death-forbidden-city-longhua-suicide-apple-iphone-brian-merchant-one-device-extract.

16 Luc Fransen and Genevieve LeBaron, 'Big audit firms as regulatory intermediaries in transnational labour governance', *Regulation & Governance* 13/2 (2018), p. 266; United States Census Bureau, 'San Francisco city, California – 2018 population estimate', https://factfinder.census.gov/faces/nav/jsf/pages/community_facts.xhtml.

17 Trefis Team and Great Speculations, 'Analysis of the Kraft–Heinz merger', *Forbes*, 20 March 2015, https://www.forbes.com/sites/greatspeculations/2015/03/30/analysis-of-the-kraft-heinz-merger/#41538d2c9a8a.

18 Nathan Bomey, 'Monsanto shedding name: Bayer acquisition leads to change for environmental lightning rod', *USA Today*, 4 June 2018, https://eu.usatoday.com/story/money/2018/06/04/monsanto-bayer-name/668418002/.

19 Brooke Barnes, 'Disney moves from behemoth to colossus with closing of Fox deal', *New York Times,* 20 March 2019, https://www.nytimes.com/2019/03/20/business/media/walt-disney-21st-century-fox-deal.html.

20 Madeleine Johnson, '15 of the Best Mergers and Acquisitions

of 2017', *Nasdaq*, 29 December 2017, https://www.nasdaq.com/article/15-of-the-best-mergers-acquisitions-of-2017-cm898464.

21 Lauren Feiner, 'Apple now has $245 billion case on hand, up 3% from previous quarter', *CNBC*, 29 January 2019, https://www.cnbc.com/2019/01/29/apple-now-has-tk-cash-on-hand.html.

22 Jennifer Clapp, 'Mega-mergers on the menu: Corporate concentration and the politics of sustainability in the global food system', *Global Environmental Politics* 18/2 (2018), pp. 12–33.

23 Steve Andriole, 'Apple, Google, Microsoft, Amazon and Facebook own huge market shares = technology oligarchy', *Forbes*, 26 September 2018, https://www.forbes.com/sites/steveandriole/2018/09/26/apple-google-microsoft-amazon-and-facebook-own-huge-market-shares-technology-oligarchy/#5f7910392318.

24 Andrea Alegria, Agata Kaczanowska and Lauren Setar, 'Top 10 highly concentrated industries', *IBISWorld*, 10 February 2012, https://news.cision.com/ibisworld/r/top-10-highly-concentrated-industries,c9219248.

25 Roger L. Martin, 'The high price of efficiency', *Harvard Business Review*, January–February 2019, https://hbr.org/2019/01/rethinking-efficiency.

26 Lina M. Khan, 'Amazon's antitrust paradox', *Yale Law Journal* 126/710 (2017), p. 710.

27 Khan, 'Amazon's antitrust paradox', p. 803.

28 *The Economist*, 'The rise of the superstars', *The Economist Magazine*, 15 September 2016, https://www.economist.com/special-report/2016/09/15/the-rise-of-the-superstars. See also Gerald Davis, *The Vanishing American Corporation: Navigating the Hazards of a New Economy* (Oakland, CA: Berrett-Koehler Publishers, 2016).

29 See Jennifer Clapp, 'Global environmental governance for corporate responsibility and accountability', *Global Environmental Politics* 5/33 (2005), p. 23; UNCTAD, *World Investment Report 2011 – Web Table 34: Number of Parent Corporations and Foreign Affiliates, by Region and Economy 2010*, https://unctad.org/Sections/dite_dir/docs/WIR11_web%20tab%2034.pdf, quoted in John Mikler, *The Political Power of Global Corporations* (Cambridge: Polity, 2018), p. 5.

30 See, for instance, Jan Fichtner and Eelke M. Heemskerk, 'The new permanent universal owners: Index funds, (im)patient capital, and the claim of long-termism', Working Paper, November (Amsterdam: CORPNET, 2018), https://papers.ssrn.com/sol3/papers.cfm?abstract_id=3321597.

31 For instance, see William Milberg, 'Shifting sources and uses of profits: Sustaining US financialization within global value chains', *Economy & Society* 37 (2008), pp. 420–451.

32 Jennifer Clapp and S. Ryan Isakson, *Speculative Harvests: Financialization, Food, and Agriculture* (Halifax: Fernwood Publishing, 2018), p. 2.

33 See, for instance, Susanne Soederberg, *Corporate Power and Ownership in Contemporary Capitalism: The Politics of Resistance and Domination* (Abingdon: Routledge, 2010); Gerald A. Epstein, ed., *Financialization and the World Economy* (Cheltenham: Edward Elgar Publishing, 2005); Greta Krippner, *Capitalizing on Crisis: The Political Origins of the Rise of Finance* (Cambridge, MA: Harvard University Press, 2011); Thomas I. Palley, 'Financialization: What it is and why it matters', Working Paper No. 52 (Washington, DC: Levy Economics Institute, 2007).

34 CORPNET, 'About', https://corpnet.uva.nl/.

35 Fichtner and Heemskerk, 'The new permanent universal owners'.

36 Fichtner and Heemskerk, 'The new permanent universal owners', p. 2.

37 Jan Fichtner, Eelke M. Hemmskerk and Javier Garcia-Bernardo, 'Hidden power of the Big Three? Passive index funds, re-concentration of corporate ownership, and new financial risk', *Business and Politics* 19/2 (2017), p. 303.

38 Patrick Jahnke, 'Ownership concentration and institutional investors' governance through voice and exit', *Business and Politics* (2019), pp. 1–24.

39 Fichtner, Hemmskerk and Garcia-Bernardo, 'Hidden power of the Big Three?', p. 303; see also Alicia McElhaney, 'Research: Asset management giants don't walk the walk on long-termism', *Institutional Investor*, 11 February 2019, https://www.institutionalinvestor.com/article/b1d323cdkjjj29/Research-Asset-Management-Giants-Don-t-Walk-the-Walk-On-Long-Termism.

40 Jacob Greenspon, 'How big a problem is it that a few

shareholders own stock in so many competing companies?', *Harvard Business Review*, 19 February 2019, https://hbr.org/2019/02/how-big-a-problem-is-it-that-a-few-share-holders-own-stock-in-so-many-competing-companies.

41 Jacob Greenspon, 'How big a problem is it that a few share-holders own stock in so many competing companies?'. See also Clapp and Isakson, *Speculative Harvests*; Jennifer Clapp, 'The rise of financial investment and common ownership in agrifood firms', *Review of International Political Economy*, https://www.tandfonline.com/doi/full/10.1080/096922 90.2019.1597755; Clapp, 'Mega-mergers on the menu: Corporate concentration and the politics of sustainability in the global food system'.

42 See, for instance, Eileen Appelbaum and Rosemary Batt, *Private Equity at Work: When Wall Street Manages Main Street* (New York: Russell Sage Foundation, 2014); William Lazonick, 'Profits without prosperity', *Harvard Business Review*, September 2014, https://hbr.org/2014/09/profits-without-prosperity.

43 See, for instance, Laura Horn, 'The finacialization of the corporation', in Grietje Baars and Andre Spicer, eds., *The Corporation: A Critical, Multi-Disciplinary Handbook* (Cambridge: Cambridge University Press, 2017), pp. 281–290; Glenn Morgan, 'Financialization and the multi-national corporation', *Transfer* 20/2, pp. 183–197; William W. Bratton and Joseph A. McCahery, eds., *Institutional Investor Activism: Hedge Funds and Private Equity, Economic and Regulation* (Oxford: Oxford University Press, 2015); Gail Weinstein, Warren S. de Wied and Philip Richter, 'The road ahead for shareholder activism', *Harvard Law School Forum on Corporate Governance and Financial Regulation*, 13 February 2019, https://corpgov.law.harvard.edu/2019/02/13/the-road-ahead-for-shareholder-activism/.

44 See Greta R. Krippner, 'The financialization of the American economy', *Socio-Economic Review* 3 (2005), pp. 173–208; Horn, 'The financialization of the corporation'.

45 Steve Denning, 'Making sense of shareholder value: "The world's dumbest idea"', *Forbes*, 17 July 2017, https://www.forbes.com/sites/stevedenning/2017/07/17/making-sense-of-shareholder-value-the-worlds-dumbest-idea/#60640e2f2a7e.

46 For an explanation of 'neoliberal', see Jamie Peck,

Constructions of Neoliberal Reason (Oxford: Oxford University Press, 2010); Jamie Peck and Nik Theodore, Fast Policy: Experimental Statecraft at the Thresholds of Neoliberalism (Minneapolis: University of Minnesota Press, 2015).

47 Frank H. Easterbrook and Daniel R. Fischel, 'The corporate contract', Columbia Law Review 1416 (1989), p. 1425.

48 See, for instance, Ken-Hou Lin, 'The rise of finance and firm employment dynamics, 1982–2005', SSRN Electronic Journal (2017), http://recursos.march.es/web/ceacs/actividades/miembros/kenhoulin.pdf; Ken-Hou Lin and Donald Tomaskovic-Devey 'Financialization and US income inequality, 1970–2008', American Journal of Sociology 118/5 (2013), pp. 1284–1329.

49 Lenore Palladino, Corporate Financialization and Worker Prosperity: A Broken Link (Roosevelt Institute, 2018), p. 11, http://rooseveltinstitute.org/wp-content/uploads/2018/01/Financialization-Primer-Report_FINAL.pdf.

50 Benjamin Selwyn, 'Harsh labour: Bedrock of global capitalism', in Genevieve LeBaron and Neil Howard, eds., Forced Labour in the Global Economy (London: openDemocracy, 2014), p. 48, https://www.opendemocracy.net/en/bts-short-course/.

51 Daniel Vaughan-Whitehead and Luis Pinedo Caro, 'Purchasing practices and working conditions in global supply chains: Global survey results', in Work Issue Brief No. 10 (Geneva: International Labour Office, 2017), pp. 1–11, https://www.ilo.org/travail/info/fs/WCMS_556336/lang--en/index.htm.

52 Mark Anner, 'Squeezing workers' rights in global supply chains: Purchasing practices in the Bangladesh garment export sector in comparative perspective', Review of International Political Economy (2019), p. 1.

53 Anner, 'Squeezing workers' rights in global supply chains', p. 18.

54 Lawrence Mishel and Julia Wolfe, 'CEO compensation has grown 940% since 1978', Economic Policy Institute, 14 August 2019, https://www.epi.org/publication/ceo-compensation-2018/.

55 For example, see Petra Dunhaupt, The Effect of Financialization on Labor's Share of Income (Berlin:

Institute for International Political Economy, 2013), https://www.econstor.eu/bitstream/10419/68475/1/734374437.pdf; Özlem Onaran and Alexander Guschanski, 'The causes of falling wage share: sectoral and firm level evidence from developed and developing countries: What have we learned?' (Greenwich Political Economy Research Centre, 2018), https://gala.gre.ac.uk/id/eprint/19373/7/19373%20ONARAN_The_Causes_of_Falling_Wage_Share_2018.pdf.

56 Onaran and Guschanski, 'The causes of falling wage share', p. 5.

57 Floyd Norris, 'Corporate profits grow and wages slide', *New York Times*, 4 April 2014, https://www.nytimes.com/2014/04/05/business/economy/corporate-profits-grow-ever-larger-as-slice-of-economy-as-wages-slide.html.

58 Genevieve LeBaron and Nicola Phillips, 'States and the political economy of unfree labour', *New Political Economy* 24/1 (2019), p. 5.

59 Soederberg, *Corporate Power and Ownership in Contemporary Capitalism*; Susan Strange, *States and Markets* (London: Bloomsbury, 2015); Susan Strange, *The Retreat of the State: The Diffusion of Power in the World Economy* (Cambridge: Cambridge University Press, 1996); Peck, *Constructions of Neoliberal Reason*.

60 A. Claire Cutler, Virginia Haufler and Tony Porter, eds., *Private Authority and International Affairs* (New York: State University of New York Press, 1999), pp. 3–4. See also Tim Bartley, *Rules without Rights: Land, Labor, and Private Authority in the Global Economy* (Oxford: Oxford University Press, 2018).

61 See, for instance Genevieve LeBaron and Andreas Rühmkorf, 'The domestic politics of corporate accountability legislation: Struggles over the 2015 Modern Slavery Act', *Socio-Economic Review* (2017), pp. 1–35; Fransen and LeBaron, 'Big audit firms as regulatory intermediaries in transnational labor governance'.

62 See Global Business Coalition Against Human Trafficking, 'About GBCAT', https://www.gbcat.org/overview-history.

63 See Consumer Goods Forum, 'Our members', https://www.theconsumergoodsforum.com/who-we-are/our-members/.

64 See Stronger Together, 'About us', https://www.stronger-2gether.org/about-us/.

65 See UN Global Compact, 'Who we are', https://www. unglobalcompact.org/what-is-gc.
66 See UN Global Compact, 'Forced labour risks in global supply chains: How to address risks, react to challenges and respond to dilemmas', https://www.unglobalcompact. org/take-action/events/1361-forced-labour-risks-in-global-supply-chains-how-to-address-risks-react-to-challenges-and-respond-to-dilemmas.
67 See UK Government Department for International Development, 'UK aid to help over half a million people at risk of slavery', https://www.gov.uk/government/news/uk-aid-to-help-over-half-a-million-people-at-risk-of-slavery; US Department of State, 'Program to end modern slavery', https://www.state.gov/program-to-end-modern-slavery/; Global Fund to End Modern Slavery, 'Our approach', https://www.gfems.org/approach.
68 Peter Dauvergne and Genevieve LeBaron, *Protest Inc.: The Corporatization of Activism* (Cambridge: Polity, 2014).
69 Interview with industry association representative overseeing forced labour programmes, 9 January 2018, Sheffield, UK.
70 See LeBaron and Rühmkorf, 'Steering CSR through home state regulation', p. 18.
71 As quoted in LeBaron and Rühmkorf, 'The domestic politics of corporate accountability legislation', p. 15.
72 LeBaron and Rühmkorf, 'Steering CSR through home state regulation', p. 26.
73 Quoted in LeBaron and Rühmkorf, 'The domestic politics of corporate accountability legislation', pp. 21–22.
74 Interview with industry actor leading NGO outreach, London, March 2012, quoted in LeBaron and Rühmkorf, 'The domestic politics of corporate accountability legislation', p. 22.
75 LeBaron and Rühmkorf, 'The domestic politics of corporate accountability legislation', p. 22.
76 LeBaron and Rühmkorf, 'The domestic politics of corporate accountability legislation', p. 22.
77 Quoted in LeBaron and Rühmkorf, 'The domestic politics of corporate accountability legislation', p. 23.
78 Quoted in LeBaron and Rühmkorf, 'The domestic politics of corporate accountability legislation', p. 23.
79 Fransen and LeBaron, 'Big audit firms as regulatory

intermediaries in transnational labor governance', pp. 269, 274.

80 Quoted in LeBaron and Rühmkorf, 'The domestic politics of corporate accountability legislation', p. 25.

81 LeBaron and Rühmkorf, 'The domestic politics of corporate accountability legislation'.

82 For analysis on why legislation is stronger or weaker across various jurisdictions, see LeBaron and Rühmkorf, 'Steering CSR through home state regulation'; LeBaron and Rühmkorf, 'The domestic politics of corporate accountability legislation'. See also: Alice Evans, 'Overcoming the global despondency trap: Strengthening corporate accountability in supply chains', *Review of International Political Economy*, https://www.tandfonline.com/doi/abs/10.1080/09 692290.2019.1679220.

Chapter 4   The Recruitment Industry

1 Southern Poverty Law Center, 'Signal international lawsuits', August 2019, https://www.splcenter.org/seeking-justice/ case-docket/signal-international-lawsuits.

2 *New York Times Editorial*, 'They pushed back', 28 June 2010, https://www.nytimes.com/2010/06/29/opinion/29tue3. html?searchResultPosition=9.

3 Southern Poverty Law Center, 'Case 2:08-cv-01220-SM-DEK Document 1706', https://www.splcenter.org/sites/default/ files/d6_legacy_files/downloads/case/david_v._signal_sixth_ amended_complaint.pdf.

4 Southern Poverty Law Center, 'Signal international lawsuits', August 2019.

5 Southern Poverty Law Center, 'Case 2:08-cv-01220-SM-DEK Document 1706'.

6 *Reuters*, 'Indian workers awarded millions after US firm found guilty of trafficking', *Guardian,* 19 February 2015, https:// www.theguardian.com/world/2015/feb/19/indian-workers- awarded-millions-after-us-firm-found-guilty-of-trafficking.

7 David vs. Signal International, US District Court for the Eastern District of Louisiana, Case 2:08-cv-01220-SM0DEK, https://www.splcenter.org/sites/default/files/d6_legacy_files/ downloads/case/david_v._signal_sixth_amended_complaint. pdf.

8 Philip Martin, *Merchants of Labor: Recruiters and International Labor Migration* (Oxford: Oxford University Press), p. 3.

9 UN Office on Drugs and Crime, *The Role of Recruitment Fees and Abusive and Fraudulent Practices of Recruitment Agencies in Trafficking in Persons* (2015), p. 6, https://www.unodc.org/documents/human-trafficking/2015/Recruitment_Fees_Report-Final-22_June_2015_AG_Final.pdf.

10 Alliance 8.7, *Global Estimates of Modern Slavery: Forced Labour and Forced Marriage* (Geneva: International Labour Office, 2017).

11 Genevieve LeBaron, 'Reconceptualizing debt bondage: Debt as a class-based form of labor discipline', *Critical Sociology* 40/5 (2014), pp. 763–780.

12 The No Project, 'Recruiters/traffickers', https://www.thenoproject.org/slavery/traffickers/.

13 Martin, *Merchants of Labor*, p. 99.

14 Rocio Bonet, Peter Cappelli and Monika Hamori, 'Labor market intermediaries and the new paradigm for human resources', *Academy of Management Annals* (2013), p. 339.

15 Recruitment International, 'Global employment industry turnover up to €491 billion in 2016, WEC finds', https://www.recruitment-international.co.uk/blog/2018/04/global-employment-industry-turnover-up-to-491-euros-billion-in-2016-wec-finds.

16 Jean Allain, Andrew Crane, Genevieve LeBaron and Laya Behbahani, *Forced Labour's Business Models and Supply Chains* (York: Joseph Rowntree Foundation, 2013).

17 Andrew Davidson, 'Migrant workers killed in crash were "breadwinners"', CBC News, 8 February 2012, https://www.cbc.ca/news/canada/migrant-workers-killed-in-crash-were-breadwinners-1.1142487.

18 Owen Gibson and Pete Pattisson, 'Death toll among Qatar's 2022 World Cup workers revealed', *Guardian*, 23 December 2014, https://www.theguardian.com/world/2014/dec/23/qatar-nepal-workers-world-cup-2022-death-toll-doha.

19 See, for instance, Leila Simona Talani and Simon McMahon, eds., *Handbook of the International Political Economy of Migration* (Cheltenham: Edward Elgar, 2015); Nicola

Phillips, *Migration in the Global Political Economy* (Boulder, CO: Lynne Rienner Publishers, 2011).

20 Nicola Phillips, 'Migration as development strategy? The new political economy of dispossession and inequality in the Americas', *Review of International Political Economy* 16/2 (2009), p. 240. 'Export commodity' is a phrase referred to by Phillips and is originally from K. Hewison, 'Thai workers in Hong Kong', in K. Hewison and K. Young, eds., *Transnational Migration and Work in Asia* (London, Routledge: 2006), p. 94.

21 The World Bank, 'Record high remittances sent globally in 2018', 8 April 2019, https://www.worldbank.org/en/news/press-release/2019/04/08/record-high-remittances-sent-globally-in-2018.

22 The Freedom Fund & Verité, *An Exploratory Study on the Role of Corruption in International Labor Migration* (2016), p. 6, available at: http://www.verite.org/wp-content/uploads/2016/11/Verite-Report-Intl-Labour-Recruitment.pdf.

23 Fereica Cocco, Jonathan Wheatley, Jane Pong, David Blood and Aendrew Rininsland, 'Remittances: The hidden engine of globalisation', 28 August 2019, *Financial Times*, https://ig.ft.com/remittances-capital-flow-emerging-markets/.

24 Martin, *Merchants of Labor*, p. 7.

25 UN Office on Drugs and Crime, *The Role of Recruitment Fees and Abusive and Fraudulent Practices of Recruitment Agencies in Trafficking in Persons* (2015), https://www.unodc.org/documents/human-trafficking/2015/Recruitment_Fees_Report-Final-22_June_2015_AG_Final.pdf; UN.GIFT, *Human Trafficking and Business: Good Practices to Prevent and Combat Human Trafficking* (2010), https://publications.iom.int/system/files/pdf/un.gift_private_sector.pdf.

26 Thanks to an anonymous reviewer for this point.

27 Jean Allain, Andrew Crane, Genevieve LeBaron and Laya Behbahani, *Forced Labour's Business Models and Supply Chains* (York: Joseph Rowntree Foundation, 2013), p. 27.

28 Allain et al., *Forced Labour's Business Models and Supply Chains*, p. 33.

29 Tom Barnes, Krishna Shekhar Lal Das and Surendra Pratap, 'Labour contractors and global production networks: The

case of India's auto supply chain', *Journal of Development Studies* 51/4 (2015), pp. 355–369.

30 Stephanie Barrientos, '"Labour chains": Analysing the role of labour contractors in global production networks', *Journal of Development Studies* 49/8 (2013), p. 1065.

31 Verité, *Forced Labor in the Production of Electronic Goods in Malaysia: A Comprehensive Study of Scope and Characteristics* (2014), https://www.verite.org/wp-content/uploads/2016/11/VeriteForcedLaborMalaysianElectronics2014.pdf.

32 Christina Stringer, D. Hugh Whittaker and Glenn Simmons, 'New Zealand's turbulent waters: The use of forced labour in the fishing industry', *Global Networks* 16/1, (2016), pp. 3–24.

33 Allain et al., *Forced Labour's Business Models and Supply Chains*.

34 See, for instance, Judy Fudge and Kendra Strauss, eds., *Temporary Work, Agencies and Unfree Labour: Insecurity in the New World of Work* (New York: Routledge, 2014); Andrew Gardner, Silvia Pessoa and Laura Harkness, *Labour Migrants and Access to Justice in Contemporary Qatar* (London: Middle East Centre, London School of Economics, 2014); Louise Waite, Gary Craig, Hannah Lewis and Klara Skrivankova, eds., *Vulnerability, Exploitation and Migrants: Insecure Work in a Globalised Economy* (Basingstoke: Palgrave Macmillan, 2015).

35 Jennifer Gordon, 'Regulating the human supply chain', *Iowa Law Review* 102 (2017), p. 452.

36 Martin, *Merchants of Labor*, pp. 3, 16.

37 Fudge and Strauss, eds., *Temporary Work, Agencies and Unfree Labour*; Leah Vosko, *Temporary Work: The Gendered Rise of a Precarious Employment Relationship* (Toronto: University of Toronto Press, 2000); Judy Fudge, 'Modern slavery, unfree labour and the labour market: The social dynamics of legal characterization', *Social & Legal Studies* 27/4 (2018), pp. 414–434.

38 Annette Bernhardt, Heather Boushey, Laura Dresser and Chris Tilly, eds., *The Gloves-Off Economy: Workplace Standards. At the Bottom of America's Labor Market* (Champaign, IL: Labor and Employment Relations Association, 2008).

39 Sonovate, 'UK recruitment industry growth 2008–2018',

https://www.sonovate.com/blog/uk-recruitment-growth-2008-2018/.

40 American Staffing Association, 'Staffing industry statistics', https://americanstaffing.net/staffing-research-data/fact-sheets-analysis-staffing-industry-trends/staffing-industry-statistics/; American Staffing Association, 'Fact sheet: Staffing and recruiting industry sales increased 3.9% to $167 Billion in 2018', https://d2m21dzi54s7kp.cloudfront.net/wp-content/uploads/2019/05/Staffing-and-Recruiting-Sales_2003-2018.pdf.

41 Genevieve LeBaron and Nicola Phillips, 'States and the political economy of unfree labour', *New Political Economy* 24/1 (2019).

42 The Human Trafficking Legal Center, *Federal Human Trafficking Civil Litigation: 15 Years of the Private Right of Action*, http://www.htlegalcenter.org/wp-content/uploads/Federal-Human-Trafficking-Civil-Litigation-1.pdf, p. 12. See also National Guestworker Alliance, *Raising the Floor for Supply Chain Workers: Perspectives from US Seafood Supply Chains* (2016), https://asia.floorwage.org/workersvoices/reports/raising-the-floor-for-supply-chain-workers-perspective-from-u-s-seafood-supply-chains/view.

43 BBC News, 'Migrant workers "exploited" in Japan', 25 August 2019, https://www.bbc.co.uk/news/av/world-asia-49448757/migrant-workers-exploited-in-japan.

44 LeBaron and Phillips, 'States and the political economy of unfree labour'.

45 The Freedom Fund and Verité, *An Exploratory Study on the Role of Corruption in International Labor Migration* (2016), http://www.verite.org/wp-content/uploads/2016/11/Verite-Report-Intl-Labour-Recruitment.pdf. See also Priya Deshingkar, C. R. Abrar, Mirza Taslima Sultana, Kazi Nurmohammad Hossainul Haque and Md Selim Reza, 'Producing ideal Bangladeshi migrants for precarious construction work in Qatar', *Journal of Ethnic and Migration Studies* (2018), https://doi.org/10.1080/1369183X.2018.1528104; David Picherit, 'Labour migration brokerage and Dalit politics in Andhra Pradesh: A Dalit fabric of labour circulation', *Journal of Ethnic*

and Migration Studies (2018), https://doi.org/10.1080/136
9183X.2018.1528101.

46 The Freedom Fund and Verité, *An Exploratory Study on the Role of Corruption in International Labor Migration*, p. 6.

47 The Freedom Fund and Verité, *An Exploratory Study on the Role of Corruption in International Labor Migration*, p 2.

48 Responsible Recruitment Gateway, https://www.ihrb.org/ employerpays/leadership-group-for-responsible-recruitment.

49 Institute for Human Rights and Business, 'Leadership group for responsible recruitment: The Employer Pays Principle', https://www.ihrb.org/uploads/news-uploads/ Employer_Pays_Principle_-_Leadership_Group_for_ Responsible_Recruitment_updated2.pdf

50 World Employment Confederation, *Promoting Fair Recruitment and Employment Practices: Code of Conduct*, https://www.wecglobal.org/uploads/2019/07/2017_WEC_ Code-Conduct.pdf.

51 Verité and ManpowerGroup, *An Ethical Framework for Cross-Border Labor Recruitment*, https://www.verite.org/ wp-content/uploads/2016/12/ethical_framework_paper.pdf.

52 Stronger Together, https://www.stronger2gether.org/ about-us/.

53 Interfaith Center on Corporate Responsibility, 'The "No Fees" Initiative', https://www.iccr.org/no-fees-initiative.

54 Complyer, https://www.complyer.co.uk/.

55 Clearview, https://irp-cdn.multiscreensite.com/b64bd780/ files/uploaded/Clearview%20Scheme%20overview%20 brochure%20-%20September%202017.pdf.

56 Responsible Business Alliance, 'The Responsible Workplace and Responsible Recruitment Programs', https://www. responsiblebusiness.org/media/docs/RWP-RRP.pdf.

57 Bassina Farbenblum, Laurie Berg and Angela Kintominas, *Transformative Technology for Migrant Workers: Opportunities, Challenges, and Risks*, https://www. opensocietyfoundations.org/publications/transformative- technology-migrant-workers-opportunities-challenges-and- risks#publications_download.

58 ILO, 'Fair Recruitment Initiative', https://www.ilo. org/wcmsp5/groups/public/---ed_norm/---declaration/ documents/publication/wcms_320405.pdf.

59 International Organization for Migration, 'Factsheet 1:

Overview of IRIS', https://iris.iom.int/sites/default/files/Factsheet%201%20-%20Overview%20of%20IRIS.pdf.

60 Interview with ethical recruitment expert, Geneva, 12 December 2017.

61 Farbenblum, Berg and Kintominas, *Transformative Technology for Migrant Workers*, p. 7.

62 Gillian B. White, 'All your clothes are made with exploited labor', *The Atlantic*, 3 June 2015, https://www.theatlantic.com/business/archive/2015/06/patagonia-labor-clothing-factory-exploitation/394658/.

63 White, 'All your clothes are made with exploited labor'.

64 Verité, 'How Patagonia is addressing forced labor in its supply chain', 30 June 2015, https://www.verite.org/how-patagonia-is-addressing-forced-labor-in-its-supply-chain/.

65 BBC News, 'Apple bans "bonded servitude" for factory workers', 12 February 2015, https://www.bbc.co.uk/news/technology-31438699.

66 Apple, *Supplier Responsibility 2015 Progress Report*, p. 18, https://www.apple.com/supplier-responsibility/pdf/Apple_SR_2015_Progress_Report.pdf.

67 Apple, *Supplier Responsibility 2019 Progress Report*, p. 5.

68 See, for instance: ILO, *Fair Recruitment Initiative*, https://www.ilo.org/wcmsp5/groups/public/---ed_norm/---declaration/documents/publication/wcms_320405.pdf. See also the ILO website for details of government ratifications of conventions.

69 Ligia Kiss, J. Mak and B. Sijapati, *South Asia Work in Freedom Three-Country Evaluation: A Theory-Based Intervention Evaluation to Promote Safer Migration of Women and Girls in Nepal, India and Bangladesh* (London: London School of Hygiene and Tropical Medicine, 2019), p. 4.

70 Kiss, Mak and Sijapati, *South Asia Work in Freedom Three-Country Evaluation*.

71 Interview with fair recruitment organization representative, Geneva, 12 December 2017.

72 TÜVRheinland, 'RBA-based auditing', https://www.tuv.com/world/en/rba-based-auditing.html.

73 Clearview, 'Clearview fee schedule', https://irp-cdn.multi-screensite.com/b64bd780/files/uploaded/Clearview%20Fee%20Schedule.pdf.

74 Lisa Rende Taylor and Elena Shih, 'Worker feedback technologies and combatting modern slavery in global supply chains: Examining the effectiveness of remediation-oriented and due-diligence-oriented technologies in identifying and addressing forced labour and human trafficking', *Journal of the British Academy* 7S1 (2019), pp. 131–165.

75 ILRWG, *The American Dream Up for Sale: A Blueprint for Ending International Labor Recruitment Abuse*, https://fairlaborrecruitment.files.wordpress.com/2013/01/final-e-version-ilrwg-report.pdf.

76 ILRWG, 'Core principles', https://fairlaborrecruitment.wordpress.com/about-ilrwg/eight-principles/. Further information is available on the ILRWG website.

77 Interview with civil servant, British Columbia human trafficking office, Vancouver, 2013.

Chapter 5   The Enforcement Industry

1 Chris Baynes, 'US company cuts ties with Chinese factory in Muslim internment camp', *Independent*, 10 January 2019, https://www.independent.co.uk/news/world/americas/china-uighur-muslim-camp-badger-sportswear-factory-forced-labour-xinjiang-a8720831.html. For information on Ali Enterprises, see AFL-CIO, *Responsibility Outsourced: Social Audits, Workplace Certification and Twenty Years of Failure to Protect Workers Rights* (2013), p. 37, https://aflcio.org/sites/default/files/2017-03/CSReport.pdf.

2 See, for instance, Tim Bartley, *Rules without Rights: Land, Labor, and Private Authority in the Global Economy* (Oxford: Oxford University Press, 2018); Carlos Oya, Florian Schafer and Dafni Skalidou, 'The effectiveness of agricultural certification in developing countries: A systematic review', *World Development* 112 (2018), pp. 282–312; Genevieve LeBaron, *Report of Findings: The Global Business of Forced Labour* (Sheffield: SPERI/University of Sheffield, 2018).

3 SGS, *Leadership and Innovation since 1878*, p. 6, https://www.sgs.co.uk/-/media/global/documents/brochures/sgs-group-history-en.pdf.

4 Fortune 500, https://fortune.com/fortune500/2019.

5 SGS, 'SGS in brief', https://www.sgs.com/en/our-company/about-sgs/sgs-in-brief.

6 SGS, 'Sustainability', https://www.sgs.com/en/sustainability.
7 SGS, '2019 group profile', https://www.sgs.co.uk/-/media/global/documents/brochures/group-profiles/sgs-group-profile-en.pdf.
8 Bureau Veritas, *2018 Registration Document*, p. 3, https://group.bureauveritas.com/sites/g/files/zypfnx196/files/media/document/2018_Registration_Document.pdf.
9 Bureau Veritas, 'Consumer products and retail: Meeting the needs of global supply chains', https://group.bureauveritas.com/markets-services/consumer-products-retail.
10 Bureau Veritas, 'Social audit', https://www.bureau-veritas.com/home/about-us/our-business/cps/our-services/csr-services/social-audit.
11 RINA, *Annual Report 2017*, https://shared.rina.org/SCresources/Documents/annual_report_2017.pdf, quotes from p. 35. Figures on certification from RINA website. See, for instance: https://www.rina.org/en/business/certification (taken 30 November 2019).
12 Intertek, *2018 Annual Report: Even Better, Even Stronger, Solutions for a Safer World*, http://www.intertek.com/2018AR/assets/pdf/Intertek_Group_plc_Annual_Report_2018_interactive.pdf.
13 TÜVRheinland, *Corporate Report 2018: Values That Count*, p. 2, https://www.tuv.com/content-media-files/master-content/about-us/tuv-rheinland-corporate-report-2018-en.pdf.
14 ELEVATE, 'About Elevate', https://www.elevatelimited.com/about-elevate/.
15 SGS, 'Stock and Bond Information', https://www.sgs.com/en/our-company/investor-relations/stock-and-bond-information, 3 September 2019. Calculations on file with author.
16 Bureau Veritas, 'Cours de l'action', https://group.bureau-veritas.com/fr/investisseurs/laction-bureau-veritas/cours-de-laction, 3 September 2019.
17 Intertek, 'History', https://www.intertek.com/about/history/.
18 NPR, 'Factory audits and safety don't always go hand in hand', 1 May 2013, https://www.npr.org/2013/05/01/180103898/foreign-factory-audits-profitable-but-flawed-business?t=1563552098029.
19 ProPublica Nonprofit Explorer, 'Fair Labor Association: Full text of "Form 990" for fiscal year ending Dec. 2017',

https://projects.propublica.org/nonprofits/organizations/522183112/201803199349310835/IRS990.

20 WRAP, http://www.wrapcompliance.org/. Quote from: Boody, 'Eco & ethics', https://boody.co.uk/pages/eco-ethics.

21 WRAP, 'Form 990: Return of Organization Exempt From Income Tax, Public Disclosure Copy', http://www.wrapcompliance.org/upload/Documents/documents/2017%20WRAP%20Form%20990%20-%20PD.PDF.

22 Stefanie Clifford and Steven Greenhouse, 'Fast and flawed inspections of factories abroad', *New York Times*, 1 September 2013, https://www.nytimes.com/2013/09/02/business/global/superficial-visits-and-trickery-undermine-foreign-factory-inspections.html.

23 AFL-CIO, *Responsibility Outsourced*, p. 4.

24 Clifford and Greenhouse, 'Fast and flawed inspections of factories abroad'.

25 Clifford and Greenhouse, 'Fast and flawed inspections of factories abroad'.

26 Quoted in Jean Allain, Andrew Crane, Genevieve LeBaron and Laya Behbahani, *Forced Labour's Business Models and Supply Chains* (York: Joseph Rowntree Foundation, 2013), p. 60.

27 UK Parliament, 'Joint Committee on the draft Modern Slavery Bill – Publications', https://www.parliament.uk/business/committees/committees-a-z/joint-select/draft-modern-slavery-bill/written-evidence/?type=Oral#pnlPublicationFilter.

28 Carolijn Terwindt and Miriam Saage-Maass, *Liability of Social Auditors in the Textile Industry* (Berlin: European Centre for Constitutional and Human Rights, 2016), p. 10, https://www.business-humanrights.org/sites/default/files/documents/Policy%20Paper_Liability%20of%20Social%20Auditors%20in%20the%20Textile%20Industry%202016%20.pdf.

29 Interview with audit firm representative, 30 November 2017.

30 Interview with representative of ethical certification organization, Accra, 6 March 2018.

31 Interview with lawyer involved in litigation against audit firm, Berlin, 28 December 2017.

32 Interview with auditor, 13 March 2013, London.

33 Interview with auditor, 13 March 2013, London; interview with audit firm representative, 30 November 2017.
34 Interview with brand retailer, 12 July 2013, Seattle.
35 Quoted in Allain et al., *Forced Labour's Business Models and Supply Chains*, p. 58.
36 Walmart, *Audit and Assessment Policy & Guidance*, https://corporate.walmart.com/media-library/document/audit-and-assessment-policy-guidance-june-2019/_proxyDocument?id=0000016b-9ab0-dfef-abeb-bab602f20000; Walmart, 'Audits', https://corporate.walmart.com/article/audits.
37 H&M Group, *Sustainability Report 2017*, pp. 73–86, https://about.hm.com/content/dam/hmgroup/groupsite/documents/masterlanguage/CSR/reports/2017%20Sustainability%20report/HM_group_SustainabilityReport_2017_FullReport.pdf.
38 H&M Group, *Sustainability Report 2017*, p. 83.
39 Sedex, 'Marco Baren: Sustainability at Philips interviewed at Sedex Conference 2018', 19 March 2018, https://www.youtube.com/watch?v=5rt8XkZayqk.
40 Interview with head of sustainability, MNC, Sheffield, 2 October 2017.
41 Clifford and Greenhouse, 'Fast and flawed inspections of factories abroad'.
42 Remi Edwards, Tom Hunt and Genevieve LeBaron, *Corporate Commitments to Living Wages in the Garment Industry* (Sheffield: SPERI, 2019), p. 22.
43 Interview with tea worker 51, Kerala, 5 March 2017.
44 Quoted in Allain et al., *Forced Labour's Business Models and Supply Chains*, p. 58.
45 Genevieve LeBaron, Jane Lister and Peter Dauvergne, 'Governing global supply chain sustainability through the ethical audit regime', *Globalizations* 14/6 (2017), p. 970.
46 UK Parliament, 'Oral evidence: Draft Modern Slavery Bill, HC [1019], Tuesday 11 March 2014', http://data.parliament.uk/writtenevidence/committeeevidence.svc/evidencedocument/draft-modern-slavery-bill-committee/draft-modern-slavery-bill/oral/7465.html.
47 China Labor Watch, 'China Labor Watch's announcement as to its lawsuit against Intertek Group PLC', 9 December 2011, http://www.chinalaborwatch.org/newscast/157.

48 Avram Piltch, 'Labor Activist: Apple best at auditing factories, still not doing enough', *Laptop Magazine*, 3 February 2012, https://www.laptopmag.com/articles/labor-activist-apple-best-at-auditing-factories-still-not-doing-enough.

49 Jonathan Vit, 'Greenwashing? RSPO audits rife with "mistakes and fraud", report finds', *Mongabay*, 16 November 2015, https://news.mongabay.com/2015/11/greenwashing-rspo-audits-rife-with-mistakes-and-fraud-report-finds/; Environmental Investigation Agency, *Who Watches the Watchmen? Auditors and the Breakdown of Oversight in the RSPO* (London: EIA, 2015).

50 Clifford and Greenhouse, 'Fast and flawed inspections of factories abroad'.

51 Interview with labour NGO representative, London, 8 March 2013.

52 As quoted in Allain et al., *Forced Labour's Business Models and Supply Chains,* p. 60.

53 Steven Greenhouse, 'In-house audit says Wal-Mart violated labor laws', *New York Times*, 13 January 2004, https://www.nytimes.com/2004/01/13/us/in-house-audit-says-wal-mart-violated-labor-laws.html?rref=collection%2Fbyline%2Fsteven-greenhouse.

54 Quoted in Allain et al., *Forced Labour's Business Models and Supply Chains*, p. 60.

55 Social & Labor Convergence, https://slconvergence.org/.

56 Sedex, 'Marco Baren: Sustainability at Philips interviewed at Sedex Conference 2018', 19 March 2018, https://www.youtube.com/watch?v=5rt8XkZayqk.

57 Unilever, *Unilever Responsible Sourcing Policy 2017: Working in Partnership with Our Suppliers*, https://www.unilever.com/Images/responsible-sourcing-policy-interactive-final_tcm244-504736_en.pdf.

58 For an overview of key aspects of the debate during this period, see Thomas Hemphill, 'The White House Apparel Industry Partnership Agreement: Will self-regulation be successful?', *Business and Society Review* 104/2 (2002), pp. 121–137.

59 Dara O'Rourke, *Smoke from a Hired Gun: A Critique of Nike's Labor and Environmental Auditing in Vietnam as Performed by Ernst & Young* (San Francisco, CA: Transnational Resource and Action Center), p. 5, https://nature.berkeley.edu/orourke/PDF/smoke.pdf.

60 Steven Greenhouse, 'Report says global accounting firm overlooks factory abuses', *New York Times*, 28 September 2000, https://www.nytimes.com/2000/09/28/world/report-says-global-accounting-firm-overlooks-factory-abuses.html?rref=collection%2Fbyline%2Fsteven-greenhouse&action=click&contentCollection=undefined&region=stream&module=stream_unit&version=search&contentPlacement=10&pgtype=collection.

61 O'Rourke, *Smoke from a Hired Gun*.

62 Samanth Subramanian, 'Is fair trade finished?', *Guardian*, 23 July 2019, https://www.theguardian.com/business/2019/jul/23/fairtrade-ethical-certification-super-markets-sainsburys.

63 Rainforest Alliance, 'About the Rainforest Alliance', https://www.rainforest-alliance.org/about.

64 Fairtrade Foundation, 'What Fairtrade does', https://www.fairtrade.org.uk/What-is-Fairtrade/What-Fairtrade-does.

65 Julia Lernoud, Jason Potts, Gregory Sampson, Salvador Garibay, Matthew Lynch, Vivek Voora, Helga Willer and Joseph Wozniak, *The State of Sustainable. Markets – Statistics and Emerging Trends 2017* (Geneva: International Trade Centre), http://www.intracen.org/uploadedFiles/intracenorg/Content/Publications/State-of-Sustainable-Market-2017_web.pdf, pp. 27, 28, 31.

66 Carlos Oya, Florian Schafer and Dafni Skalidou, 'The effectiveness of agricultural certification in developing countries: A systematic review', *World Development* 112 (2018), abstract.

67 Oya, Schafer and Skalidou, 'The effectiveness of agricultural certification in developing countries', p. 292.

68 SAI, 'SA8000® Standard', http://www.sa-intl.org/index.cfm?fuseaction=Page.ViewPage&PageID=1689.

69 Tim Bartley, *Rules without Rights: Land, Labor, and Private Authority in the Global Economy* (Oxford: Oxford University Press, 2018), pp. 180–188.

70 Thomas Dietz, Andrea Estrella Chong, Janina Grabs and Bernard Kilian, 'How effective is multiple certification in improving the economic conditions of smallholder farmers? Evidence from an impact evaluation in Colombia's coffee belt', *Journal of Development Studies*, DOI: 10.1080/00220388.2019.1632433.

71 LeBaron, *Report of Findings: The Global Business of Forced Labour.*

72 Interview with ethical certification organization representative, Amsterdam, 22 November 2017.

73 Interview with cocoa seller, Kumasi, 2 March 2018.

74 Interview with representative of ethical certification organization, Accra, 6 March 2018.

75 Interview with director of research, MNC, Sheffield, 2 October 2017.

76 Interview with head of sustainability, MNC, Sheffield, 2 October 2017.

77 Interview with director of research, MNC, Sheffield, 2 October 2017.

78 Interview with enforcement industry professional association, via Skype, 28 December 2017.

79 Interview with head of sustainability, MNC, Sheffield, 2 October 2017.

80 Interview with director of research, MNC, Sheffield, 2 October 2017.

81 Interview with international organization representative, Geneva, 21 December 2017.

Chapter 6   Protecting Twenty-First-Century Workers

1 See, for instance, the work of those at Brown University's conference 'Whitewashing abolition: Race, displacement, and combatting human trafficking', https://www.brown.edu/initiatives/slavery-and-justice/news/2018-03/whitewashing-abolition-race-displacement-and-combating-human-trafficking.

2 Global Alliance Against Trafficking in Women, *Collateral Damage: The Impact of Anti-Trafficking Measures on Human Rights around the World* (Bangkok: GAATW, 2007), http://www.gaatw.org/Collateral%20Damage_Final/singlefile_CollateralDamagefinal.pdf. See also Elena Shih, 'The anti-trafficking rehabilitation complex: Commodity activism and slave-free goods', 19 August 2015, *openDemocracy*, https://www.opendemocracy.net/en/beyond-trafficking-and-slavery/antitrafficking-rehabilitation-complex-commodity-activism-and-slavefree-goo/.

3 See, for instance, Richard Appelbaum and Nelson

Lichtenstein, eds., *Achieving Workers' Rights in the Global Economy* (Ithaca, NY: Cornell University Press, 2016); Mark Anner, 'Squeezing workers' rights in global supply chains: Purchasing practices in the Bangladesh garment export sector in comparative perspective', *Review of International Political Economy*, https://www.tandfonline.com/doi/full/10.1080/09692290.2019.1625426; Mark Anner, 'CSR participation committees, wildcat strikes and the sourcing squeeze in global supply chains', *British Journal of Industrial Relations* 56/1 (2018), pp. 75–98; Mark Anner, 'Monitoring workers' rights: The limits of voluntary social compliance initiatives in labor repressive regimes', *Global Policy* 8/3 (2017), pp. 56–65; Tim Bartley, *Rules without Rights: Land, Labor, and Private Authority in the Global Economy* (Oxford: Oxford University Press, 2018); Andrew Crane, Vivek Soundararajan, Michael Bloomfield, Laura Spence and Genevieve LeBaron, *Decent Work and Economic Growth in the South Indian Garment Industry* (Bath: University of Bath, 2019).

4 Remi Edwards, Tom Hunt and Genevieve LeBaron, *Corporate Commitments to Living Wages in the Garment Industry* (Sheffield: SPERI, 2019).

5 See Chapter 5. See also Genevieve LeBaron and Jane Lister, 'Ethical audits and the supply chains of global corporations', SPERI Global Political Economy Policy Brief No. 1 (Sheffield: SPERI, 2016); Genevieve LeBaron and Jane Lister, 'Benchmarking global supply chains: The power of the "ethical audit" regime', *Review of International Studies* 41/5 (2015), pp. 905–924; Genevieve LeBaron, Jane Lister, and Peter Dauvergne, 'Governing global supply chain sustainability through the ethical audit regime', *Globalizations* 14/6 (2017), pp. 958–975.

6 Genevieve LeBaron, *Report of Findings: The Global Business of Forced Labour* (Sheffield: SPERI/University of Sheffield, 2018); Thomas Dietz, Andrea Estrella Chong, Janina Grabs and Bernard Kilian, 'How effective is multiple certification in improving the economic conditions of small-holder farmers? Evidence from an impact evaluation in Colombia's coffee belt', *Journal of Development Studies*, DOI: 10.1080/00220388.2019.1632433; Carlos Oya, Florian Schafer and Dafni Skalidou, 'The effectiveness

of agricultural certification in developing countries: A systematic review', *World Development* 112 (2018), pp. 282–312; Michael J. Bloomfield and Philip Schleifer, 'Tracing failure of coral reef protection in nonstate market-driven governance', *Global Environmental Politics* 17/1 (2017), pp. 127–146.

7 Genevieve LeBaron and Andreas Ruhmkorf, 'Steering CSR through home state regulation: A comparison of the impact of the UK Bribery Act and Modern Slavery Act on global supply chain governance', *Global Policy* 8/3 (2017), pp. 14–28. See also the articles in the special issue of *Global Policy Journal* edited by Brian Burgoon and Luc Fransen, including their introduction: 'Introduction to the special issue: Public and private labor standards policy in the global economy', *Global Policy* 3/S3 (2017), pp. 1–10.

8 See, for instance, 'Core standards', 'Enduring relation-ships and fair terms of trade', all sections in Taylors of Harrogate's Commitment to Ethical Trading, https://www.bettysandtaylors.co.uk/wp-content/uploads/2016/02/Taylors-of-Harrogate-Ethical-Trading-Commitments.pdf/. Also see the website of chocolate company Tony's Chocolonely, which has developed long-term partner-ships with the cocoa farms from which it buys beans, using long-term contracts to support its suppliers so they experience fewer pressures to resort to forced or child labour.

9 Fair Food Program, 'Participating buyers', https://www.fairfoodprogram.org/partners/; *NYT* Editors, 'One penny more a pound', 3 December 2010, *New York Times*, https://www.nytimes.com/2010/12/04/opinion/04sat3.html.

10 Fair Food Program, *Fair Food 2017 Annual Report*, http://fairfoodstandards.org/2017-annual-report.pdf.

11 See Coalition of Immokalee Workers, http://ciw-online.org/fair-food-program.

12 Luis Fabiano de Assis, 'The Decent Work SmartLab: A knowledge management initiative in Brazil', *Delta 8.7*, 9 August 2018, https://delta87.org/2018/08/the-decent-work-smartlab-a-knowledge-management-initiative-in-brazil/.

13 Janice Fine, *Co-Production: Bringing Together the Unique Capabilities of Government and Society for Stronger Labor Standards Enforcement* (LIFT Fund, 2015),

p. 5, http://theliftfund.org/wp-content/uploads/2015/09/LIFT ReportCoproductionOct_ExecSumm-rf_4.pdf.

14 For an overview, see Fine, *Co-Production: Bringing Together the Unique Capabilities of Government and Society for Stronger Labor Standards Enforcement*, pp. 552–585.

15 Illinois News, 'Gov. Pritzker signs legislation creating worker protection unit in Attorney General's office', 23 August 2019, Illinois.gov, https://www2.illinois.gov/Pages/news-item.aspx?ReleaseID=20532.

16 For instance, see the policy agenda laid out in Annette Bernhardt, Ruth Milkman, Nik Theodore, Douglas Heckathorn, Mirabai Auer, James DeFilippis, Ana Luz González, Victor Narro, Jason Perelshteyn, Diana Polson and Michael Spiller, *Broken Laws, Unprotected Workers: Violations of Employment and Labor Laws in America's Cities* (New York: National Employment Law Project, 2009).

17 See UN, *Guiding Principles on Business and Human Rights: Implementing the United Nations 'Protect, Respect and Remedy' Framework* (Geneva: United Nations, 2011), pp. 17–19. See also Andreas Rühmkorf and Lena Walker, *Assessment of the Concept of 'Duty of Care' in European Legal Systems* (Amnesty International, 2018).

18 Slavery & Trafficking Risk Template, https://www.social-responsibilityalliance.org/strt/.

19 See, for instance, ILO, 'International Labour Conference Provisional Record, 105th Session, Geneva May–June 2016, Fourth item on the agenda: Decent work in global supply chains', https://www.ilo.org/wcmsp5/groups/public/---ed_norm/---relconf/documents/meetingdocument/wcms_489117.pdf.

20 Nicola Phillips, Genevieve LeBaron and Sara Wallin, 'Mapping and measuring the effectiveness of labour-related disclosure requirements for global supply chains', ILO Research Department Working Paper No. 32, June (Geneva: International Labour Office, 2018); see also Michael Bloomfield and Genevieve LeBaron, 'The UK Modern Slavery Act: Transparency through disclosure', *E-International Relations*, 21 September 2018, https://www.e-ir.info/2018/09/21/the-uk-modern-slavery-act-transparency-through-disclosure-in-global-governance/;

Genevieve LeBaron, 'How to spur corporate accountability with modern slavery legislation', 8 May 2019, *United Nations Delta 8.7*, https://delta87.org/2019/05/how-spur-corporate-accountability-modern-slavery-legislation/.

21 Genevieve LeBaron and Andreas Ruhmkorf, 'Steering CSR through home state regulation: A comparison of the impact of the UK Bribery Act and Modern Slavery Act on global supply chain governance', *Global Policy* 8/3 (2017).

22 Mark Anner, Jennifer Bair and Jeremy Blasi, 'Toward joint liability in global supply chains: Addressing the root causes of labor violations in international subcontracting networks', *Comparative Labor Law and Policy Journal* 31/1 (2013), pp. 1–43.

23 For an overview of legislation, see Thomas Hemphill, 'The White House Apparel Industry Partnership Agreement: Will self-regulation be successful?', *Business and Society Review* 104/2 (1999), pp. 121–137.

24 For an overview, see Jennifer Gordon, *Global Labour Recruitment in a Supply Chain Context* (Geneva: ILO Fundamentals Working Paper, 2015), https://papers.ssrn.com/sol3/papers.cfm?abstract_id=2518519.

25 ITUC, 'Joint corporate liability in labour trafficking cases: Court decision example (Belgium)', https://www.ituc-csi.org/joint-corporate-liability-in.

26 J. J. Rosenbaum, 'Guest post: 2016 steps forward on joint employer liability', *On Labor*, 2 February 2016, https://onlabor.org/guest-post-2016-steps-forward-on-joint-employer-liability/.

27 See Jennifer Gordon's publications, https://www.fordham.edu/info/23139/jennifer_gordon/5402/selected_publications.

28 Rosenbaum, 'Guest post: 2016 steps forward on joint employer liability'.

29 David Weil, *The Fissured Workplace: Why Work Became So Bad for So Many and What Can Be Done to Improve It* (Cambridge, MA: Harvard University Press, 2014), p. 289.

30 See, for instance, Andreas Rühmkorf, *Corporate Social Responsibility, Private Law and Global Supply Chains* (Cheltenham: Edward Elgar Publishing, 2015); see also trade union and worker organizations like Jobs with Justice, United Workers Congress, ITUC, Asia Floor Wage, the US National Employment Law Project and Amnesty International.

31 Global Labor Justice, https://www.globallaborjustice.org/labor-migration/.

32 Carolijn Terwindt and Miriam Saage-Maass, *Liability of Social Auditors in the Textile Industry* (Berlin: European Center for Constitutional and Human Rights, 2016), https://www.business-humanrights.org/sites/default/files/documents/Policy%20Paper_Liability%20of%20Social%20Auditors%20in%20the%20Textile%20Industry%202016%20.pdf.

33 Felix Hadwiger, 'Background paper: International Framework Agreements – Achieving decent work in global supply chains', Geneva: International Labour Office, 2015, https://www.ilo.org/wcmsp5/groups/public/---ed_dialogue/---actrav/documents/meetingdocument/wcms_434248.pdf.

34 WSR Network, 'What is WSR?', https://wsr-network.org/what-is-wsr/.

35 WSR Network, 'What is WSR?'.

36 Worker Rights Consortium, 'Press release: Leading apparel brands, trade unions, and women's rights organizations sign binding agreements to combat gender-based violence and harassment at key supplier's factories in Lesotho', 15 August 2019, https://www.workersrights.org/press-release/leading-apparel-brands-trade-unions-and-womens-rights-organizations-sign-binding-agreements-to-combat-gender-based-violence-and-harassment-at-key-suppliers-factories-in-lesotho/.

37 ILO, 'Social protection floor', https://www.ilo.org/secsoc/%20areas-of-work/policy-development-and-applied-research/%20social-protection-floor/lang--ja/index.htm.

38 Benjamin Davis, Sudhanshu Handa, Nicola Hypher, Natalia Winder Rossi, Paul Winters and Jennifer Yablonski, eds., *From Evidence to Action: The Story of Cash Transfers and Impact Evaluation in Sub Saharan Africa* (Oxford: FAO, UNICEF and Oxford University Press).

39 Living Wage Foundation, https://www.livingwage.org.uk/what-real-living-wage.

40 Fine, *Co-Production: Bringing Together the Unique Capabilities of Government and Society for Stronger Labor Standards Enforcement*, p. 11.

41 See, for instance, the TUC's series *The Added Value of Trade Unions*, https://www.tuc.org.uk/added-value-trade-unions.

42 AFL-CIO Solidarity Center, 'Labor migration and human trafficking', https://www.solidaritycenter.org/what-we-do/migration-and-human-trafficking/.

43 ITUC, *How to Combat Forced Labour and Trafficking: Best Practices Manual for Trade Unions* (Brussels: ITUC, 2010), p. 24.

44 ITUC, *How to Combat Forced Labour and Trafficking*.

45 Personal communication with J. J. Rosenbaum, 6 September 2019.

46 National Domestic Workers Alliance, https://www.domestic-workers.org/bill-rights.

47 Global Labor Justice, https://www.globallaborjustice.org/labor-migration/

48 Jennifer Gordon, 'Regulating the human supply chain', *Iowa Law Review* 102 (2017).

Index